Learning OpenGL ES for iOS

Learning OpenGL ES for iOS

A Hands-On Guide to
Modern 3D Graphics Programming

Erik M. Buck

✦✦Addison-Wesley

Upper Saddle River, NJ • Boston • Indianapolis • San Francisco
New York • Toronto • Montreal • London • Munich • Paris • Madrid
Cape Town • Sydney • Tokyo • Singapore • Mexico City

The publisher offers excellent discounts on this book when ordered in quantity for bulk purchases or special sales, which may include electronic versions and/or custom covers and content particular to your business, training goals, marketing focus, and branding interests. For more information, please contact:

U.S. Corporate and Government Sales

(800) 382-3419

corpsales@pearsontechgroup.com

For sales outside the United States, please contact:

International Sales

international@pearsoned.com

Visit us on the Web: informit.com/aw

Library of Congress Cataloging-in-Publication Data is on file.

ISBN-13: 978-0-32-174183-7

ISBN-10: 0-32-174183-8

Text printed in the United States on recycled paper at R.R. Donnelley in Crawfordsville, Indiana.

First printing, August 2012

Editor-in-Chief
Mark Taub

Acquisitions Editor
Trina MacDonald

Development Editor
Sheri Cain

Managing Editor
Kristy Hart

Project Editor
Andy Beaster

Copy Editor
Paula Lowell

Indexer
Christine Karpeles

Proofreader
Sarah Kearns

Technical Reviewers
Scott Yelich
Mike Daley
Patrick Burleson

Editorial Assistant
Olivia Basegio

Cover Designer
Chuti Prasertsith

Compositor
Gloria Schurick

❖

I dedicate this tome to my beloved wife, Michelle. She is always right in matters of fact or memory (seriously, never bet against her) and makes life possible. May her tireless support and understanding bring her just commendation.

❖

Contents at a Glance

Table of Contents

Preface

OpenGL ES technology underlies the user interface and graphical capabilities exhibited by Apple's iOS devices, iPhone, iPod Touch, and iPad. The "ES" stands for Embedded Systems, and the same technology applies to video game consoles and aircraft cockpit displays, as well as a wide range of cell phones from almost every manufacturer. OpenGL ES is a subset of the OpenGL versions used with desktop operating systems. As a result, OpenGL ES applications are often adaptable to desktop systems, too.

This book introduces modern graphics programming and succinctly explains the effective uses of OpenGL ES for iOS devices. Numerous example programs demonstrate graphics programming concepts. The website at http://opengles.cosmicthump.com/ hosts the examples, related articles, and any errata discovered after publication. This book serves as a gentle but thorough explanation of graphics technology from the lowest-level bit manipulation to advanced topics.

A significant challenge to learning graphics programming manifests the first time you try to sort through piles of misleading information and out-of-date examples littering the Internet. OpenGL started as a small software library for state-of-the-art graphics workstations in 1992. Graphics hardware improved so much so quickly that handheld devices now outperform the best systems money could buy when OpenGL was new. As hardware advanced, some of the compromises and assumptions made by the designers of OpenGL lost relevance. At least 12 different versions of the OpenGL standard exist, and modern OpenGL ES omits support for many techniques that were common in previous versions. Unfortunately, obsolete code, suboptimal approaches, and anachronistic practices built up over decades remain high in Google search results. This book focuses on modern, efficient approaches and avoids distractions from irrelevant and obsolete practices.

Audience

The audience for this book includes programming students and programmers who are expert in other disciplines and want to learn about graphics. No prior experience with computer graphics is required. You do need to be familiar with C or C++ and object-oriented programming concepts. Prior experience with iOS, the Objective-C programming language, and the Cocoa Touch frameworks is beneficial but not essential. After finishing this book, you will be ready to apply advanced computer graphics technology in your iOS applications.

Example Code

Many of the examples provided in this book serve as a launch point for your own projects. Computer source code for examples accompanying this book can be downloaded from http:// opengles.cosmicthump.com/learning-opengl-es-sample-code/ under the terms of the permissive MIT software license: http://www.opensource.org/licenses/mit-license.html.

Examples are built with Apple's free developer tools, the Objective-C programming language, and Apple's Cocoa Touch object-oriented software frameworks. The OpenGL ES Application Programming Interface (API) consists of American National Standards Institute (ANSI) / International Organization for Standardization (ISO) C programming language data types and functions. As a superset of ANSI/ISO C, Objective-C programs natively interact with OpenGL ES.

Every application for iOS contains at least a small dependence on Apple's Objective-C–based Cocoa Touch frameworks. Some developers minimize application integration with Cocoa Touch by reusing existing libraries of cross-platform code written in C or C++. As a derivative of UNIX operating systems, iOS includes the standard C libraries and UNIX APIs making it surprisingly easy to re-host cross-platform code to Apple devices. OpenGL ES itself partly consists of a cross-platform C library. Nevertheless, in almost every case, developers who shun Cocoa Touch and Objective-C do themselves a disservice. Apple's object-oriented frameworks promote unprecedented programmer productivity. More importantly, Cocoa Touch provides much of the tight platform integration and polish users expect from iOS applications.

This book embraces Objective-C and Cocoa Touch. Apple's Objective-C–based GLKit framework is so compellingly powerful and elegant that it clearly establishes the future direction of graphics programming. This book could hardly claim to teach modern techniques by avoiding GLKit and focusing solely on low-level C interfaces to the operating system and OpenGL ES.

Objective-C

Like ANSI/ISO C, Objective-C is a very small language. Experienced C programmers generally find Objective-C easy to learn in a few hours at most. Objective-C adds minimally to the C language while enabling an expressive object-oriented programming style. This book emphasizes graphics programming with descriptions of Objective-C language features provided as needed. You don't need to be an Objective-C or Cocoa Touch expert to get started, but you do need to be familiar with C or C++ and object-oriented programming concepts. You will find that implementing application logic with Objective-C is easy and elegant. Cocoa Touch often simplifies application design particularly when responding to user input.

C++

The ANSI/ISO C++ programming language is not quite a perfect superset of ANSI/ISO C, but it can almost always be intermixed freely with C. OpenGL ES works seamlessly with C++, and the OpenGL Architectural Review Board (ARB) guards the OpenGL ES specification to assure future compatibility with C++.

The C++ programming language is one of the most popular choices for graphics programmers. However, C++ is a very large programming language replete with idioms and subtlety. Developing an intermediate mastery of C++ can take many years. Graphics programming with C++ has advantages. For example, the mathematics used in graphics programs can often be expressed most succinctly using the C++ operator overloading feature.

There are no obstacles to mixing C++ code with Objective-C. Apple's developer tools even support Objective-C++ allowing mixed C++ and Objective-C code within a single statement. However, Objective-C is the primary programming language for iOS. You'll find Objective-C in almost all iOS sample code available from Apple and third parties. C++ is available if you want it but covering it falls outside the scope of this book.

Using GLKit as a Guide

This book leverages exploration of Apple's GLKit to provide a guided tour of modern graphics programming concepts. In several cases, chapters explain and demonstrate technology by partially reimplementing GLKit objects. The approach serves several purposes: Using GLKit simplifies the steps needed to get started. You'll have three OpenGL ES applications up and running on your iOS device by the end of Chapter 2, "Make the Hardware Work for You." From chapter to chapter, topics build upon each other, creating a reusable infrastructure of knowledge and code. When investing effort to build from scratch, having a clear notion of the desired end result helps. GLKit sets a high-quality modern benchmark for worthy end results.

This book dispels any mystery about how GLKit can be implemented and extended using OpenGL ES. By the end of the book, you'll be a GLKit expert armed with thorough understanding and ability to apply GLKit in your iOS applications. GLKit demonstrates best current practices for OpenGL ES and can even serve as a template for your own cross-platform library if you decide you need one.

Errata

This book's website, http://opengles.cosmicthump.com/learning-opengl-es-errata/, provides a list of errata discovered after publication. This book has been extensively reviewed and examples tested. Every effort has been made to avoid defects and omissions. If you find something in the book or examples that you believe is an error, please report the problem via the user comment and errata discussion features of the errata list.

Acknowledgments

Writing a book requires the support of many people. First and foremost, my wife, Michelle, and children, Joshua, Emma, and Jacob, deserve thanks for their patient understanding and support. The publisher, editors, and reviewers provided invaluable assistance. Many people guide me academically, professionally, spiritually, morally, and artistically through life. I cannot thank them enough.

About the Author

Erik M. Buck is a serial entrepreneur and author. He co-wrote *Cocoa Programming* in 2003 and *Cocoa Design Patterns* in 2009. He founded his first company, EMB & Associates, Inc., in 1993 and built the company into a leader in the aerospace and entertainment software industries. Mr. Buck has also worked in construction, taught science to 8th graders, exhibited oil on canvas portraits, and developed alternative fuel vehicles. Mr. Buck sold his company in 2002 and took the opportunity to pursue other interests, including his latest startup, cosmicthump.com. Mr. Buck is an Adjunct Professor of Computer Science at Wright State University and teaches iOS programming courses. He received a BS in Computer Science from the University of Dayton in 1991.

1

Using Modern Mobile Graphics Hardware

This chapter introduces the modern approach for drawing three-dimensional (3D) graphics with embedded graphics hardware. Embedded systems encompass a wide range of devices, from aircraft cockpits to vending machines. The vast majority of 3D-capable embedded systems are handheld computers such as Apple's iPhone, iPod Touch, and iPad or phones based on Google's Android operating system. Handheld devices from Sony, Nintendo, and others also include powerful built-in 3D graphics capabilities.

OpenGL for Embedded Systems (OpenGL ES) defines the standard for embedded 3D graphics. Apple's iPhone, iPod Touch, and iPad devices running iOS 5 support OpenGL ES version 2.0. Apple's devices also support the older OpenGL ES version 1.1. A software framework called GLKit introduced with iOS 5 simplifies many common programming tasks and partially hides the differences between the two supported OpenGL ES versions. This book focuses on OpenGL ES version 2.0 for iOS 5 with GLKit.

OpenGL ES defines an application programming interface (API) for use with the American National Standards Institute (ANSI) C programming language. The C++ and Objective-C programming languages commonly used to program Apple's products seamlessly interact with ANSI C. Special translation layers or "bindings" exist so OpenGL ES may be used from languages such as JavaScript and Python. Emerging web programming standards such as WebGL from the non-profit Web3D Consortium are poised to enable standardized cross-platform access to the OpenGL ES API from within web pages, too. The 3D graphics concepts explained within this book apply to all 3D-capable embedded systems.

Without diving into specific programming details, this chapter explains the general approach to producing 3D graphics with OpenGL ES and iOS 5. Modern hardware-accelerated 3D graphics underlie all the visual effects produced by advanced mobile products. Reading this chapter is the first step toward squeezing the best possible 3D graphics and visual effects out of mobile hardware.

What Is 3D Rendering?

A graphics processing unit (GPU) is a hardware component that combines data describing geometry, colors, lights, and other information to produce an image on a screen. The screen only has two dimensions, so the trick to displaying 3D data is generating an image that fools the eye into seeing the missing third dimension, as in the example in Figure 1.1.

Figure 1.1   A sample image generated from 3D data.

The generation of a 2D image from 3D data is called *rendering*. The image on a computer display is composed of rectangular dots of color called *pixels*. Figure 1.2 shows an enlarged portion of an image to show the individual pixels. If you examine your display through a magnifying glass, you will see that each pixel is composed of three color elements: a red dot, a green dot, and a blue dot. Figure 1.2 also shows a further enlarged single pixel to depict the individual color elements. On a full-color display, pixels always have red, green, and blue color elements, but the elements might be arranged in different patterns than the side-by-side arrangement shown in Figure 1.2.

Figure 1.2 Images are composed of pixels that each have red, green, and blue elements.

Images are stored in computer memory using an array containing at least three values for each pixel. The first value specifies the red color element's intensity for the pixel. The second value is the green intensity, and the third value is the blue intensity. An image that contains 10,000 pixels can be stored in memory as an array of 30,000 intensity values—one value for each of the three color elements in each pixel. Combinations of red, green, and blue at different intensities are sufficient to produce every color of the rainbow. If all three elements have zero intensity, the resulting color is black. If all three elements have full intensity, the perceived color is white. Yellow is formed by mixing red and green without any blue. The Mac OS X standard Color panel user interface shown in Figure 1.3 contains graphical sliders to adjust relative Red, Green, Blue (RGB) intensities.

Figure 1.3   User interface to adjust Red, Green, and Blue color component intensities.

Rendering 3D data into a 2D image typically occurs in several separate steps involving calculations to set the red, green, and blue intensities of every pixel in the image. Taken as a whole, this book describes how programs best take advantage of OpenGL ES and graphics hardware at each step in the rendering process. The first step is to supply the GPU with 3D data to process.

Supplying the Graphics Processor with Data

Programs store the data for 3D scenes in hardware random access memory (RAM). The embedded system's central processing unit (CPU) has access to some RAM that is dedicated for its own exclusive use. The GPU also has RAM dedicated for exclusive use during graphics processing. The speed of rendering 3D graphics with modern hardware depends almost entirely on the ways the different memory areas are accessed.

OpenGL ES is a software technology. Portions of OpenGL ES execute on the CPU and other parts execute on the GPU. OpenGL ES straddles the boundary between the two processors and coordinates data exchanges between the memory areas. The arrows in Figure 1.4 identify data exchanges between the hardware components involved in 3D rendering. Each of the arrows also represents a bottleneck to rendering performance. OpenGL ES usually coordinates data exchanges efficiently, but the ways programs interact with OpenGL ES can dramatically increase or decrease the number and types of data exchanges needed. With regard to rendering speed, the fastest data exchange is the one that is avoided.

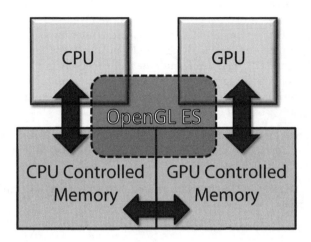

Figure 1.4   Relationships between hardware components and OpenGL ES.

First and foremost, copying data from one memory area to another is relatively slow. Even worse, unless care is taken, neither the GPU nor CPU can use the memory for anything else while memory copying takes place. Therefore, copying between memory areas needs to be avoided when possible.

Second, all memory accesses are relatively slow. A current embedded CPU can readily complete about a billion operations per second, but it can only read or write memory about 200 million times per second. That means that unless the CPU can usefully perform five or more operations on each piece of data read from memory, the processor is performing sub-optimally and is called "data starved." The situation is even more dramatic with GPUs, which complete several billion operations per second under ideal conditions but can still only access memory about 200 million times per second. GPUs are almost always limited by memory access performance and can usually perform 10 to 30 operations on each piece of data without degradation in overall graphics output.

One way to summarize the difference between modern OpenGL ES and older versions of OpenGL is that OpenGL ES dropped support for archaic and inefficient memory copying operations in favor of new streamlined approaches. If you have ever programmed desktop OpenGL the old way, forget those experiences now. Most of the worst techniques don't work in modern embedded systems anyway. OpenGL ES still provides several ways to supply data to the graphics processor, but only one "best" way exists, and it's used consistently in this book.

Buffers: The Best Way to Supply Data

OpenGL ES defines the concept of *buffers* for exchanging data between memory areas. A buffer is a contiguous range of RAM that the graphics processor can control and manage. Programs copy data from the CPU's memory into OpenGL ES buffers. After the GPU takes ownership of a buffer, programs running on the CPU ideally avoid touching the buffer again. By exclusively controlling the buffer, the GPU reads and writes the buffer memory in the most efficient way possible. The graphics processor applies its number-crunching power to buffers asynchronously and concurrently, which means the program running on the CPU continues to execute while the GPU simultaneously works on data in buffers.

Nearly all the data that programs supply to the GPU should be in buffers. It doesn't matter if a buffer stores geometric data, colors, hints for lighting effects, or other information. The seven steps to supply data in a buffer are

1. **Generate**—Ask OpenGL ES to generate a unique identifier for a buffer that the graphics processor controls.

2. **Bind**—Tell OpenGL ES to use a buffer for subsequent operations.

3. **Buffer Data**—Tell OpenGL ES to allocate and initialize sufficient contiguous memory for a currently bound buffer—often by copying data from CPU-controlled memory into the allocated memory.

4. **Enable or Disable**—Tell OpenGL ES whether to use data in buffers during subsequent rendering.

5. **Set Pointers**—Tell OpenGL ES about the types of data in buffers and any memory offsets needed to access the data.

6. **Draw**—Tell OpenGL ES to render all or part of a scene using data in currently bound and enabled buffers.

7. **Delete**—Tell OpenGL ES to delete previously generated buffers and free associated resources.

Ideally, each generated buffer is used for a long time (possibly the entire lifetime of the program). Generating, initializing, and deleting buffers sometimes require time-consuming synchronization between the graphics processor and the CPU. Delays are incurred because the GPU must complete any pending operations that use the buffer before deleting it. If a program generates and deletes buffers thousands of times per second, the GPU might not have time to accomplish any rendering.

OpenGL ES defines the following C language functions to perform each step in the process for using one type of buffer and provides similar functions for other types of buffer.

- `glGenBuffers()`—Asks OpenGL ES to generate a unique identifier for a buffer that the graphics processor controls.

- `glBindBuffer()`—Tells OpenGL ES to use a buffer for subsequent operations.

- `glBufferData()` or `glBufferSubData()`—Tells OpenGL ES to allocate and initialize sufficient contiguous memory for a currently bound buffer.

- `glEnableVertexAttribArray()` or `glDisableVertexAttribArray()`—Tells OpenGL ES whether to use data in buffers during subsequent rendering.

- `glVertexAttribPointer()`—Tells OpenGL ES about the types of data in buffers and any offsets in memory needed to access data in the buffers.

- `glDrawArrays()` or `glDrawElements()`—Tells OpenGL ES to render all or part of a scene using data in currently bound and enabled buffers.

- `glDeleteBuffers()`—Tells OpenGL ES to delete previously generated buffers and free associated resources.

Note

The C functions are only mentioned here to present a flavor of the way the OpenGL ES 2.0 API function names map to the underlying concepts. Various examples throughout this book explain the C functions, so don't worry about memorizing them now.

The Frame Buffer

The GPU needs to know where to store rendered 2D image pixel data in memory. Just like buffers supply data to the GPU, other buffers called *frame buffers* receive the results of rendering. Programs generate, bind, and delete frame buffers like any other buffers. However, frame buffers don't need to be initialized because rendering commands replace the content of the buffer when appropriate. Frame buffers are implicitly enabled when bound, and OpenGL ES automatically configures data types and offsets based on platform-specific hardware configuration and capabilities.

Many frame buffers can exist at one time, and the GPU can be configured through OpenGL ES to render into any number of frame buffers. However, the pixels on the display are controlled by the pixel color element values stored in a special frame buffer called the *front frame buffer*. Programs and the operating system seldom render directly into the front frame buffer because that would enable users to see partially completed images while rendering takes place. Instead, programs and the operating system render into other frame buffers including the *back frame buffer*. When the rendered back frame buffer contains a complete image, the front frame buffer and the back frame buffer are swapped almost instantaneously. The back frame buffer becomes the new front frame buffer and the old front frame buffer becomes the back frame buffer. Figure 1.5 illustrates the relationships between the pixels onscreen, the front frame buffer, and the back frame buffer.

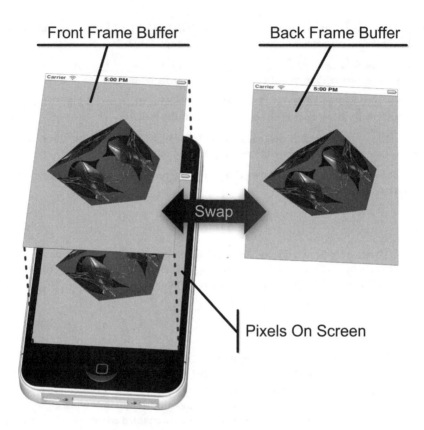

Figure 1.5   The front frame buffer controls pixel colors on the display and is swapped with the back frame buffer.

The OpenGL ES Context

The information that configures OpenGL ES resides in platform-specific software data structures encapsulated within an OpenGL ES *context*. OpenGL ES is a state machine, which means that after a program sets a configuration value, the value remains set until the program changes the value. Information within a context may be stored in memory controlled by the CPU or in memory controlled by the GPU. OpenGL ES copies information between the two memory areas as needed, and knowing when copying happens helps to optimize programs. Chapter 9, "Optimization," describes optimization techniques.

The internal implementation of OpenGL ES Contexts depends on the specific embedded system and the particular GPU hardware installed. The OpenGL ES API provides ANSI C language functions called by programs to interact with contexts so that programs don't need to know much if any system-specific information.

The OpenGL ES context keeps track of the frame buffer that will be used for rendering. The context also keeps track of buffers for geometric data, colors, and so on. The context determines whether to use features such as textures and lighting, described in Chapter 3, "Textures," and Chapter 4, "Shedding Some Light." The context defines the current coordinate system for rendering, as described in the next section.

The Geometry of a 3D Scene

Many kinds of data, such as lighting information and colors, can be optionally omitted when supplying data to the GPU. The one kind of data that OpenGL ES must have when rendering a scene is geometric data specifying the shapes to be rendered. Geometric data is defined relative to a 3D coordinate system.

Coordinate System

Figure 1.6 depicts the OpenGL coordinate system. A coordinate system is an imaginary set of guides to help visualize the relationships between positions in space. Each arrow in Figure 1.6 is called an *axis*. OpenGL ES always starts with a rectangular Cartesian coordinate system. That means the angle between any two axes is 90 degrees. Each position in space is called a *vertex*, and each vertex is defined by its locations along each of three axes called X, Y, and Z.

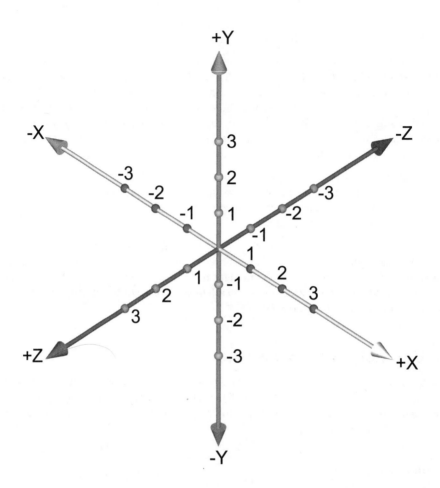

Figure 1.6   X, Y, and Z axes define the OpenGL coordinate system.

Figure 1.7 shows the vertex at position {1.5, 3.0, 0.0} relative to the axes. The vertex is defined by its position, 1.5, along the X axis; its position, 3.0, along the Y axis; and its position, 0.0, along the Z axis. Dashed lines in Figure 1.7 show how the vertex aligns with the axes.

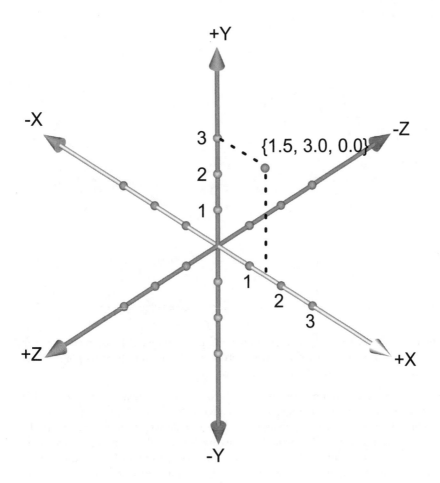

Figure 1.7   The vertex at position {1.5, 3.0, 0.0} relative to the axes.

The locations along each axis are called *coordinates,* and three coordinates are needed to specify a vertex for use with 3D graphics. Figure 1.8 illustrates more vertices and their relative positions within the OpenGL coordinate system. Dashed lines show how the vertices align with the axes.

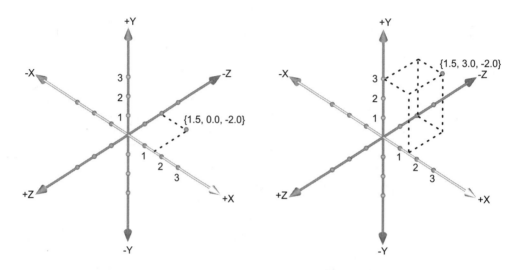

Figure 1.8   The relative positions of vertices within a coordinate system.

OpenGL ES coordinates are best stored as floating-point numbers. Modern GPUs are optimized for floating point and will usually convert vertex coordinates into floating-point values even when vertices are specified with some other data type.

One of the keys to using and understanding the coordinate system is to remember that it's merely an imaginary tool of mathematics. Chapter 5, "Changing Your Point of View," explains the dramatic effects produced by changing the coordinate system. In a purely mathematic sense, lots of non-Cartesian coordinate systems are possible. For example, a polar coordinate system identifies positions in 3D space by imagining where a point falls on the surface of a sphere using two angles and a radius. Don't worry about the math for non-Cartesian coordinate systems now. Embedded GPUs don't support most non-Cartesian coordinate systems in hardware, and none of the book's examples use non-Cartesian coordinate systems. If the need arises in your projects, positions expressed in any coordinate system can be converted into the OpenGL ES default coordinate system as needed.

The OpenGL ES coordinate system has no units. The distance between vertex {1, 0, 0} and {2, 0, 0} is 1 along the X axis, but ask yourself, "One what—is that one inch, or one millimeter, or one mile, or one light-year?" The answer is that it doesn't matter; or more precisely, it's up to you. You are free to imagine that a distance of 1 represents a centimeter or any other unit in your 3D scene.

> **Note**
>
> Leaving units undefined can be very convenient for 3D graphics, but it also introduces a challenge if you ever want to print your 3D scenes. Apple's iOS supports Quartz 2D for two-dimensional drawing compatible with the standard Portable Document Format (PDF) and defines units in terms of real-world measurements. Real-world measurements enable you to draw geometric objects and know what size the objects will be on a printed page regardless of the resolution of the printer. In contrast, no resolution-independent way exists to specify or render OpenGL geometry.

Vectors

Vectors are another math concept used frequently in graphics programming. In one sense, vectors are an alternative way of interpreting vertex data. A vector is a description of a direction and a distance. The distance is also called the magnitude. Every vertex can be defined by its direction and distance from the origin, {0, 0, 0}, in the OpenGL ES coordinate system. Figure 1.9 uses a solid arrow to depict the vector from the origin to the vertex at {1.5, 3.0, -2.0}. Dashed lines show how the vertex aligns with the axes.

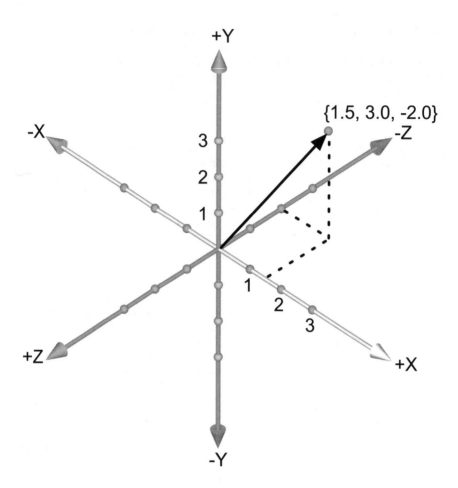

Figure 1.9   A vector in the 3D coordinate system.

Calculating a vector between any two vertices is possible using the differences between the individual coordinates of each vertex. The vector between a vertex at {1.5, 3.0, -2.0} and the origin is {1.5 − 0.0, 3.0 − 0.0, -2.0 − 0.0}. The vector between vertex V1 and vertex V2 in Figure 1.10 equals {v2.x − v1.x, v2.y − v1.y, v2.z − v1.z}.

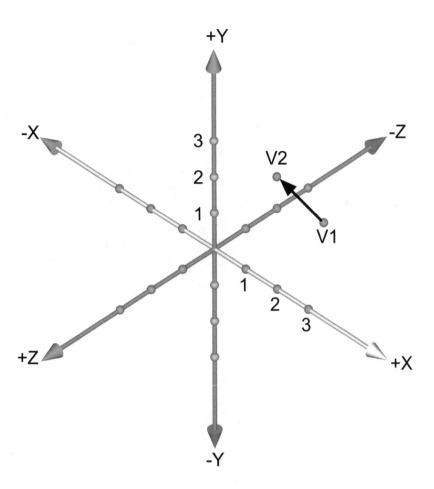

Figure 1.10   The vector between two vertices, V1 and V2.

Vectors can be added together to produce a new vector. The vector between the origin and any vertex is the sum of three axis-aligned vectors, as shown in Figure 1.11. Vectors A + B + C equal vector D (as shown in the following), which also defines the vertex at {1.5, 3.0, -2.0}.

```
D.x = A.x + B.x + C.x = 1.5 + 0.0 + 0.0  = 1.5
D.y = A.y + B.y + C.y = 0.0 + 3.0 + 0.0  = 3.0
D.z = A.z + B.z + C.z = 0.0 + 0.0 + -2.0 = -2.0
```

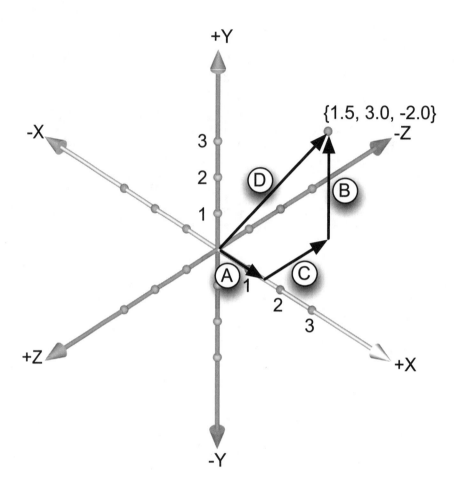

Figure 1.11   The sum of axis-aligned vectors.

Vectors are key to understanding modern GPUs because graphics processors are massively parallel vector processing engines. The GPU is able to manipulate multiple vectors simultaneously, and vector calculations define the results of rendering. Several critical vector operations besides addition and subtraction are explained as needed in later chapters. The OpenGL ES default coordinate system, vertices, and vectors provide enough math to get started specifying geometric data to be rendered.

> **Note**
>
> An entire field of mathematics called *linear algebra* deals with math operations using vectors. Linear algebra is related to trigonometry, but it primarily uses simple operations such as addition and multiplication to build and manipulate complex geometry. Computer graphics rely on linear algebra because computers and particularly GPUs excel at simple math operations. Linear algebra concepts are introduced gradually throughout this book as needed.

Points, Lines, and Triangles

OpenGL ES uses vertex data to specify *points, line segments,* and *triangles.* One vertex defines the position of a point in the coordinate system. Two vertices define a line segment. Three vertices define a triangle. OpenGL ES only renders points, line segments, and triangles, so every complex 3D scene is constructed from combinations of points, line segments, and triangles. Figure 1.12 shows how complex geometric objects are built using many triangles.

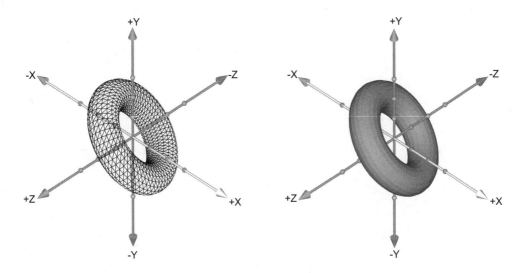

Figure 1.12   Vertex data rendered as line segments and triangles.

Summary

OpenGL ES is the standard for accessing the hardware accelerated 3D graphics capabilities of modern embedded systems such as the iPhone and iPad. The process of converting geometric data supplied by programs into an image on the screen is called rendering. Buffers controlled by the GPU are the key to efficient rendering. Buffers containing geometric data define the points, line segments, and triangles to be rendered. The OpenGL ES 3D default coordinate system, vertices, and vectors provide the mathematic basis for specifying geometric data. Rendering results are always stored in a frame buffer. Two special frame buffers, the front frame buffer and back frame buffer, control the final colors of pixels on the display. The OpenGL ES context stores OpenGL ES state information including identification of buffers to supply data for rendering and buffers to receive the results.

Chapter 2, "Making the Hardware Work for You," introduces a simple program to draw 3D graphics with an iPhone, iPod Touch, or iPad using Apple's Xcode development tools and Cocoa Touch object-oriented frameworks. Examples in Chapter 2 form the basis for subsequent examples in this book.

Making the Hardware Work for You

This chapter explains how to set up and use OpenGL ES graphics within iOS 5 applications. An initial example program applies graphics concepts from Chapter 1, "Using Modern Mobile Graphics Hardware," to make the embedded hardware render an image. The initial example is then extended to produce two additional versions exploring relationships between Apple's GLKit technology introduced in iOS 5 and underlying OpenGL ES functions.

Drawing a Core Animation Layer with OpenGL ES

Chapter 1 introduced OpenGL ES frame buffers. The iOS operating system won't let applications draw directly into the front frame buffer or the back frame buffer nor can applications directly control swapping the front frame buffer with the back frame buffer. The operating system reserves those operations for itself so it can always control the final appearance of the display using a system component called the *Core Animation Compositor*.

Core Animation includes the concept of *layers*. There can be any number of layers at one time. The Core Animation Compositor combines layers to produce the final pixel colors in the back frame buffer and then swaps buffers. Figure 2.1 shows two layers combined to produce the color data in the back frame buffer.

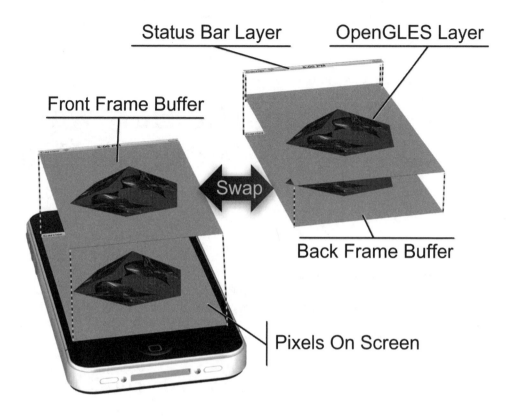

Figure 2.1   Core Animation layers combine to produce the color data in the back frame buffer.

A mix of layers provided by applications and layers provided by the operating system combine to produce the final display appearance. For example, in Figure 2.1, the OpenGL ES layer showing a rotated cube is generated by an application, but the layer showing the status bar at the top of the display is produced and controlled by the operating system. Most applications use several layers. Every iOS native user interface object has a corresponding Core Animation layer, so an application that displays several buttons, text fields, tables, images, and so on automatically uses many layers.

Layers store the results of all drawing operations. For example, iOS provides software objects to efficiently draw video onto layers. There are layers that display images with special effects like fade-in and fade-out. Layer content can be drawn with Apple's Core Graphics framework for 2D including rich font support. Applications like the examples in this chapter render layer content with OpenGL ES.

> **Note**
>
> Apple's Core Animation Compositor uses OpenGL ES to control the graphics processing unit (GPU), mix layers, and swap frame buffers with maximum efficiency. Graphics programmers often use the term *compositing* to describe the process of mixing images to form a composite result. All drawing to the display passes through the Core Animation Compositor and therefore ultimately involves OpenGL ES.

Frame buffers store the results of OpenGL ES rendering, so to render onto a Core Animation layer, programs need a frame buffer connected to a layer. In a nutshell, each program configures a layer with enough memory to store pixel color data and then creates a frame buffer that uses the layer's memory to store rendered images. Figure 2.2 depicts the relationship between an OpenGL ES frame buffer and a layer.

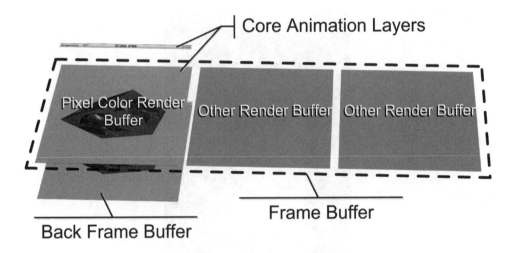

Figure 2.2   A frame buffer can share pixel storage with a layer.

Figure 2.2 shows a *pixel color render buffer* and two extra buffers each labeled "Other Render Buffer." In addition to pixel color data, OpenGL ES and the GPU sometimes produce useful data as a byproduct of rendering. Frame buffers can be configured with multiple buffers called *render buffers* to receive multiple types of output. Frame buffers that share data with a layer must have a pixel color render buffer. Other render buffers are optional and not used in this chapter. Figure 2.2 shows the other render buffers for completeness and because most non-trivial OpenGL ES programs use at least one extra render buffer, as explained in Chapter 5, "Changing Your Point of View."

Combining Cocoa Touch with OpenGL ES

This chapter's first example application, OpenGLES_Ch2_1, provides the starting point for examples in this book. The program configures OpenGL ES to render an image onto a Core Animation layer. The iOS Core Animation Compositor then automatically combines the rendered layer content with other layers to produce pixel color data stored in the back frame buffer and ultimately shown onscreen.

Figure 2.3 shows the image rendered by OpenGLES_Ch2_1. Only one triangle is drawn, but the steps to perform OpenGL ES rendering are the same for more complex scenes. The example applies Apple's Cocoa Touch technology and the Xcode Integrated Development Environment (IDE). Apple's developer tools for iOS including Xcode are part of the iOS Software Development Kit (SDK) at http://developer.apple.com/technologies/ios/.

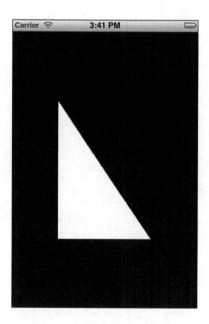

Figure 2.3   Final display produced by the OpenGLES_Ch2_1 example.

Cocoa Touch

Cocoa Touch consists of reusable software objects and functions for creating and running applications. Apple's iOS comprises a nearly complete UNIX-like operating system similar to Mac OS X, which runs on Apple's Macintosh line of computers. Google's Linux-based Android OS is also similar to UNIX. Cocoa Touch builds on top of the underlying UNIX system to integrate many disparate capabilities ranging from network connections to Core Animation and the graphical user interface objects required for users to start, stop, see, and interact with applications. Writing a program for iOS without using Cocoa Touch is technically possible by using only the American National Standards Institute (ANSI) C programming language, UNIX command-line tools, and UNIX application programming interfaces (APIs). However, most users have no way to start such a program, and Apple does not accept such applications for distribution via Apple's App Store.

Cocoa Touch is implemented primarily with the Objective-C programming language. Objective-C adds a small number of syntactic elements and an object-oriented runtime system to the ANSI C programming language. Cocoa Touch provides access to underlying ANSI C–based technologies including OpenGL ES, but even the simplest applications such as the OpenGLES_Ch2_1 example require Objective-C. Cocoa Touch provides many standard capabilities for iOS applications and frees developers to concentrate on the features that make applications unique. Every iOS programmer benefits from learning and using Cocoa Touch and Objective-C. However, this book focuses on OpenGL ES and barely scratches the surface of the Cocoa Touch technology.

Using Apple's Developer Tools

Xcode runs on Mac OS X and includes a syntax-aware code editor, compilers, debuggers, performance tools, and a file management user interface. Xcode supports software development using the ANSI C, C++, Objective-C, and Objective-C++ languages, and it works with a variety of external source code management systems. Apple builds its own software using Xcode. More information is available at http://developer.apple.com/iphone/library/referencelibrary/ GettingStarted/URL_Tools_for_iPhone_OS_Development/index.html.

Figure 2.4 shows Xcode loaded with the `OpenGLES_Ch2_1.xcodeproj` configuration file defining the resources needed to build the OpenGLES_Ch2_1 example. Xcode has features similar to most other IDEs such as the open source Eclipse IDE and Microsoft's Visual Studio IDE. The list on the left side in Figure 2.4 identifies the files to be compiled and linked into the application. The toolbar at the top of the Xcode window provides buttons for building and running the application under development. The rest of the user interface consists primarily of a source code editor.

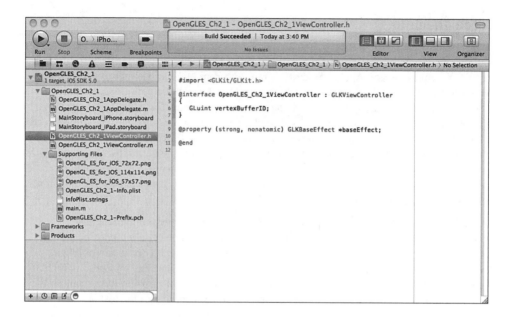

Figure 2.4   The example Xcode project.

Cocoa Touch Application Architecture

Figure 2.5 identifies the major software components within all modern Cocoa Touch applications that use OpenGL ES. Arrows indicate the typical flow of information between components. Cocoa Touch provides the shaded components in Figure 2.5, and applications typically use the shaded components unmodified. The white components in Figure 2.5 are unique to each application. More complex applications contain additional application-specific software. Don't be overwhelmed by the complexity of Figure 2.5. Much of the time, only the two white components, the application delegate and root view controller, require any programmer attention. The other components are part of the infrastructure providing standard iOS application behavior without any programmer intervention.

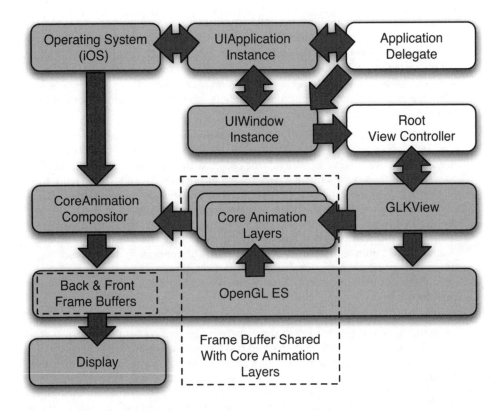

Figure 2.5   The software architecture of Cocoa Touch OpenGL ES applications.

The operating system controls access to hardware components and sends events such as user touches on the display to Cocoa Touch–based applications. Cocoa Touch implements standard graphical components including the touch-sensitive keyboard and the status bar, so individual applications don't need to reproduce those components. Apple provides a diagram and explains typical Cocoa Touch application components at http://developer.apple.com/ library/ios/documentation/iPhone/Conceptual/iPhoneOSProgrammingGuide/AppArchitecture/ AppArchitecture.html. Apple's diagram omits OpenGL ES and Core Animation layers for brevity but provides additional rationale for Cocoa Touch application design.

Chapter 1 introduces the roles of the OpenGL ES and frame buffer components shown in Figure 2.5. This chapter introduces Core Animation layers and the Core Animation Compositor. The remaining components in Figure 2.5 implement standard Cocoa Touch behaviors.

- **UIApplication:** Each application contains a single instance of the UIApplication class. UIApplication is an Objective-C Cocoa Touch object that provides bidirectional communication between an application and iOS. Applications request services from iOS and the system provides information such as the current orientation of the display to the running application. UIApplication also communicates with one or more Cocoa Touch UIWindow instances and an application-specific Delegate to route user input events to the correct application-specific objects.

- **Application delegate:** A *delegate* object is given an opportunity to react to changes in another object or influence the behavior of another object. The basic idea is that two objects coordinate to solve a problem. One object, such as UIApplication, is very general and intended for reuse in a wide variety of situations. It stores a reference to another object, its delegate, and sends messages to the delegate at critical times. The messages might just inform the delegate that something has happened, giving the delegate an opportunity to perform extra processing, or the messages might ask the delegate for critical information that will control what happens. The delegate is typically a custom object unique to a particular application. The application delegate receives messages about all important changes to the environment in which the Cocoa Touch application runs including when the application has finished launching and when it's about to terminate.

- **UIWindow:** Cocoa Touch applications always have at least one UIWindow instance created automatically that covers the full display. UIWindow instances control rectangular areas of the display, and they can be overlapped and layered so that one window covers another window. Cocoa Touch applications seldom directly access windows other than the one that covers the full display. Cocoa Touch automatically uses other UIWindows as needed to display alerts or status information to users. UIWindows contain one or more UIView instances that provide the graphical content of the window. An important role of windows within the application architecture is to collect user input events from the UIApplication instance and redirect those events to the right UIView instances on a case-by-case basis. For example, the UIWindow determines which UIView instance was touched by the user and sends the appropriate event directly to that instance.

- **Root view controller:** Each window optionally has a root view controller. View controllers are instances of the Cocoa Touch UIViewController class and tie together the design of most iOS applications. View controllers coordinate the presentation of an associated view and support rotating views in response to device orientation changes. The root view controller identifies the UIView instance that fills the entire window. The default behavior of the UIViewController class handles much of the standard visual behavior of iOS applications. The GLKViewController class is a built-in subclass of UIViewController that additionally supports OpenGL ES–specific behavior and animation timing. The OpenGLES_Ch2_1 example creates an OpenGLES_Ch2_1ViewController subclass of GLKViewController to provide all the example's application-specific behavior.

- **GLKView:** This is a built-in subclass of the Cocoa Touch UIView class. GLKView simplifies the effort required to create an OpenGL ES application by automatically creating and managing a frame buffer and render buffers sharing memory with a Core Animation layer. GLKView's associated GLKViewController instance is the view's delegate and receives messages whenever the view needs to be redrawn. Creating your own subclasses of UIView or GLKView to implement application-specific drawing is possible, but OpenGLES_Ch2_1 adopts a simpler approach and uses GLKView unmodified. The OpenGLES_Ch2_1 example implements all application-specific behavior including drawing in the OpenGLES_Ch2_1ViewController class.

Note

The *GLK* prefix in the names of classes like GLKView and GLKViewController indicates that the classes are part of the GLKit framework introduced in iOS 5. A framework is a collection of compiled code, interface declarations, and resources such as images or data files used by the compiled code. Frameworks effectively organize reusable shared libraries and might contain multiple versions of the libraries in some cases. GLKit provides classes and functions to simplify the use of OpenGL ES with iOS. GLKit is part of Cocoa Touch along with several other frameworks including the User Interface Kit (UIKit) framework that contains classes such as UIApplication, UIWindow, and UIView.

The OpenGLES_Ch2_1 Example

You can download example code for this book from http://opengles.cosmicthump.com/learning-opengl-es-sample-code/. Xcode projects and all the files needed to build this book's examples are provided. A file called OpenGLES_Ch2_1.xcodeproj stores information about the project itself. When Apple's iOS 5 software development kit (SDK) and Xcode 4.2 or later are installed on your computer, double-clicking the OpenGLES_Ch2_1.xcodeproj file starts Xcode and loads the project. After it's loaded, clicking the Run button in Xcode's toolbar compiles and links the files in the project and then launches Apple's iPhone simulator to run the OpenGLES_Ch2_1 application.

Note

All the examples in this book use Apple's Automatic Reference Counting (ARC) technology to manage memory for Objective-C objects. ARC is enabled by default in newly created Xcode projects for iOS. Using ARC avoids the need to manually manage memory for objects and simplifies example code.

Figure 2.6 lists the files built and linked in the example. The remainder of this section describes the content and purpose of each file.

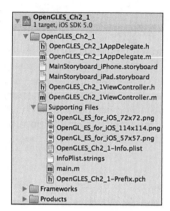

Figure 2.6   The files in the OpenGLES_Ch2_1 Xcode project.

The OpenGLES_Ch2_1 Xcode project was created using Xcode's standard "Single View Application" template. The template configures the new project to build a simple application composed of a single UIView (or subclass) instance filling the entire display. Other templates provide a starting point for other types of iOS applications. The Single View Application template generated a custom application delegate class named OpenGLES_Ch2_1AppDelegate and a custom view controller class named OpenGLES_Ch2_1ViewController.

The OpenGLES_Ch2_1AppDelegate Class

The OpenGLES_Ch2_1AppDelegate.h file was automatically generated by Xcode when the project was first created. OpenGLES_Ch2_1AppDelegate.h contains the Objective-C declaration for the OpenGLES_Ch2_1AppDelegate class. The OpenGLES_Ch2_1 example uses the generated class without any modifications.

The OpenGLES_Ch2_1AppDelegate.m file was also automatically generated by Xcode when the project was first created. OpenGLES_Ch2_1AppDelegate.m contains the Objective-C implementation for the OpenGLES_Ch2_1AppDelegate class. The generated code contains "stubbed" implementations of several methods commonly implemented by application delegates. The OpenGLES_Ch2_1 example uses the generated class without any modifications.

Storyboards

The MainStoryboard_iPhone.storyboard and MainStoryboard_iPad.storyboard files are also generated by the Xcode Single View Application template. These files are edited graphically in Xcode to define the user interface. The iPad and iPhone have different-sized screens and therefore benefit from different user interfaces. The OpenGLES_Ch2_1 example automatically reads whichever storyboard file is appropriate for the device when the example runs. Storyboards chain UIViewController instances and the UIView instances associated with each controller. Storyboards specify transitions from view controller to view controller and back to automate much of an application's user interaction design and potentially eliminate code that would otherwise need to be written. However, the OpenGLES_Ch2_1 example is so simple that it only uses one view controller, an instance of the OpenGLES_Ch2_1ViewController class.

The OpenGLES_Ch2_1ViewController Class Interface

The OpenGLES_Ch2_1ViewController.h file was originally generated by Xcode when the project was first created but is modified for this example. OpenGLES_Ch2_1ViewController.h contains the modified Objective-C declaration for the OpenGLES_Ch2_1ViewController class. The bold code identifies the principal changes from the generated code.

```
//
//  OpenGLES_Ch2_1ViewController.h
//  OpenGLES_Ch2_1
//

#import <GLKit/GLKit.h>

@interface OpenGLES_Ch2_1ViewController : GLKViewController
{
    GLuint vertexBufferID;
}

@property (strong, nonatomic) GLKBaseEffect *baseEffect;

@end
```

The file begins with an identifying comment. The interface for the Cocoa Touch GLKit framework is imported by the #import compiler directive, which is similar to the ANSI C #include directive. Both directives insert the contents of the specified file into the compilation of the file containing the directive. Objective-C's #import directive automatically prevents the same file contents from being inserted more than once per compilation and is preferred even though #include also works with Objective-C.

OpenGLES_Ch2_1ViewController is a subclass of the built-in GLKViewController class and inherits many standard capabilities from GLKViewController, which in turn inherits capabilities from its super class, UIViewController. In particular, GLKViewController automatically reconfigures OpenGL ES and the application's GLKView instance in response to device orientation changes and visual transitions such as fade-in and fade-out.

The vertexBufferID variable declared in the interface of OpenGLES_Ch2_1ViewController stores the OpenGL ES identifier for a buffer to contain vertex data used in the example. The implementation of the OpenGLES_Ch2_1ViewController class explains initialization and use of the buffer identifier.

The `baseEffect` *property* in the interface of `OpenGLES_Ch2_1ViewController` declares a pointer to a `GLKBaseEffect` instance. Objective-C properties declare values similar to instance variables. Properties of Objective-C objects can be accessed using the language's "dot notation"; for example, `someObject.baseEffect`, or by methods that follow a special naming convention of `-set<PropertyName>` for methods that set the property and `-<propertyName>` for methods that return the property. The specially named methods are called *accessors*. The accessor that returns the value of `OpenGLES_Ch2_1ViewController`'s `baseEffect` property is `-baseEffect`. The accessor for setting its value is `-setBaseEffect:`. Properties in general are not always implemented as instance variables; their values may be calculated on demand or loaded from databases and so on. The property syntax in Objective-C provides a way to declare that an object provides values without revealing in the class declaration how the values are stored. When the dot notation is used to get or set the value of a property, the Objective-C compiler automatically substitutes calls to the appropriately named assessor methods. Objective-C also provides a way to automatically generate the accessor method implementations as explained in the `OpenGLES_Ch2_1ViewController` implementation.

`GLKBaseEffect` is another built-in class provided by GLKit. `GLKBaseEffect` exists to simplify many common operations performed with OpenGL ES. `GLKBaseEffect` hides many of the differences between the multiple OpenGL ES versions supported by iOS devices. Using `GLKBaseEffect` in your application reduces the amount of code you need to write. The implementation of `OpenGLES_Ch2_1ViewController` explains `GLKBaseEffect` in more detail.

The OpenGLES_Ch2_1ViewController Class Implementation

The `OpenGLES_Ch2_1ViewController.m` file was originally generated by Xcode when the project was first created but is modified for the example. `OpenGLES_Ch2_1ViewController.m` contains the Objective-C implementation for the `OpenGLES_Ch2_1ViewController` class. Only three methods are defined in the implementation: `-viewDidLoad`, `-glkView:drawInRect:`, and `-viewDidUnload`. This section explains the three methods in detail. Examples in this chapter and subsequent chapters reuse and build upon code from this example. The implementation starts as follows:

```
//
//  OpenGLES_Ch2_1ViewController.m
//  OpenGLES_Ch2_1
//

#import "OpenGLES_Ch2_1ViewController.h"

@implementation OpenGLES_Ch2_1ViewController

@synthesize baseEffect;
```

The @synthesize baseEffect; expression directs the Objective-C compiler to automatically generate accessor methods for the baseEffect property. An alternative to using the @synthesize expression is to explicitly implement appropriately named accessor methods in code. No reason exists to explicitly implement the accessors for this example because all the standard accessor behaviors apply. The accessors should only be explicitly written when storage for the property needs to be handled specially or changes to the property's value invoke custom application logic.

The next code in OpenGLES_Ch2_1ViewController.m defines the SceneVertex type as a C structure that stores a positionCoords member of type GLKVector3. Recall from Chapter 1 that vertex positions can be expressed in the form of a vector from the coordinate system origin. GLKit's GLKVector3 type stores three coordinates: X, Y, and Z.

The vertices variable is as an ordinary C array initialized with vertex data to define a triangle.

```
/////////////////////////////////////////////////////////////////
// This data type is used to store information for each vertex
typedef struct {
    GLKVector3  positionCoords;
}
SceneVertex;


/////////////////////////////////////////////////////////////////
// Define vertex data for a triangle to use in example
static const SceneVertex vertices[] =
{
    {{-0.5f, -0.5f, 0.0}}, // lower left corner
    {{ 0.5f, -0.5f, 0.0}}, // lower right corner
    {{-0.5f,  0.5f, 0.0}}  // upper left corner
};
```

The vertex position coordinates for this example are chosen because the default visible coordinate system for an OpenGL context stretches from –1.0 to 1.0 along each of the X, Y, and Z axes. The example triangle's coordinates place it in the center of the visible coordinate system and aligned with the plane formed by the X and Y axes. Figure 2.7 shows the triangle defined by vertices[] within a cube that represents the visible portion of the default OpenGL ES coordinate system.

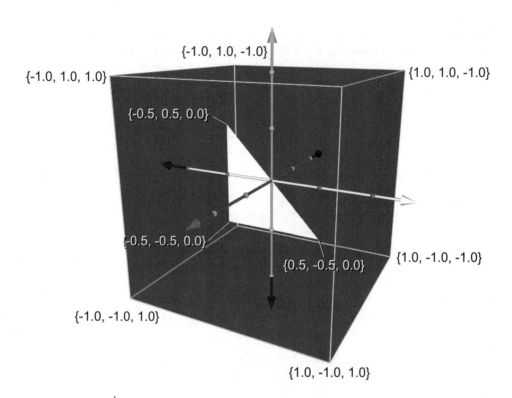

{-1.0, 1.0, -1.0}

{-1.0, 1.0, 1.0}

{1.0, 1.0, -1.0}

{-0.5, 0.5, 0.0}

{-0.5, -0.5, 0.0}

{0.5, -0.5, 0.0}

{1.0, -1.0, -1.0}

{-1.0, -1.0, 1.0}

{1.0, -1.0, 1.0}

Figure 2.7   Triangle vertices in the default OpenGL ES coordinate system.

-viewDidLoad

The following –viewDidLoad method provides the triangle's vertex data to OpenGL
ES. The –viewDidLoad method is inherited from the GLKViewController class and
is called automatically when the application's GLKView instance associated with the
GLKViewController is loaded from a storyboard file. OpenGLES_Ch2_1ViewController
provides its own implementation of –viewDidLoad that first calls the inherited super class's
implementation:

```
/////////////////////////////////////////////////////////////////
// Called when the view controller's view is loaded
// Perform initialization before the view is asked to draw
- (void)viewDidLoad
{
   [super viewDidLoad];
```

```
// Verify the type of view created automatically by the
// Interface Builder storyboard
GLKView *view = (GLKView *)self.view;
NSAssert([view isKindOfClass:[GLKView class]],
    @"View controller's view is not a GLKView");

// Create an OpenGL ES 2.0 context and provide it to the
// view
view.context = [[EAGLContext alloc]
    initWithAPI:kEAGLRenderingAPIOpenGLES2];

// Make the new context current
[EAGLContext setCurrentContext:view.context];

// Create a base effect that provides standard OpenGL ES 2.0
// Shading Language programs and set constants to be used for
// all subsequent rendering
self.baseEffect = [[GLKBaseEffect alloc] init];
self.baseEffect.useConstantColor = GL_TRUE;
self.baseEffect.constantColor = GLKVector4Make(
    1.0f, // Red
    1.0f, // Green
    1.0f, // Blue
    1.0f);// Alpha

// Set the background color stored in the current context
glClearColor(0.0f, 0.0f, 0.0f, 1.0f); // background color

// Generate, bind, and initialize contents of a buffer to be
// stored in GPU memory
glGenBuffers(1,               // STEP 1
    &vertexBufferID);
glBindBuffer(GL_ARRAY_BUFFER,  // STEP 2
    vertexBufferID);
glBufferData(                 // STEP 3
    GL_ARRAY_BUFFER,  // Initialize buffer contents
    sizeof(vertices), // Number of bytes to copy
    vertices,         // Address of bytes to copy
    GL_STATIC_DRAW);  // Hint: cache in GPU memory
}
```

The −viewDidLoad method casts the value of its inherited view property to the GLKView class. Subclasses of GLKViewController like OpenGLES_Ch2_1ViewController only work correctly with GLKView instances or instances of GLKView subclasses. However, the example's storyboard files define which view is associated with the application's GLKViewController instance. A run-time check using the NSAssert() function verifies that the view loaded from a storyboard at runtime is indeed the correct kind of view. NSAssert() sends an error message to the debugger or iOS device console if the condition to be verified is false. NSAssert() also generates an NSInternalInconsistencyException that halts the application if not handled. In this example, there is no way to recover from an incorrect view loaded from a storyboard, so the best behavior is to halt the application at the point where the error is detected at runtime.

As introduced in Chapter 1, an OpenGL ES context stores the OpenGL ES state and controls how the GPU performs rendering operations. OpenGLES_Ch2_1ViewController's −viewDidLoad method allocates and initializes an instance of the built-in EAGLContext class, which encapsulates a platform-specific OpenGL ES context. The origin of the EAGL prefix has not been documented by Apple, but it presumably stands for "Embedded Apple GL." Apple's OpenGLES framework declares Objective-C classes and functions prefixed with EAGL and included with the iOS.

The context property of the application's GLKView instance needs to be set and made current before any other OpenGL ES configuration or rendering can occur. EAGLContext instances support either OpenGL ES version 1.1 or version 2.0. The examples in this book use version 2.0. The following lines allocate a new instance of EAGLContext and initialize it for OpenGL ES 2.0 using the constant in bold before assigning the view's context property:

```
view.context = [[EAGLContext alloc]
    initWithAPI:kEAGLRenderingAPIOpenGLES2];

// Make the new context current
[EAGLContext setCurrentContext:view.context];
```

It's possible for a single application to use multiple contexts. The EAGLContext method, +setCurrentContext:, sets the context that will be used for subsequent OpenGL ES operations. The "+" before the +setCurrentContext: method indicates that +setCurrentContext: is a "class method." In Objective-C, class methods are methods that can be called for the class itself even if there are no instances of the class.

Apple's OpenGLES.framework defines the kEAGLRenderingAPIOpenGLES2 constant used with EAGLContext's −initWithAPI: method. A kEAGLRenderingAPIOpenGLES1 constant exists as well. The OpenGL ES 2.0 standard differs substantially from earlier versions. In particular, OpenGL ES 2.0 omits many features and application support infrastructure defined in prior standards. Instead, OpenGL ES 2.0 provides a new, more flexible concept of programmable GPUs. Apple recommends using OpenGL ES 2.0 for new applications because of the flexibility. Before the introduction of Apple's GLKit, OpenGL ES 2.0 required extra work up-front to program the GPU and recreate some of the convenient features missing from version 2.0 that version 1.1 includes by default. GLKit now replaces most of the OpenGL ES 1.1 infrastructure missing from the 2.0 standard and makes OpenGL ES 2.0 as easy to start using as version 1.1.

The −viewDidLoad method next sets the OpenGLES_Ch2_1ViewController's baseEffect property to an allocated and initialized instance of the class GLKBaseEffect and sets some of the GLKBaseEffect instance's properties to values appropriate for the example.

```
// Create a base effect that provides standard OpenGL ES 2.0
// Shading Language programs and set constants to be used for
```

```
// all subsequent rendering
self.baseEffect = [[GLKBaseEffect alloc] init];
self.baseEffect.useConstantColor = GL_TRUE;
```

The GLKBaseEffect class provides methods that control OpenGL ES rendering regardless of the OpenGL ES version being used. Under the surface, OpenGL ES 1.1 and OpenGL ES 2.0 work very differently. Version 2.0 executes specialized custom programs on the GPU. Without GLKit and the GLKBaseEffect class, writing a small GPU program in OpenGL ES 2.0 "Shading Language" would be necessary to make this simple example work. GLKBaseEffect automatically constructs GPU programs when needed and greatly simplifies the examples in this book.

Several ways exist to control the color of rendered pixels. This application's GLKBaseEffect instance uses a constant opaque white color for the triangle to be rendered. That means that every pixel in the triangle has the same color. The following code to set the constant color uses a C data structure, GLKVector4, defined in GLKit to store four color component values:

```
self.baseEffect.constantColor = GLKVector4Make(
    1.0f, // Red
    1.0f, // Green
    1.0f, // Blue
    1.0f);// Alpha

    // Set the background color stored in the current context
    glClearColor(0.0f, 0.0f, 0.0f, 1.0f); // background color
```

The first three color components are Red, Green, and Blue as described by Figure 1.2 in Chapter 1. The fourth value, Alpha, determines how opaque or translucent each pixel should be. The Alpha component is explained in more detail in Chapter 3. Setting Red, Green, and Blue to full intensity, 1.0, makes the color white. Setting the Alpha component to full intensity makes the color fully opaque. The Red, Green, Blue, and Alpha values are collectively called an *RGBA* color. The GLKVector4Make() function returns a GLKit GLKVector4 structure initialized with the specified values.

The glClearColor() function sets the current OpenGL ES context's "clear color" to opaque black. The clear color consists of RGBA color component values used to initialize the color elements of every pixel whenever the context's frame buffer is cleared.

Chapter 1 introduced the concept of buffers for exchanging data between central processor unit (CPU)-controlled memory and GPU controlled memory. The vertex position data that defines the triangle to be drawn must be sent to the GPU to be rendered. There are seven steps to creating and using a *vertex attribute array buffer* that stores vertex data. The first three steps consist of

1. Generate a unique identifier for the buffer.

2. Bind the buffer for subsequent operations.

3. Copy data into the buffer.

The following code from the implementation of –viewDidLoad performs the first three steps:

```
// Generate, bind, and initialize contents of a buffer to be
// stored in GPU memory
glGenBuffers(1,                 // STEP 1
   &vertexBufferID);
glBindBuffer(GL_ARRAY_BUFFER,   // STEP 2
   vertexBufferID);
glBufferData(                   // STEP 3
   GL_ARRAY_BUFFER,   // Initialize buffer contents
   sizeof(vertices), // Number of bytes to copy
   vertices,          // Address of bytes to copy
   GL_STATIC_DRAW);   // Hint: cache in GPU memory
```

For step 1, the glGenBuffers() function accepts a first parameter to specify the number of buffer identifiers to generate followed by a pointer to the memory where the generated identifiers are stored. In this case, one identifier is generated, and it's stored in the vertexBufferID instance variable.

In step 2, the glBindBuffer() function "binds" or makes the buffer for the specified identifier into the "current" buffer. OpenGL ES stores buffer identifiers for different types of buffers in different parts of the current OpenGL ES context. However, there can only be one buffer of each type bound at any one time. If two vertex attribute array buffers were used in this example, they could not both be bound into the context at the same time.

The first argument to glBindBuffer() is a constant identifying which type of buffer to bind. The OpenGL ES 2.0 implementation of glBindBuffer() only supports two types of buffer, GL_ARRAY_BUFFER and GL_ELEMENT_ARRAY_BUFFER. The GL_ELEMENT_ARRAY_BUFFER type is explained in Chapter 6, "Animation." The GL_ARRAY_BUFFER type specifies an array of vertex attributes such as the positions of triangle vertices used in this example. The second argument to glBindBuffer() is the identifier of the buffer to be bound.

Note

Buffer identifiers are actually unsigned integers. The value zero is reserved to mean "no buffer." Calling glBindBuffer() with 0 as the second argument configures the current context so that no buffer of the specified type is bound. Buffer identifiers are also called "names" in OpenGL ES documentation.

In step 3, the glBufferData() function copies the application's vertex data into the current context's bound vertex buffer:

```
glBufferData(                   // STEP 3
   GL_ARRAY_BUFFER,   // Initialize buffer contents
   sizeof(vertices), // Number of bytes to copy
   vertices,          // Address of bytes to copy
   GL_STATIC_DRAW);   // Hint: cache in GPU memory
```

The first argument to glBufferData() specifies which of the bound buffers in the current context to update. The second argument specifies the number of bytes to be copied into the buffer. The third argument is the address of the bytes to be copied. Finally, the fourth argument hints how the buffer is likely to be used for future operations. Providing the GL_STATIC_DRAW hint tells the context that the contents of the buffer are suitable to be copied into GPU-controlled memory once and won't be changed very often if ever. That information helps OpenGL ES optimize memory use. Using GL_DYNAMIC_DRAW as the hint tells the context that the data in the buffer changes frequently and might prompt OpenGL ES to handle buffer storage differently.

-glkView:drawInRect:

Whenever a GLKView instance needs to be redrawn, it makes the OpenGL ES context stored in the view's context property current. If necessary, the GLKView instance binds the frame buffer shared with a Core Animation layer, performs other standard OpenGL ES configuration, and sends a message to invoke OpenGLES_Ch2_1ViewController's -glkView:drawInRect: method. The -glkView:drawInRect: method is a delegate method for the GLKView class. As a subclass of GLKViewController, OpenGLES_Ch2_1ViewController automatically makes itself the delegate of the associated view loaded from a storyboard file.

The following implementation of the delegate method tells baseEffect to prepare the current OpenGL ES context for drawing with attributes and Shading Language programs generated by baseEffect. Then, a call to the OpenGL ES function, glClear(), sets the color of every pixel in the currently bound frame buffer's pixel color render buffer to the values previously set with the glClearColor() function. As described in the "Drawing a Core Animation Layer with OpenGL ES" section of this chapter, the frame buffer might have other attached buffers in addition to the pixel color render buffer, and if other buffers are used, they can be cleared by specifying different arguments to the glClear() function. Clearing effectively sets every pixel in the frame buffer to the background color.

```
/////////////////////////////////////////////////////////////////
// GLKView delegate method: Called by the view controller's view
// whenever Cocoa Touch asks the view controller's view to
// draw itself. (In this case, render into a Frame Buffer that
// shares memory with a Core Animation Layer)
- (void)glkView:(GLKView *)view drawInRect:(CGRect)rect
{
   [self.baseEffect prepareToDraw];

   // Clear Frame Buffer (erase previous drawing)
   glClear(GL_COLOR_BUFFER_BIT);

   // Enable use of currently bound vertex buffer
   glEnableVertexAttribArray(        // STEP 4
      GLKVertexAttribPosition);

   glVertexAttribPointer(            // STEP 5
```

```
    GLKVertexAttribPosition,
    3,                      // three components per vertex
    GL_FLOAT,               // data is floating point
    GL_FALSE,               // no fixed point scaling
    sizeof(SceneVertex),    // no gaps in data
    NULL);                  // NULL tells GPU to start at
                            // beginning of bound buffer

  // Draw triangles using the first three vertices in the
  // currently bound vertex buffer
  glDrawArrays(GL_TRIANGLES,       // STEP 6
    0,  // Start with first vertex in currently bound buffer
    3); // Use three vertices from currently bound buffer
}
```

After the frame buffer has been cleared, it's time to draw the example's triangle using vertex data stored in the currently bound OpenGL ES `GL_ARRAY_BUFFER` buffer. The first three steps for using a buffer were performed in the `–viewDidLoad` method. As described in Chapter 1, the `OpenGLES_Ch2_1ViewController`'s `–glkView:drawInRect:` method performs these steps:

4. Enable.

5. Set pointers.

6. Draw.

In step 4, vertex buffer rendering operations are enabled by calling `glEnableVertexAttrib-Array()`. Each of the rendering operations supported by OpenGL ES can be independently enabled or disabled with settings stored within the current OpenGL ES context.

In step 5, the `glVertexAttribPointer()` function tells OpenGL ES where vertex data is located and how to interpret the data stored for each vertex. In this example, the first argument to `glVertexAttribPointer()` specifies that the currently bound buffer contains position information for each vertex. The second argument specifies that there are three components to each position. The third argument tells OpenGL ES that each component is stored as a floating point value. The fourth argument tells OpenGL ES whether fixed point data can be scaled or not. None of the examples in this book use fixed point data, so the argument value is `GL_FALSE`.

Note

Fixed-point data types are supported by OpenGL ES as an alternative to floating point. Fixed-point types sacrifice precision to conserve memory. All modern GPUs are optimized to use floating point and end up converting supplied fixed-point data to floating-point before use. Therefore, it reduces GPU effort and improves precision to consistently use floating-point values.

The fifth argument is called the "stride." It specifies how many bytes are stored for each vertex. In other words, stride specifies the number of bytes that the GPU must skip to get from the beginning of memory for one vertex to the beginning of memory for the next vertex. Specifying the `sizeof(GLKVector3)` indicates that there are no "extra" bytes in the buffer: The vertex position data is tightly packed. It's possible for a vertex buffer to store extra data besides the X,Y, Z coordinates of each vertex position. The vertex data memory representations in Figure 2.8 show some of the options for vertex storage. The first example depicts 3D vertex position coordinates tightly backed in 12 bytes per vertex like in the OpenGLES_Ch2_1 example. An alternative arrangement shows extra bytes stored for each vertex so there are gaps in memory between the position coordinates of one vertex and the next.

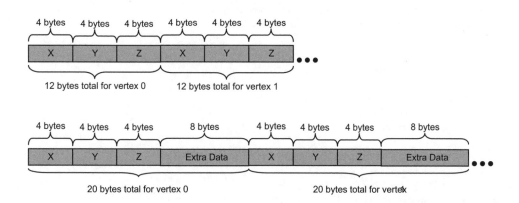

Figure 2.8   Some potential arrangements of vertex data in vertex array buffer memory.

The final argument to `glVertexAttribPointer()` is NULL, which tells OpenGL ES to access vertex data starting from the beginning of the currently bound vertex buffer.

In step 6, drawing is performed by calling `glDrawArrays()`. The first argument to `glDrawArrays()` tells the GPU what to do with the vertex data in the bound vertex buffer. This example instructs OpenGL ES to render triangles. The second and third arguments to `glDrawArrays()` respectively specify the position within the buffer of the first vertex to render and the number of vertices to render. At this point, the scene shown in Figure 2.3 has been fully rendered or at least it will be when the GPU gets around to it. Remember that the GPU operates asynchronously to the CPU. All the code in this example runs on the central processing unit (CPU) and sends commands to the GPU for future processing. The GPU may also process commands sent by iOS via Core Animation, so how much total processing the GPU has to perform at any given moment isn't always obvious.

–viewDidUnload

The last method in the implementation of `OpenGLES_Ch2_1ViewController` is –viewDidUnload. Just like –viewDidLoad is called automatically when the view controller's associated view is loaded, the –viewDidUnload method is called if the view is ever unloaded. Unloaded views can't draw, so any OpenGL ES buffers that are only needed for drawing can be safely deleted.

Step 7 is to delete the vertex buffer and context that are no longer needed. Setting vertexBufferID to 0 avoids any chance of using an identifier that is invalid after the corresponding buffer has been deleted. Setting the view's context property to nil and setting the current context to nil lets Cocoa Touch reclaim any memory or other resources used by the context.

```
/////////////////////////////////////////////////////////////////
// Called when the view controller's view has been unloaded
// Perform clean-up that is possible when you know the view
// controller's view won't be asked to draw again soon.
- (void)viewDidUnload
{
   [super viewDidUnload];

   // Make the view's context current
   GLKView *view = (GLKView *)self.view;
   [EAGLContext setCurrentContext:view.context];

   // Delete buffers that aren't needed when view is unloaded
   if (0 != vertexBufferID)
   {
      glDeleteBuffers (1,              // STEP 7
                    &vertexBufferID);
      vertexBufferID = 0;
   }

   // Stop using the context created in -viewDidLoad
   ((GLKView *)self.view).context = nil;
   [EAGLContext setCurrentContext:nil];
}

@end
```

Supporting Files

The group of .png files shown in Figure 2.6 are the OpenGLES_Ch2_1 application's icons. The operating system selects the correct icon whether running on iPhone, iPod Touch, or iPad. The OpenGL_ES_for_iOS_72x72.png file contains the image of the icon used on the iPad. The OpenGL_ES_for_iOS_114x114.png and OpenGL_ES_for_iOS_57x57.png files contain icon images used on the iPod Touch and iPhone. The .png extension stands for Portable Network Graphics (PNG). PNG files are natively supported by iOS devices and store images according to the International Organization for Standardization (ISO 15948) specification.

The OpenGLES_Ch2_1 Example

The `OpenGLES_Ch2_1-Info.plist` file is generated automatically by Xcode when a new project is created. `OpenGLES_Ch2_1-Info.plist` stores configuration information such as the application's version number, the names of storyboard files to use, and the names of icon files. Adding application-specific information to the file is possible, but the OpenGLES_Ch2_1 application doesn't need any nonstandard information. The configuration file is read once by the application each time the application starts.

The `InfoPlist.strings` file is generated automatically by Xcode when a new project is created. `InfoPlist.strings` contains localized versions of strings used in `OpenGLES_Ch2_1-Info.plist`. Localization refers to the practice of providing text and images specialized for different language and cultural groups. `InfoPlist.strings` provides a way for the same application to present different icons and user interfaces based on the user's location.

The main() Function

The `main.m` file is automatically generated by Xcode when a new project is created and contains the implementation of the application's `main()` function. The `main()` function is called by the operating system to start ANSI C, C++, and Objective-C programs running. The generated `main.m` file contains the following code:

```
//
//  main.m
//  OpenGLES_Ch2_1
//


#import <UIKit/UIKit.h>

#import "OpenGLES_Ch2_1AppDelegate.h"

int main(int argc, char *argv[])
{
    @autoreleasepool
    {
        return UIApplicationMain(argc, argv, nil,
            NSStringFromClass([OpenGLES_Ch2_1AppDelegate class]));
    }
}
```

The `main()` function uses the Objective-C `@autoreleasepool` keyword to enable Automatic Reference Counting, a compiler-level language feature that provides automatic object memory management in Cocoa Touch applications. The `main()` function also calls the `UIApplicationMain()` function, which creates the application's key objects including the required `UIApplication` instance and starts processing user events. The `NSStringFromClass([OpenGLES_Ch2_1AppDelegate class])` expression specifies the name of the class of the application delegate to be used with the newly created `UIApplication` instance. `UIApplication` creates a `UIWindow` that fills the whole display and loads one or more storyboard files to construct the application's user interface. The `UIApplicationMain()` function hands off execution to `UIApplication` and doesn't return until the application quits.

Pre-Compiled Header

The `OpenGLES_Ch2_1-Prefix.pch` file is generated automatically by Xcode and improves the speed of compiling the example application. The `.pch` extension stands for "pre-compiled header."

Frameworks and Products

Frameworks are system libraries and resources used by iOS applications. The Frameworks folder in the Xcode files list specifies which frameworks are used by an application. The OpenGLES_Ch2_1 example uses the `OpenGLES.framework`, `QuartzCore.framework`, `GLKit.framework`, `UIKit.framework`, `Foundation.framework`, and `CoreGraphics.framework`.

The Products folder contains the results produced by Xcode when compiling the application(s) specified in the Xcode project.

Deep Dive: How Does GLKView Work?

Prior to the introduction of GLKit with iOS 5, it was necessary for each developer to create a `UIView` subclass similar to `GLKView`. Apple doesn't provide source code for GLKit classes, but deducing how the major features of a class like `GLKView` might be implemented in terms of OpenGL ES is possible. The remainder of this section and the OpenGLES_Ch2_2 example introduce the `AGLKView` class and its partial reimplementation of `GLKView`. The `AGLKView` class shouldn't be used in production code; it's provided solely to dispel some mystery regarding the interaction of `GLKView`, Core Animation, and OpenGL ES. For almost every purpose, relying on Apple's optimized, tested, and future-proof implementation of GLKit is best. Feel free to skip to the next section if a deep dive into `GLKView` doesn't interest you.

> **Note**
>
> If you choose not to use Apple's GLKit in your applications, you will need to use this `AGLKView` example or create a similar class yourself. The rest of the examples in this book assume GLKit is used. Therefore, `AGLKView` does not appear in any other examples in this book.

`AGLKView` in the OpenGLES_Ch2_2 example subclasses the Cocoa Touch `UIView` class and declares the following interface, similar to Apple's `GLKView` class interface:

```
//
//   AGLKView.h
//   OpenGLES_Ch2_1
//

#import <UIKit/UIKit.h>
```

```
#import <OpenGLES/ES2/gl.h>
#import <OpenGLES/ES2/glext.h>

@class EAGLContext;
@protocol AGLKViewDelegate;


/////////////////////////////////////////////////////////////////
// This subclass of the Cocoa Touch UIView class uses OpenGL ES
// to render pixel data into a Frame Buffer that shares pixel
// color storage with a Core Animation Layer.
@interface AGLKView : UIView
{
    EAGLContext    *context;
    GLuint         defaultFrameBuffer;
    GLuint         colorRenderBuffer;
    GLint          drawableWidth;
    GLint          drawableHeight;
}

@property (nonatomic, weak) IBOutlet id <AGLKViewDelegate> delegate;
@property (nonatomic, retain) EAGLContext *context;
@property (nonatomic, readonly) NSInteger drawableWidth;
@property (nonatomic, readonly) NSInteger drawableHeight;

- (void)display;

@end


#pragma mark - AGLKViewDelegate

@protocol AGLKViewDelegate <NSObject>

@required
- (void)glkView:(AGLKView *)view drawInRect:(CGRect)rect;

@end
```

The AGLKViewDelegate protocol specifies one method that any delegate of an AGLKView must implement. Each AGLKView instance sends the –glkView:drawInRect: message to its delegate if the view's delegate property is not nil.

The implementation of AGLKView is straightforward but overrides several methods from UIView and adds some methods to support drawing with OpenGL ES:

```
//
//  AGLKView.m
```

```
//  OpenGLES_Ch2_1
//

#import "AGLKView.h"
#import <QuartzCore/QuartzCore.h>


@implementation AGLKView

@synthesize delegate;
@synthesize context;

/////////////////////////////////////////////////////////////////
// This method returns the CALayer subclass to be used by
// CoreAnimation with this view
+ (Class)layerClass
{
    return [CAEAGLLayer class];
}
```

Every UIView instance has an associated Core Animation layer that is automatically created by Cocoa Touch as needed. Cocoa Touch calls the +layerClass method to find out what type of layer to create. In this sample, the AGLKView class overrides the implementation inherited from UIView. When Cocoa Touch calls AGLKView's implementation of +layerClass, it's told to use an instance of the CAEAGLLayer class instead of an ordinary CALayer. CAEAGLLayer is one of the standard layer classes provided by Core Animation. CAEAGLLayer shares its pixel color storage with an OpenGL ES frame buffer.

The next blocks of code in AGLKView.m implement the −initWithFrame:context: method and override the inherited −initWithCoder: method. The −initWithFrame:context: method initializes instances allocated manually through code. The −initWithCoder: method is one of the Cocoa Touch standard methods for initializing objects. Cocoa Touch automatically calls −initWithCoder: as part of the process of un-archiving an object that was previously archived into a file. Archiving and un-archiving operations are called serializing and deserializing in other popular object-oriented frameworks such as Java and Microsoft's .NET. The instance of AGLKView used in this example is automatically loaded (also known as un-archived) from the application's storyboard files when the OpenGLES_Ch2_2 application is launched.

The code in the following two methods is nearly identical. Only one or the other of the methods is called for each instance initialized. Both methods first give the super class, UIView, a chance to perform initialization, and then the methods perform one-time initialization of Core Animation and the OpenGL ES context needed for the example. The first step is to initialize a local pointer to the view's Core Animation layer as follows:

```
CAEAGLLayer *eaglLayer = (CAEAGLLayer *)self.layer;
```

The (CAEAGLLayer *) C Language cast is needed because UIView's –layer method returns a pointer to a CALayer instance. Within the implementation of the AGLKView class, it's known that the true layer type is CAEAGLLayer, so the cast forcing the compiler to accept the CAEAGLLayer type is safe.

```objc
/////////////////////////////////////////////////////////////////
// This method is designated initializer for the class
- (id)initWithFrame:(CGRect)frame context:(EAGLContext *)aContext;
{
   if ((self = [super initWithFrame:frame]))
   {
      CAEAGLLayer *eaglLayer = (CAEAGLLayer *)self.layer;

      eaglLayer.drawableProperties =
         [NSDictionary dictionaryWithObjectsAndKeys:
            [NSNumber numberWithBool:NO],
            kEAGLDrawablePropertyRetainedBacking,
            kEAGLColorFormatRGBA8,
            kEAGLDrawablePropertyColorFormat,
            nil];

      self.context = aContext;
   }

   return self;
}


/////////////////////////////////////////////////////////////////
// This method is called automatically to initialize each Cocoa
// Touch object as the object is unarchived from an
// Interface Builder .xib or .storyboard file.
- (id)initWithCoder:(NSCoder*)coder
{
   if ((self = [super initWithCoder:coder]))
   {
      CAEAGLLayer *eaglLayer = (CAEAGLLayer *)self.layer;

      eaglLayer.drawableProperties =
         [NSDictionary dictionaryWithObjectsAndKeys:
            [NSNumber numberWithBool:NO],
            kEAGLDrawablePropertyRetainedBacking,
            kEAGLColorFormatRGBA8,
            kEAGLDrawablePropertyColorFormat,
            nil];
```

```
    }

    return self;
}
```

Each of AGLKView's initialization methods uses a temporary NSDictionary instance to set eaglLayer's drawableProperties property. Dictionaries store collections of key value pairs. Each value can be quickly retrieved using the corresponding key. NSDictionary is a Cocoa Touch class used in this case by instances of the CAEAGLLayer class to store information about the type of OpenGL ES frame buffer to be used with the layer.

```
eaglLayer.drawableProperties =
    [NSDictionary dictionaryWithObjectsAndKeys:
        [NSNumber numberWithBool:NO],
        kEAGLDrawablePropertyRetainedBacking,
        kEAGLColorFormatRGBA8,
        kEAGLDrawablePropertyColorFormat,
        nil];
```

The example sets the kEAGLDrawablePropertyRetainedBacking key's value to NO and sets the kEAGLDrawablePropertyColorFormat key's value to kEAGLColorFormatRGBA8. Not using "retained" backing tells Core Animation to redraw the entire content of the layer whenever any part of the layer needs to be presented onscreen. In other words, the code tells Core Animation, "Don't retain any prior drawing for reuse later." The RGBA8 color format tells Core Animation to store RGBA values using 8 bits for each color component of every pixel in the layer.

Two manually implemented accessor methods set and return the view's platform-specific OpenGL ES context. Setting the context causes several side effects because AGLKView instances need to create and configure a frame buffer and a pixel color render buffer for use with the view's Core Animation layer. The context stores the buffers. Therefore, changing the view's context invalidates any previously created buffers and requires creation and configuration of new buffers.

The context affected by the buffer operations is made the current context before OpenGL ES functions are called. Notice in the following code that creating frame buffers and render buffers follows some of the same steps applied to other types of buffer, including the vertex array buffer in the OpenGLES_Ch2_1 example. A new step calls the glFramebufferRenderbuffer() function to configure the currently bound frame buffer for storing rendered pixel colors in colorRenderBuffer.

```
/////////////////////////////////////////////////////////////////
// This method sets the receiver's OpenGL ES Context. If the
// receiver already has a different Context, this method deletes
// OpenGL ES Frame Buffer resources in the old Context and the
// recreates them in the new Context.
- (void)setContext:(EAGLContext *)aContext
{
```

```
    if(context != aContext)
    {   // Delete any buffers previously created in old Context
        [EAGLContext setCurrentContext:context];

        if (0 != defaultFrameBuffer)
        {
            glDeleteFramebuffers(1, &defaultFrameBuffer); // Step 7
            defaultFrameBuffer = 0;
        }

        if (0 != colorRenderBuffer)
        {
            glDeleteRenderbuffers(1, &colorRenderBuffer); // Step 7
            colorRenderBuffer = 0;
        }

        context = aContext;

        if(nil != context)
        {   // Configure the new Context with required buffers
            context = aContext;
            [EAGLContext setCurrentContext:context];

            glGenFramebuffers(1, &defaultFrameBuffer);    // Step 1
            glBindFramebuffer(                            // Step 2
                GL_FRAMEBUFFER,
                defaultFrameBuffer);

            glGenRenderbuffers(1, &colorRenderBuffer);    // Step 1
            glBindRenderbuffer(                           // Step 2
                GL_RENDERBUFFER,
                colorRenderBuffer);

            // Attach color render buffer to bound Frame Buffer
            glFramebufferRenderbuffer(
                GL_FRAMEBUFFER,
                GL_COLOR_ATTACHMENT0,
                GL_RENDERBUFFER,
                colorRenderBuffer);
        }
    }
}


/////////////////////////////////////////////////////////////////
// This method returns the receiver's OpenGL ES Context
- (EAGLContext *)context
```

```
{
   return context;
}
```

The following −display method makes the view's context current, tells OpenGL ES that rendering fills the entire frame buffer, calls the view's −drawRect: method to actually draw using OpenGL ES functions, and then tells the context to coordinate presentation and mixing of the frame buffer's pixel color render buffer with any other pertinent layers via the Core Animation Compositor.

```
/////////////////////////////////////////////////////////////////
// Calling this method tells the receiver to redraw the contents
// of its associated OpenGL ES Frame Buffer. This method
// configures OpenGL ES and then calls -drawRect:
- (void)display;
{
   [EAGLContext setCurrentContext:self.context];
   glViewport(0, 0, self.drawableWidth, self.drawableHeight);

   [self drawRect:[self bounds]];

   [self.context presentRenderbuffer:GL_RENDERBUFFER];
}
```

The glViewport() function can be used to control rendering to a subset of the frame buffer, but in this example uses the entire frame buffer.

The −drawRect: method calls the delegate's -glkView:drawInRect: if the view's delegate property is not nil. Without a delegate, AGLKView doesn't draw anything. A subclass of AGLKView could override the inherited implementation of −drawRect: to draw even when no delegate is assigned. The arguments to -glkView:drawInRect: are the view to be drawn and a rectangle encompassing the entire area of the view.

```
/////////////////////////////////////////////////////////////////
// This method is called automatically whenever the receiver
// needs to redraw the contents of its associated OpenGL ES
// Frame Buffer. This method should not be called directly. Call
// -display instead which configures OpenGL ES before calling
// -drawRect:
- (void)drawRect:(CGRect)rect
{
   if(self.delegate)
   {
      [self.delegate glkView:self drawInRect:[self bounds]];
   }
}
```

Cocoa Touch calls the following —layoutSubviews method whenever the receiving view resizes. The view's attached frame buffer and pixel color render buffer depend on the size of the view. Views automatically resize associated layers. The context's —renderbufferStorage:fromDrawable: method resizes the view's buffers to match the layer's new size.

```
/////////////////////////////////////////////////////////////////
// This method is called automatically whenever a UIView is
// resized including just after the view is added to a UIWindow.
- (void)layoutSubviews
{
   CAEAGLLayer   *eaglLayer = (CAEAGLLayer *)self.layer;

   // Initialize the current Frame Buffer's pixel color buffer
   // so that it shares the corresponding Core Animation Layer's
   // pixel color storage.
   [context renderbufferStorage:GL_RENDERBUFFER
      fromDrawable:eaglLayer];

   // Make the Color Render Buffer the current buffer for display
   glBindRenderbuffer(GL_RENDERBUFFER, colorRenderBuffer);

   // Check for any errors configuring the render buffer
   GLenum status = glCheckFramebufferStatus(
      GL_FRAMEBUFFER) ;

   if(status != GL_FRAMEBUFFER_COMPLETE)
   {
      NSLog(@"failed to make complete frame buffer object %x",
         status);
   }
}
```

The —drawableWidth and —drawableHeight methods are accessors for their respective properties. They are implemented to obtain and return the dimensions of the current context's frame buffer's pixel color render buffer via the OpenGL ES glGetRenderbufferParameteriv() function.

```
/////////////////////////////////////////////////////////////////
// This method returns the width in pixels of current context's
// Pixel Color Render Buffer
- (NSInteger)drawableWidth;
{
   GLint          backingWidth;

   glGetRenderbufferParameteriv(
      GL_RENDERBUFFER,
      GL_RENDERBUFFER_WIDTH,
```

```
        &backingWidth);

    return (NSInteger)backingWidth;
}



/////////////////////////////////////////////////////////////////
// This method returns the height in pixels of current context's
// Pixel Color Render Buffer
- (NSInteger)drawableHeight;
{
    GLint          backingHeight;

    glGetRenderbufferParameteriv(
        GL_RENDERBUFFER,
        GL_RENDERBUFFER_HEIGHT,
        &backingHeight);

    return (NSInteger)backingHeight;
}
```

Finally, Cocoa Touch automatically calls the –dealloc method whenever an object can be de-allocated and its resources returned to the operating system. AGLKView implements –dealloc to make sure the view's context does not remain current and then sets the context property to nil. If the view's context isn't being used anywhere else when the property becomes nil, the context is automatically de-allocated, too.

```
/////////////////////////////////////////////////////////////////
// This method is called automatically when the reference count
// for a Cocoa Touch object reaches zero.
- (void)dealloc
{
    // Make sure the receiver's OpenGL ES Context is not current
    if ([EAGLContext currentContext] == context)
    {
        [EAGLContext setCurrentContext:nil];
    }

    // Deletes the receiver's OpenGL ES Context
    context = nil;
}
```

@end

That's all there is to the AGLKView class. Example OpenGLES_Ch2_2 also contains an AGLKViewController class similar to GLKit's GLKViewController class. OpenGLES_Ch2_2 is identical to OpenGLES_Ch2_1 except that AGLKView and AGLKViewController are used instead of GLKit classes to show what the GLKit classes do behind the scenes.

Like GLKit's `GLKViewVontroller` class, `AGLKViewController` uses a Core Animation `CADisplayLink` object to schedule and perform periodic redraw of the controller's associated view. `CADisplayLink` is essentially a timer synchronized to the display update and can be configured to send a message on every display update or every other update, and so on. The period of the `CADisplayLink` timer is measured in display updates.

The display update rate is usually determined by the hardware of embedded devices and establishes the maximum number times per second that the contents of a frame buffer can be represented by pixels onscreen. Therefore, messages from `CADisplayLink` provide the ideal trigger to re-render a scene. Rendering any faster than the display refresh rate is a waste of effort because the user will never see the extra frame buffer updates between display refreshes.

Extrapolating from GLKit

GLKit classes encapsulate and simplify common interactions between Cocoa Touch applications and OpenGL ES. Just like speculating about how existing GLKit classes might be implemented is instructional, following Apple's precedent established with GLKit to create new classes is also possible.

The OpenGLES_Ch2_1 example in this chapter uses GLKit and only adds direct OpenGL ES function calls to accomplish two goals: clear the frame buffer, and use a vertex array buffer to draw. Just like GLKit's `GLKView` encapsulates frame buffer and layer management, example OpenGLES_Ch2_3 refactors the reusable OpenGL ES code from OpenGLES_Ch2_1 into two new classes: `AGLKContext` and `AGLKVertexAttribArrayBuffer`. This book uses the *AGLK* prefix on classes and functions to identify "additional" GLKit-like classes. It's entirely possible that a future version of GLKit might contain classes similar to the AGLK classes. Apple doesn't typically pre-announce enhancements to its frameworks, and even if Apple eventually implements classes with features of this book's AGLK classes, there's no guarantee Apple will do it in the same way.

The `AGLKContext` class is a simple subclass of the built-in `EAGLContext` class used in example OpenGLES_Ch2_1. For this example, `AGLKContext` only adds the `clearColor` property and a `–clear:` method that tells OpenGL ES to set every pixel color in the context's frame buffer to the component values of `clearColor`.

```
//
//  GLKContext.h
//  OpenGLES_Ch2_3
//

#import <GLKit/GLKit.h>

@interface AGLKContext : EAGLContext
{
    GLKVector4 clearColor;
}
```

```
@property (nonatomic, assign) GLKVector4
   clearColor;

- (void)clear:(GLbitfield)mask;

@end
```

The implementation of AGLKContext implements the —clear: method and accessors for the clearColor property. Setting the clearColor property results in a call to the OpenGL ES glClearColor() function. The —clear: method implementation calls glClear().

```
//
//  GLKContext.m
//  OpenGLES_Ch2_3
//

#import "AGLKContext.h"

@implementation AGLKContext

/////////////////////////////////////////////////////////////////
// This method sets the clear (background) RGBA color.
// The clear color is undefined until this method is called.
- (void)setClearColor:(GLKVector4)clearColorRGBA
{
   clearColor = clearColorRGBA;

   NSAssert(self == [[self class] currentContext],
      @"Receiving context required to be current context");

   glClearColor(
      clearColorRGBA.r,
      clearColorRGBA.g,
      clearColorRGBA.b,
      clearColorRGBA.a);
}


/////////////////////////////////////////////////////////////////
// Returns the clear (background) color set via -setClearColor:.
// If no clear color has been set via -setClearColor:, the
// return clear color is undefined.
- (GLKVector4)clearColor
{
   return clearColor;
}
```

```
/////////////////////////////////////////////////////////////
// This method instructs OpenGL ES to set all data in the
// current Context's Render Buffer(s) identified by mask to
// colors (values) specified via -setClearColor: and/or
// OpenGL ES functions for each Render Buffer type.
- (void)clear:(GLbitfield)mask
{
   NSAssert(self == [[self class] currentContext],
      @"Receiving context required to be current context");

   glClear(mask);
}

@end
```

The `GLKVertexAttribArrayBuffer` class encapsulates all seven steps for using OpenGL ES 2.0 vertex attribute array buffers (or just "vertex buffers" for short). The class reduces the number of OpenGL ES function calls that applications need to make. Reusing the `AGLKVertexAttribArrayBuffer` class in the examples for subsequent chapters shrinks the overall size of example code while minimizing the possibility for application errors related to the seven buffer management steps.

```
//
//  GLKVertexAttribArrayBuffer.h
//  OpenGLES_Ch2_3
//

#import <GLKit/GLKit.h>

@class AGLKElementIndexArrayBuffer;


@interface AGLKVertexAttribArrayBuffer : NSObject
{
   GLsizeiptr    stride;
   GLsizeiptr    bufferSizeBytes;
   GLuint        glName;
}

@property (nonatomic, readonly) GLuint
   glName;
@property (nonatomic, readonly) GLsizeiptr
   bufferSizeBytes;
@property (nonatomic, readonly) GLsizeiptr
   stride;

- (id)initWithAttribStride:(GLsizeiptr)stride
```

```
       numberOfVertices:(GLsizei)count
       data:(const GLvoid *)dataPtr
       usage:(GLenum)usage;

- (void)prepareToDrawWithAttrib:(GLuint)index
       numberOfCoordinates:(GLint)count
       attribOffset:(GLsizeiptr)offset
       shouldEnable:(BOOL)shouldEnable;

- (void)drawArrayWithMode:(GLenum)mode
       startVertexIndex:(GLint)first
       numberOfVertices:(GLsizei)count;
```

@end

The following implementation wraps the seven buffer management steps in three methods. The AGLKVertexAttribArrayBuffer class includes some error-checking code but otherwise comprises a straightforward reuse and refactoring of the buffer management code from example OpenGLES_Ch2_1. In addition to the three methods declared in the class interface, a —dealloc method implementation deletes an associated OpenGL ES buffer identifier.

```
//
//   GLKVertexAttribArrayBuffer.m
//   OpenGLES_Ch2_3
//

#import "AGLKVertexAttribArrayBuffer.h"

@interface AGLKVertexAttribArrayBuffer ()

@property (nonatomic, assign) GLsizeiptr
   bufferSizeBytes;

@property (nonatomic, assign) GLsizeiptr
   stride;

@end


@implementation AGLKVertexAttribArrayBuffer

@synthesize glName;
@synthesize bufferSizeBytes;
@synthesize stride;


/////////////////////////////////////////////////////////////////
```

```
// This method creates a vertex attribute array buffer in
// the current OpenGL ES context for the thread upon which this
// method is called.
- (id)initWithAttribStride:(GLsizeiptr)aStride
   numberOfVertices:(GLsizei)count
   data:(const GLvoid *)dataPtr
   usage:(GLenum)usage;
{
   NSParameterAssert(0 < aStride);
   NSParameterAssert(0 < count);
   NSParameterAssert(NULL != dataPtr);

   if(nil != (self = [super init]))
   {
      stride = aStride;
      bufferSizeBytes = stride * count;

      glGenBuffers(1,                   // STEP 1
         &glName);
      glBindBuffer(GL_ARRAY_BUFFER,    // STEP 2
         self.glName);
      glBufferData(                    // STEP 3
         GL_ARRAY_BUFFER,  // Initialize buffer contents
         bufferSizeBytes,  // Number of bytes to copy
         dataPtr,          // Address of bytes to copy
         usage);           // Hint: cache in GPU memory

      NSAssert(0 != glName, @"Failed to generate glName");
   }

   return self;
}


/////////////////////////////////////////////////////////////////
// A vertex attribute array buffer must be prepared when your
// application wants to use the buffer to render any geometry.
// When your application prepares an buffer, some OpenGL ES state
// is altered to allow bind the buffer and configure pointers.
- (void)prepareToDrawWithAttrib:(GLuint)index
   numberOfCoordinates:(GLint)count
   attribOffset:(GLsizeiptr)offset
   shouldEnable:(BOOL)shouldEnable
{
   NSParameterAssert((0 < count) && (count < 4));
   NSParameterAssert(offset < self.stride);
   NSAssert(0 != glName, @"Invalid glName");
```

```
    glBindBuffer(GL_ARRAY_BUFFER,      // STEP 2
        self.glName);

    if(shouldEnable)
    {
        glEnableVertexAttribArray(     // Step 4
            index);
    }

    glVertexAttribPointer(             // Step 5
        index,                // Identifies the attribute to use
        count,                // number of coordinates for attribute
        GL_FLOAT,             // data is floating point
        GL_FALSE,             // no fixed point scaling
        self.stride,          // total num bytes stored per vertex
        NULL + offset);       // offset from start of each vertex to
                              // first coord for attribute
}


/////////////////////////////////////////////////////////////////
// Submits the drawing command identified by mode and instructs
// OpenGL ES to use count vertices from the buffer starting from
// the vertex at index first. Vertex indices start at 0.
- (void)drawArrayWithMode:(GLenum)mode
    startVertexIndex:(GLint)first
    numberOfVertices:(GLsizei)count
{
    NSAssert(self.bufferSizeBytes >=
        ((first + count) * self.stride),
        @"Attempt to draw more vertex data than available.");

    glDrawArrays(mode, first, count); // Step 6
}


/////////////////////////////////////////////////////////////////
// This method deletes the receiver's buffer from the current
// Context when the receiver is deallocated.
- (void)dealloc
{
    // Delete buffer from current context
    if (0 != glName)
    {
        glDeleteBuffers (1,            // STEP 7
                         &glName);
        glName = 0;
```

```
    }
}

@end
```

Examine the implementation of the `OpenGLES_Ch2_3ViewController` class in example OpenGLES_Ch2_3 and compare it to the `OpenGLES_Ch2_1ViewController` class in example OpenGLES_Ch2_1. There are no direct OpenGL ES function calls in `OpenGLES_Ch2_3ViewController`. Additionally, some minor code style inconsistencies that you might have noticed in OpenGLES_Ch2_1 no longer exist. For example, OpenGLES_Ch2_1 uses a `GLKVector4` structure to set the constant color, but the OpenGL ES function call to set the clear color accepts RGBA color component values directly:

```
self.baseEffect.constantColor = GLKVector4Make(
    1.0f, // Red
    1.0f, // Green
    1.0f, // Blue
    1.0f);// Alpha

// Set the background color stored in the current context
glClearColor(0.0f, 0.0f, 0.0f, 1.0f); // background color
```

The `AGLKVertexAttribArrayBuffer` and `AGLKContext` classes extend the code style introduced by GLKit. Consequently, the OpenGLES_Ch2_3 example uses a consistent style:

```
self.baseEffect.constantColor = GLKVector4Make(
    1.0f, // Red
    1.0f, // Green
    1.0f, // Blue
    1.0f);// Alpha

// Set the background color stored in the current context
((AGLKContext *)view.context).clearColor = GLKVector4Make(
    0.0f, // Red
    0.0f, // Green
    0.0f, // Blue
    1.0f);// Alpha
```

The minor stylistic consistency improvement makes application code cleaner, but more importantly, wrapping OpenGL ES code in Objective-C classes enables easier code reuse. There is less chance of programmer error each time a new buffer is created and used. Applications that use multiple buffers have less code overall to write, test, and debug.

Summary

All graphical iOS applications contain Core Animation layers. All drawing occurs on layers. The Core Animation Compositor combines layers from the current application and the operating system to produce the final pixel colors in the OpenGL ES back frame buffer. The Core Animation Compositor then swaps the front and back buffers to make the combined content of the layers visible on the screen.

Native iOS applications use Apple's Cocoa Touch framework and are built using the Xcode IDE. An Xcode-generated `main.m` file contains code that sets up the Cocoa Touch application architecture and loads the application's user interface from storyboard files. A standard set of Cocoa Touch objects provides all the standard iOS application features. Application-specific features are implemented by modifying the application delegate or root view controller objects within the standard application architecture. Complex applications add many additional files to the Xcode project.

Cocoa Touch applications that use OpenGL ES either configure a custom `UIView` with a Core Animation layer that shares memory with an OpenGL ES frame buffer or use the built-in `GLKView` class. Apple's GLKit framework provides the `GLKView` to handle the details so developers aren't constantly reinventing `UIView` subclasses. An OpenGL ES context stores the current OpenGL ES state and controls the GPU hardware. Each `GLKView` instance requires a context.

The OpenGLES_Ch2_1 example in this chapter provides the basis for subsequent examples. All the code unique to the example is implemented in the `OpenGLES_Ch2_1ViewController` class. The application's storyboard files specify `GLKView` instances, which use the root view controller as a delegate. Delegates receive messages from other objects and perform application-specific operations or control other objects in response.

The example's `OpenGLES_Ch2_1ViewController` implementation contains three methods: one automatically called when the view is loaded from a storyboard file, one automatically called every time the view needs to be redrawn, and one automatically called when the view is unloaded. The three methods respectively initialize OpenGL ES by creating the necessary context and vertex buffer, use the context and vertex buffer to draw into a `GLKView`'s frame buffer that shares memory with a Core Animation layer, and delete the context and vertex buffer.

The `GLKBaseEffect` class hides many of the differences between OpenGL ES versions supported by iOS. When used with OpenGL ES 2.0, `GLKBaseEffect` generates Shading Language programs that run directly on the GPU. `GLKBaseEffect` enables programmers to focus on application features and graphics concepts without needing to learn Shading Language at the same time.

The OpenGLES_Ch2_3 example in this chapter refactors OpenGL ES function calls from example OpenGLES_Ch2_1 into the `AGLKVertexAttribArrayBuffer` and `AGLKContext` classes.

Chapter 3, "Textures," extends OpenGLES_Ch2_1 to make triangle rendering more interesting and powerful.

3

Textures

The examples in Chapter 2, "Making the Hardware Work for You," demonstrate how to render and display a white triangle with OpenGL ES 2.0. Real-life objects are seldom composed solely of white or any other solid color. OpenGL ES provides a way to specify different colors for every vertex in your geometry, but in practice, even triangles with multi-color vertices don't provide a sense of realism in rendered scenes. This chapter introduces a graphics technique called *texturing* that controls the color of every pixel in a rendered triangle.

Texturing is one of the most complex topics in computer graphics. This chapter introduces the concepts that underlay texturing and explains the commonly used options. Several examples progressively demonstrate the techniques.

What Is a Texture?

A *texture* is an OpenGL ES buffer that stores the color element values of an image. Figure 3.1 shows an image used as a texture by the examples in this chapter. Textures can be based on images of anything, including trees, faces, bricks, clouds, or machinery. Rendered scenes appear more natural when textures are applied to geometry so that complex combinations of triangles seem to be real objects instead of just colored facets.

Figure 3.1　An image used as an OpenGL ES texture.

The color values stored in a texture buffer potentially consume a lot of memory. Each embedded system defines a maximum memory size limit for textures. All iPhones and iPod Touch versions support textures generated from images with dimensions up to 1024 x 1024 pixels. All iPads and the most recent generations of the iPhone and iPod Touch support textures even larger. However, due to the relatively small amount of available memory in embedded systems, using the smallest image that still produces acceptable rendered results is a good practice.

When a texture buffer is initialized from an image, each pixel in the image becomes a *texel* in the texture. Like pixels, texels store color information. The distinction between pixels and texels is subtle: The term *pixel* typically describes an actual colored dot on a computer display, and as a result, pixels are often used as a unit of measurement. Saying that an image is 256 pixels wide and 256 pixels tall is correct. In contrast, texels exist in an imaginary mathematic coordinate system that has no size. Figure 3.2 shows a texture in the OpenGL ES texture coordinate system.

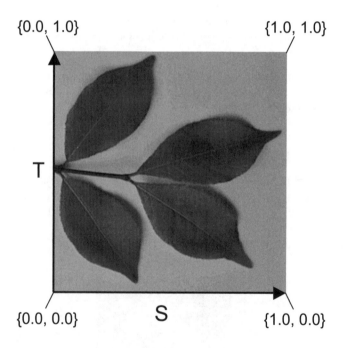

Figure 3.2   The OpenGL ES texture coordinate system.

The texture coordinate system has 2D axes named S and T. No matter how many texels are in a texture, the texture's dimensions are always 0.0 to 1.0 on the S axis and 0.0 to 1.0 on the T axis. A texture initialized from an image that is 1 pixel tall and 64 pixels wide will have one texel that stretches along the entire T axis and 64 texels spread along the S axis.

> **Note**
>
> The examples in this book use 2D textures, but some OpenGL implementations support 1D and 3D textures, too. A 1D texture is equivalent to a 2D texture that only has one texel along the T axis, so a 1D texture with 64 texels is the same as a 2D texture initialized from a 64 x 1 image. 3D textures are like layer cakes with multiple 2D textures stacked along the R axis in a coordinate system with R, S, and T axes. 1D and 3D textures are very handy for certain specialized applications, but 2D textures are by far the most common.

Aligning Textures with Geometry

OpenGL ES requires information about how to color geometric objects using a texture. Figure 3.3 illustrates the simple triangle from the examples in Chapter 2, but this time it's drawn with a texture. The first thing to notice about Figure 3.3 is that the triangle is drawn taller than it is wide. The triangle is defined by vertices at `{-0.5f, -0.5f, 0.0}`, `{0.5f, -0.5f, 0.0}`, and `{-0.5f, 0.5f, 0.0}`, which make the triangle's width the same as its height within the mathematic OpenGL ES coordinate system. However, the example's frame buffer matches the screen size in pixels. During rendering, the graphics processing unit (GPU) transforms the X, Y, Z coordinates of every vertex from the purely mathematic OpenGL ES coordinate system into the corresponding real pixel locations in the frame buffer. The pixel positions in the frame buffer are called *viewport* coordinates. The viewport is briefly mentioned in the "Deep Dive: How Does GLKView Work?" section of Chapter 2. The result of the transformation into viewport coordinates stretches all the drawn geometry to fit the screen, which is taller than it is wide. Chapter 5, "Changing Your Point of View," explains how to control the transformations performed by the GPU.

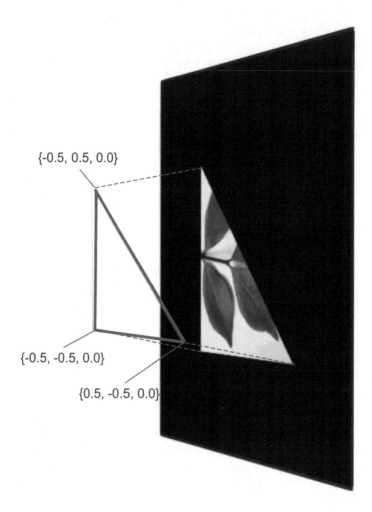

{-0.5, 0.5, 0.0}

{-0.5, -0.5, 0.0}

{0.5, -0.5, 0.0}

Figure 3.3   A textured triangle rendered into the frame buffer.

Note

Transforming each geometric coordinate within a scene consumes a dozen vector math operations, but GPUs routinely perform billions of vector operations per second. The transformation is so fast compared to reading memory that transformations are almost never a performance bottleneck in real applications.

After the X, Y, Z coordinates of each vertex are transformed into viewport coordinates, the GPU sets the color of each pixel within the resulting transformed triangle. The rendering step that converts geometric shape data into colored pixels in the frame buffer is called *rasterizing,* and each colored pixel is called a *fragment*. When OpenGL ES isn't using textures, the GPU calculates the color of each fragment based on the colors of the vertices of the object that contains the fragment. When configured to use textures, the GPU looks at the texels in the currently bound texture buffer to calculate the color of each fragment.

Programs specify how to align the texture with vertices so that the GPU knows which texels contribute color to each fragment. Alignment is also called *mapping* and is accomplished by extending the information stored for each vertex: In addition to X, Y, Z coordinates, each vertex is given U and V coordinate values. Each U coordinate maps the vertex's ultimate position in the viewport to a position along the S axis in the texture. The V coordinate maps to the T axis. Figure 3.4 helps to visualize texture mapping demonstrated by the OpenGLES_Ch3_1 example introduced in the "The OpenGLES_Ch3_1 Example" section of this chapter.

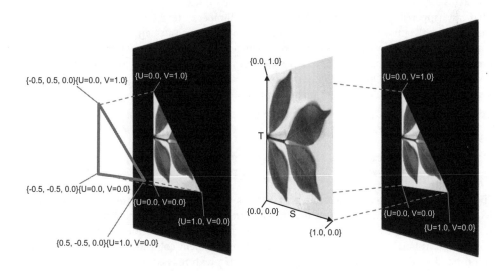

Figure 3.4   Texture mapping to transformed vertices.

Texture Sampling Modes

The U and V coordinates of each vertex remain attached to the final position of each vertex in viewport coordinates. The GPU then selects texels from within the bound texture based on the calculated U,V position of each fragment. The selection process is called *sampling*. Sampling aligns the texture's S and T coordinate system with the U,V coordinates of each rendered triangle's vertices. As shown in Figure 3.4, the texel closest to position {0, 0} in the S and T coordinate system is mapped to the fragment corresponding to the vertex that has U and V coordinates of {0, 0}. Each subsequent fragment position corresponds to a position along the S and T axes proportional to the fragment's position in U and V coordinates. For example, a fragment that has U, V coordinates {0.5, 0.5} will be colored by the texel closest to the center of the currently bound texture.

> **Note**
>
> The {S, T} coordinates and {U, V} coordinates are often described interchangeably by program-mers and 3D artists. Only one practical distinction exists between them: The {U, V} coordinates may be outside the range 0.0 to 1.0. Rasterizing maps {S, T} coordinates to {U, V} coordinates outside the range 0.0 to 1.0 based on a configurable "Wrap mode" described later in this section.

Sampling might cause the texture to be stretched, compressed, or even flipped during rendering. The OpenGLES_Ch3_3 example demonstrates some of the texture distortions that can be produced.

OpenGL ES supports several different sampling modes: Consider what happens when fewer fragments are produced for a triangle than the number of texels available in the bound texture. That can happen any time the texture with a large number of texels is mapped to a triangle that covers only a few pixels in the frame buffer. The opposite can happen, too. A texture containing few texels might be mapped to a triangle that produces many fragments in the frame buffer. Programs use the glTexParameteri() function as follows to configure each bound texture so that OpenGL ES knows how to handle mismatches between the number of available texels and the number of fragments that need to be colored:

```
glTexParameteri(GL_TEXTURE_2D, GL_TEXTURE_MIN_FILTER, GL_NEAREST);
glTexParameteri(GL_TEXTURE_2D, GL_TEXTURE_MIN_FILTER, GL_LINEAR);

glTexParameteri(GL_TEXTURE_2D, GL_TEXTURE_MAG_FILTER, GL_NEAREST);
glTexParameteri(GL_TEXTURE_2D, GL_TEXTURE_MAG_FILTER, GL_LINEAR);
```

Specifying the parameter GL_TEXTURE_MIN_FILTER with the value GL_LINEAR tells OpenGL ES that whenever there are multiple texels that correspond to a fragment, sample colors from several of the suitable texels and mix the colors using linear interpolation to produce the texture's contribution for the fragment. The resulting fragment color might end up being a color that doesn't exist in the texture. For example, if a texture is composed of alternating black and white texels, linear sampling will mix the texel colors and the fragment will end up being gray. The GL_NEAREST value specified with the GL_TEXTURE_MIN_FILTER parameter produces a different result. The color of the texel that most closely corresponds to the U, V coordinate of the fragment is sampled. If a texture is composed of alternating black and white texels, the GL_NEAREST sampling mode will pick one texel or another and the fragment will end up either white or black. A later section, "The OpenGLES_Ch3_3 Example," includes Figure 3.5, which shows the effects of nearest versus linear interpolation sampling modes.

The GL_TEXTURE_MAG_FILTER parameter to glTexParameteri() configures sampling when there are not enough available texels to uniquely map one or more texels to each fragment. In this case, the GL_LINEAR value tells OpenGL ES to mix the colors from nearby texels to calculate the fragment's color. The GL_LINEAR value has the effect of magnifying the texture and making it appear blurry on the rendered triangle. The GL_NEAREST value of the GL_TEXTURE_MAG_FILTER just picks the color of the texel nearest to the U, V position of the fragment and magnifies the texture by making it appear pixelated on the rendered triangle.

In addition to minimize and magnify filtering options, programs specify what should happen when U, V coordinates have values less than zero or greater than one. The two options are either to repeat the texture as many times as needed to fill the entire U, V area mapped to the geometry, or sample edge texels from the texture whenever the fragment's U, V coordinates have values outside the texture's S, T coordinate system. Texture wrapping modes are configured separately for the S and T axes as follows:

```
glTexParameteri(GL_TEXTURE_2D, GL_TEXTURE_WRAP_S, GL_CLAMP_TO_EDGE);
glTexParameteri(GL_TEXTURE_2D, GL_TEXTURE_WRAP_S, GL_REPEAT);

glTexParameteri(GL_TEXTURE_2D, GL_TEXTURE_WRAP_T, GL_CLAMP_TO_EDGE);
glTexParameteri(GL_TEXTURE_2D, GL_TEXTURE_WRAP_T, GL_REPEAT);
```

The OpenGLES_Ch3_3 example in this chapter demonstrates some effects produced by texture parameter values.

MIP Mapping

MIP mapping is closely related to sampling. According to Wikipedia, *MIP* stands for the Latin phrase *Multum In Parvo*, which means "much in a small space." Recall that memory accesses are the Achilles' heel of modern graphics processing. When multiple texels correspond to a fragment, linear sampling causes the GPU to read the color values of multiple texels just to calculate the final color of one fragment. MIP mapping is a technique for storing textures with multiple levels of detail. Highly detailed textures store many texels along each of the S and T axes. Low detail textures store few texels along each axis. The lowest detail texture stores only one texel. Multiple levels of detail increase the probability of close correspondence between texels on the S, T axes and the U, V coordinates of each fragment. When there is close correspondence, the GPU reduces the number of sampled texels and therefore reduces the number memory accesses.

Using MIP maps often increases rendering performance by reducing the number of samples made by the GPU, but MIP maps increase the memory required for each texture by 1/3 as explained at http://en.wikipedia.org/wiki/Mipmap. On iOS devices, memory constraints might take precedence over rendering performance. Usually the best strategy is to try your applications with and without MIP mapping to determine which approach works best on a case-by-case basis.

The OpenGLES_Ch3_1 Example

Texturing involves many potentially complex options, but Apple's GLKit greatly simplifies common texturing configurations. The OpenGLES_Ch3_1 example builds upon the OpenGLES_Ch2_3 example from Chapter 2. A single file, the implementation of the OpenGLES_Ch3_1ViewController class, in OpenGLES_Ch3_1 contains all the relevant code changes from OpenGLES_Ch2_3. The following code blocks highlight the changes in bold. First, texture coordinates are added to the SceneVertex type declaration:

```
/////////////////////////////////////////////////////////////////
// This data type is used to store information for each vertex
typedef struct {
   GLKVector3  positionCoords;
   GLKVector2  textureCoords;
}
SceneVertex;
```

Texture coordinates define the texture mapping for each vertex in the geometry. The `vertices` array that stores vertex data for the example initializes texture coordinates as well as the position coordinates.

```
/////////////////////////////////////////////////////////////////
// Define vertex data for a triangle to use in example
static const SceneVertex vertices[] =
{
   {{-0.5f, -0.5f, 0.0f}, {0.0f, 0.0f}}, // lower left corner
   {{ 0.5f, -0.5f, 0.0f}, {1.0f, 0.0f}}, // lower right corner
   {{-0.5f,  0.5f, 0.0f}, {0.0f, 1.0f}}, // upper left corner
};
```

The —viewDidLoad method extends the code from example OpenGLES_Ch2_3 to leverage the GLKit-provided GLKTextureLoader class, which loads a texture image into an OpenGL ES texture buffer.

```
/////////////////////////////////////////////////////////////////
// Called when the view controller's view is loaded
// Perform initialization before the view is asked to draw
- (void)viewDidLoad
{
   [super viewDidLoad];

   // Verify the type of view created automatically by the
   // Interface Builder storyboard
   GLKView *view = (GLKView *)self.view;
   NSAssert([view isKindOfClass:[GLKView class]],
      @"View controller's view is not a GLKView");

   // Create an OpenGL ES 2.0 context and provide it to the
   // view
   view.context = [[AGLKContext alloc]
      initWithAPI:kEAGLRenderingAPIOpenGLES2];

   // Make the new context current
   [AGLKContext setCurrentContext:view.context];

   // Create a base effect that provides standard OpenGL ES 2.0
   // shading language programs and set constants to be used for
```

```
    // all subsequent rendering
    self.baseEffect = [[GLKBaseEffect alloc] init];
    self.baseEffect.useConstantColor = GL_TRUE;
    self.baseEffect.constantColor = GLKVector4Make(
        1.0f, // Red
        1.0f, // Green
        1.0f, // Blue
        1.0f);// Alpha

    // Set the background color stored in the current context
    ((AGLKContext *)view.context).clearColor = GLKVector4Make(
        0.0f, // Red
        0.0f, // Green
        0.0f, // Blue
        1.0f);// Alpha

    // Create vertex buffer containing vertices to draw
    self.vertexBuffer = [[AGLKVertexAttribArrayBuffer alloc]
        initWithAttribStride:sizeof(SceneVertex)
        numberOfVertices:sizeof(vertices) / sizeof(SceneVertex)
        data:vertices
        usage:GL_STATIC_DRAW];

    // Setup texture
    CGImageRef imageRef =
        [[UIImage imageNamed:@"leaves.gif"] CGImage];

    GLKTextureInfo *textureInfo = [GLKTextureLoader
        textureWithCGImage:imageRef
        options:nil
        error:NULL];

    self.baseEffect.texture2d0.name = textureInfo.name;
    self.baseEffect.texture2d0.target = textureInfo.target;
}
```

A CGImageRef is a C data type defined in Apple's Core Graphics framework. Core Graphics includes many powerful 2D image processing and drawing functions. The UIImage +imageNamed: method returns a UIImage instance initialized from the contents of an image file. Many different image file formats are supported. The named image must be included as part of the application for +imageNamed: to find it.

GLKTextureLoader's –textureWithCGImage:options:error: method accepts a CGImageRef and creates a new OpenGL ES texture buffer containing the pixel data from the CGImageRef. This method is deceptively powerful. Accepting a CGImageRef enables the source of the image data to be anything Core Graphics supports from individual frames of a movie to custom 2D graphics drawn by the application to the contents of an image file. The options: argument accepts an NSDictionary storing key-value pairs that specify how GLKTextureLoader interprets the loaded image data. One of the available options directs GLKTextureLoader to generate MIP maps for the loaded image.

GLKTextureLoader automatically calls glTexParameteri() to configure the OpenGL ES sampling and wrap modes for created texture buffers. If MIP maps are used, the GL_TEXTURE_MIN_FILTER is set to GL_LINEAR_MIPMAP_LINEAR, which tells OpenGL ES to sample the two most appropriate MIP map image sizes (levels of detail) using linear interpolation of the texels closest to the S, T coordinate being sampled. Then, the two samples from the MIP map are linearly interpolated to produce the final fragment color. The GL_LINEAR_MIPMAP_LINEAR filter commonly produces the highest quality rendering output but requires more computation by the GPU than other modes. Without MIP maps, GLKTextureLoader automatically sets GL_TEXTURE_MIN_FILTER to GL_LINEAR. Both GL_TEXTURE_WRAP_S and GL_TEXTURE_WRAP_T are set to GL_CLAMP_TO_EDGE.

The example's GLKBaseEffect object introduced in Chapter 2 provides built-in support for rendering with textures. After the OpenGL ES texture buffer has been created, the example configures baseEffect's texture2d0 property to use the new texture buffer.

The GLKTextureInfo class encapsulates information about the created texture buffer including its size and whether it contains MIP maps, but this example only requires the buffer's OpenGL ES identifier, name, and the OpenGL ES "target" for the texture. OpenGL ES contexts store configuration information for the various kinds of buffers separately. Frame buffers are configured separately from vertex attribute array buffers or texture buffers. In fact, multiple kinds of texture buffer are supported. For example, one kind of texture buffer contains ordinary 2D image data, and another kind stores a specially shaped image used for special effects, explained in Chapter 8, "Special Effects." GLKTextureInfo's target property identifies the type of texture buffer being configured. Some OpenGL ES implementations maintain separate texture buffer targets for 1D and 3D textures as well.

```
/////////////////////////////////////////////////////////////////
// GLKView delegate method: Called by the view controller's view
// whenever Cocoa Touch asks the view controller's view to
// draw itself. (In this case, render into a frame buffer that
// shares memory with a Core Animation Layer)
- (void)glkView:(GLKView *)view drawInRect:(CGRect)rect
{
   [self.baseEffect prepareToDraw];

   // Clear back frame buffer (erase previous drawing)
   [(AGLKContext *)view.context clear:GL_COLOR_BUFFER_BIT];

   [self.vertexBuffer prepareToDrawWithAttrib:GLKVertexAttribPosition
      numberOfCoordinates:3
      attribOffset:offsetof(SceneVertex, positionCoords)
      shouldEnable:YES];
   [self.vertexBuffer prepareToDrawWithAttrib:GLKVertexAttribTexCoord0
```

```
    numberOfCoordinates:2
    attribOffset:offsetof(SceneVertex, textureCoords)
    shouldEnable:YES];

  // Draw triangles using the first three vertices in the
  // currently bound vertex buffer
  [self.vertexBuffer drawArrayWithMode:GL_TRIANGLES
    startVertexIndex:0
    numberOfVertices:3];
}
```

The `AGLKVertexAttribArrayBuffer` class created in example OpenGLES_Ch2_3 and reused here implicitly supports any combination of attributes for each vertex. The implementation of `OpenGLES_Ch3_1ViewController`'s `-glkView:drawInRect:` method tells `vertexBuffer` to prepare OpenGL ES for rendering vertex positions just like example OpenGLES_Ch2_3 and adds a second call to `-prepareToDrawWithAttrib:numberOfCoordinates:attribOffset:shouldEnable:`. The second call tells `vertexBuffer` to prepare OpenGL ES for rendering with two texture coordinates for each vertex. The compiler replaces the ANSI C `offsetof()` macro with the memory offset within each `SceneVertex` structure of the start of texture coordinates.

After a texture has been assigned to `baseEffect` and OpenGL ES has been prepared to use both position and texture coordinate attributes, calling `AGLKVertexAttribArrayBuffer`'s `-drawArrayWithMode:startVertexIndex:numberOfVertices:` instructs OpenGL ES to render the textured triangle.

The OpenGLES_Ch3_1 implementation of the `-viewDidUnload` method remains unchanged from the implementation in OpenGLES_Ch2_3.

Deep Dive: How Does GLKTextureLoader Work?

OpenGL ES texture buffers follow the same steps enumerated for other buffers discussed in Chapter 1, "Using Modern Mobile Graphics Hardware." First a texture buffer identifier is generated using the `glGenTextures()` function. Then, the texture is bound into the current context with the `glBindTexture()` function. The third step initializes the texture buffer contents by copying image data via the `glTexImage2D()` function. The OpenGLES_Ch3_2 example shows all the steps.

Most OpenGL ES implementations either require or benefit from using textures with dimensions that are powers of 2. The image in Figure 3.1 is 256 pixels wide and 256 pixels tall. Those dimensions work with OpenGL ES because 256 is a power of 2. Powers of 2 include $2^0 = 1$, $2^1 = 2$, $2^2 = 4$, $2^3 = 8$, $2^4 = 16$, $2^5 = 32$, $2^6 = 64$, $2^7 = 128$, $2^8 = 256$, and $2^9 = 512$. A 4 x 64 texture is valid. A 128 x 128 texture works fine, as does a 1 x 64 texture. A 200 x 200 texture either won't work or causes inefficiencies during rendering depending on the OpenGL ES version being used. The constraint on texture dimensions doesn't generally cause any problems.

The OpenGLES_Ch3_2 example shows how to generate texture buffers, resize images to power of 2 dimensions as needed, and initialize texture buffers with images.

The AGLKTextureLoader class in example OpenGLES_Ch3_2 partially reimplements Apple's GLKit GLKTextureLoader class. The AGLKTextureLoader class shouldn't be used in production code; it's provided solely to dispel some mystery regarding the interaction of GLKTextureLoader, Core Graphics, and OpenGL ES.

The use of AGLKTextureLoader instead of GLKit's GLKTextureLoader comprises the only relevant difference between OpenGLES_Ch3_2ViewController in example OpenGLES_Ch3_2 and the corresponding view controller from the OpenGLES_Ch3_1 example. The AGLKTextureLoader class interface and implementation in example OpenGLES_Ch3_2 provide a subset of the capabilities provided by GLKit. In particular, GLKit's GLKTextureLoader class supports asynchronous texture loading, MIP map generation, and more exotic texture buffer types than simple flat 2D. AGLKTextureLoader only replicates the features of GLKTextureLoader used in example OpenGLES_Ch3_1.

The AGLKTextureLoader.h file in example OpenGLES_Ch3_2 declares two classes: AGLKTextureInfo and AGLKTextureLoader.

```
//
//  AGLKTextureLoader.h
//  OpenGLES_Ch3_2
//

#import <GLKit/GLKit.h>


#pragma mark -AGLKTextureInfo

@interface AGLKTextureInfo : NSObject
{
@private
   GLuint name;
   GLenum target;
   GLuint width;
   GLuint height;
}

@property (readonly) GLuint name;
@property (readonly) GLenum target;
@property (readonly) GLuint width;
@property (readonly) GLuint height;

@end



#pragma mark -AGLKTextureLoader
```

```
@interface AGLKTextureLoader : NSObject

+ (AGLKTextureInfo *)textureWithCGImage:(CGImageRef)cgImage
options:(NSDictionary *)options
   error:(NSError **)outError;

@end
```

AGLKTextureInfo is a simple class that encapsulates useful information about texture buffers such as the associated OpenGL ES texture buffer identifier and the texture's image dimensions. AGLKTextureLoader only declares one method: +textureWithCGImage:options:error:.

The implementation of AGLKTextureLoader reveals the integration of Core Graphics and OpenGL ES needed to provide features similar to GLKit's GLKTextureLoader. The OpenGL ES function calls used in the +textureWithCGImage:options:error: method accomplish the standard buffer management steps to generate, bind, and initialize a new texture buffer as shown in bold in the following code:

```
/////////////////////////////////////////////////////////////////
// This method generates a new OpenGL ES texture buffer and
// initializes the buffer contents using pixel data from the
// specified Core Graphics image, cgImage. This method returns an
// immutable AGLKTextureInfo instance initialized with
// information about the newly generated texture buffer.
//    The generated texture buffer has power of 2 dimensions. The
// provided image data is scaled (re-sampled) by Core Graphics as
// necessary to fit within the generated texture buffer.
+ (AGLKTextureInfo *)textureWithCGImage:(CGImageRef)cgImage
   options:(NSDictionary *)options
   error:(NSError **)outError;
{
   // Get the bytes to be used when copying data into new texture
   // buffer
   size_t width;
   size_t height;
   NSData *imageData = AGLKDataWithResizedCGImageBytes(
      cgImage,
      &width,
      &height);

   // Generation, bind, and copy data into a new texture buffer
   GLuint     textureBufferID;

   glGenTextures(1, &textureBufferID);                    // Step 1
   glBindTexture(GL_TEXTURE_2D, textureBufferID);         // Step 2

   glTexImage2D(                                          // Step 3
```

```
    GL_TEXTURE_2D,
    0,
    GL_RGBA,
    width,
    height,
    0,
    GL_RGBA,
    GL_UNSIGNED_BYTE,
    [imageData bytes]);

// Set parameters that control texture sampling for the bound
// texture
glTexParameteri(GL_TEXTURE_2D,
    GL_TEXTURE_MIN_FILTER,
    GL_LINEAR);

// Allocate and initialize the AGLKTextureInfo instance to be
// returned
AGLKTextureInfo *result = [[AGLKTextureInfo alloc]
    initWithName:textureBufferID
    target:GL_TEXTURE_2D
    width:width
    height:height];

return result;
}
```

The `glGenTextures()` and `glBindTexture()` functions work like the similarly named functions for vertex buffers. However, the `glTexImage2D(GLenum target, Glint level, Glint internalFormat, GLsizei width, GLsizei height, Glint border, GLenum format, GLenum type, const GLvoid *data)` function is one of the most complex in the OpenGL ES standard. It copies image pixel color data into the bound texture buffer. The first argument to `glTexImage2D()` is `GL_TEXTURE_2D` for 2D textures. The second argument specifies the MIP map level of detail that is being initialized. When MIP maps are not used, the second argument must be zero. When MIP maps are enabled, use the second argument to explicitly initialize each level of detail, but be careful because every level from full resolution down to the one-texel version must be specified or else the texture buffer will not be acceptable to the GPU.

The third argument to `glTexImage2D()` is the `internalFormat`, which specifies the amount of information to be stored by each texel within the texture buffer. For iOS devices, the texel information should always be either `GL_RGB` or `GL_RGBA`. `GL_RGB` stores Red, Green, and Blue color components for each texel. `GL_RGBA` stores an additional Alpha component that defines the opacity of each texel.

The fourth and fifth arguments to `glTexImage2D()` specify the width and height of the image. The width and height should be powers of two. The border argument has historically been used to define the size of a border around the texture's texels, but it is always set to zero for OpenGL ES. The seventh argument, `format`, identifies the information stored for each pixel in the image data being used to initialize the buffer and should always be the same as the `internalFormat` argument. Other versions of OpenGL might perform automatic image data format conversions when the `format` and `internalFormat` arguments don't match.

The second-to-last argument specifies the `type` of bit encoding to use for the buffered texel data as one of the following symbolic values: `GL_UNSIGNED_BYTE`, `GL_UNSIGNED_SHORT_5_6_5`, `GL_UNSIGNED_SHORT_4_4_4_4`, and `GL_UNSIGNED_SHORT_5_5_5_1`. Using `GL_UNSIGNED_BYTE` provides the best available color quality, but it requires one byte of storage for each color element stored per texel. As a result, a minimum of three bytes (24-bits) must be read by the GPU every time an RGB texel is sampled, and four bytes (32-bits) are read for every RGBA texel. The other texel formats use a variety of encodings to store a combination of all the color elements within only 2 bytes (16-bits) per texel. The `GL_UNSIGNED_SHORT_5_6_5` format uses 5 bits for Red, 6 bits for Green, and 5 bits for Blue but nothing for the Alpha component. The `GL_UNSIGNED_SHORT_4_4_4_4` format uses 4 bits for each of the texel color components. `GL_UNSIGNED_SHORT_5_5_5_1` uses 5 bits to store each of the Red, Green, and Blue components but only one bit for Alpha. Using `GL_UNSIGNED_SHORT_5_5_5_1` makes every texel either fully opaque or fully transparent.

Regardless of the number of bits stored for each color element, the intensity of the color element is scaled to the range 0.0 to 1.0 by the GPU. A color element at full intensity (all bits for that color element are 1s) corresponds to an intensity of 1.0. Alpha color elements with intensity 1.0 are fully opaque. Alpha intensity of 0.5 is 50% translucent, and Alpha intensity of 0.0 is fully transparent.

The last parameter to `glTexImage2D()` is the pointer to the image's pixel color data to be copied into the bound texture buffer.

The `+textureWithCGImage:options:error:` method uses the `AGLKDataWithResizedCGImageBytes()` function to obtain the bytes that initialize the texture buffer contents. `AGLKDataWithResizedCGImageBytes()` is implemented in `AGLKTextureLoader.m` and contains the code needed to transform a Core Graphics image into suitable bytes for use with OpenGL ES.

```
/////////////////////////////////////////////////////////////////
// This function returns an NSData object that contains bytes
// loaded from the specified Core Graphics image, cgImage. This
// function also returns (by reference) the power of 2 width and
// height to be used when initializing an OpenGL ES texture buffer
// with the bytes in the returned NSData instance. The widthPtr
// and heightPtr arguments must be valid pointers.
static NSData *AGLKDataWithResizedCGImageBytes(
   CGImageRef cgImage,
   size_t *widthPtr,
   size_t *heightPtr)
{
   NSCParameterAssert(NULL != cgImage);
```

```
NSCParameterAssert(NULL != widthPtr);
NSCParameterAssert(NULL != heightPtr);

size_t originalWidth = CGImageGetWidth(cgImage);
size_t originalHeight = CGImageGetWidth(cgImage);

NSCAssert(0 < originalWidth, @"Invalid image width");
NSCAssert(0 < originalHeight, @"Invalid image width");

// Calculate the width and height of the new texture buffer
// The new texture buffer will have power of 2 dimensions.
size_t width = AGLKCalculatePowerOf2ForDimension(
   originalWidth);
size_t height = AGLKCalculatePowerOf2ForDimension(
   originalHeight);

// Allocate sufficient storage for RGBA pixel color data with
// the power of 2 sizes specified
NSMutableData    *imageData = [NSMutableData dataWithLength:
   height * width * 4];  // 4 bytes per RGBA pixel

NSCAssert(nil != imageData,
   @"Unable to allocate image storage");

// Create a Core Graphics context that draws into the
// allocated bytes
CGColorSpaceRef colorSpace = CGColorSpaceCreateDeviceRGB();
CGContextRef cgContext = CGBitmapContextCreate(
   [imageData mutableBytes], width, height, 8,
   4 * width, colorSpace,
   kCGImageAlphaPremultipliedLast);
CGColorSpaceRelease(colorSpace);

// Flip the Core Graphics Y-axis for future drawing
CGContextTranslateCTM (cgContext, 0, height);
CGContextScaleCTM (cgContext, 1.0, -1.0);

// Draw the loaded image into the Core Graphics context
// resizing as necessary
CGContextDrawImage(cgContext, CGRectMake(0, 0, width, height),
   cgImage);

CGContextRelease(cgContext);

*widthPtr = width;
*heightPtr = height;
```

```
    return imageData;
}
```

Core Graphics functions draw the specified `cgImage` into the bytes provided by `imageData`. Core Graphics resizes the image to power of 2 dimensions as a side effect of drawing into a properly sized Core Graphics context. The image is also flipped while it's being drawn. Flipping the Y axis is necessary because the Core Graphics implementation for iOS stores images with the origin in the upper-left corner and Y values that increase downward. The OpenGL ES texture coordinate system places the origin in the lower-left corner with increasing Y values up. Flipping the Y axis ensures that the image bytes have the correct orientation for the texture buffer.

> **Note**
>
> Core Graphics for Mac OS X stores images with the origin in the lower left and increasing Y values up just like OpenGL ES. Apple changed the implementation of Core Graphics when creating iOS and introduced the minor incompatibility with OpenGL ES that did not exist on Mac OS X.

After the `cgImage` has been drawn into the bytes provided by `imageData`, the function returns `imageData` and the corresponding width and height for the data.

The remainder of the code in `AGLKTextureLoader.m` is self explanatory. One minor implementation detail that might be unfamiliar is the use of an Objective-C *category* for the declaration and implementation of an initializer method for the `AGLKTextureInfo` class. The category syntax is bold in the following code block:

```
/////////////////////////////////////////////////////////////////
// Instances of AGLKTextureInfo are immutable once initialized
@interface AGLKTextureInfo (AGLKTextureLoader)

- (id)initWithName:(GLuint)aName
   target:(GLenum)aTarget
   width:(size_t)aWidth
   height:(size_t)aHeight;

@end
```

Objective-C categories add methods to existing classes and make it possible for the implementation of a class to span multiple files. In this example, the category is only used to organize declaration of the `-initWithName:target:width:height:` method separately from the main class interface. Declaring the category within the `AGLKTextureLoader.m` file instead of the `.h` file signals that the method should only be used within the `AGLKTextureLoader.m` file. The category name is arbitrary, but calling it `(AGLKTextureLoader)` further emphasizes that the added method is for use within the `AGLKTextureLoader` class.

The OpenGLES_Ch3_3 Example

Play with the user interface presented by example OpenGLES_Ch3_3. It demonstrates the effects of texture sampling modes, texture wrapping modes, and image distortions produced when a texture is mapped to vertices with changing positions in the viewport. Figure 3.5 illustrates several of the effects.

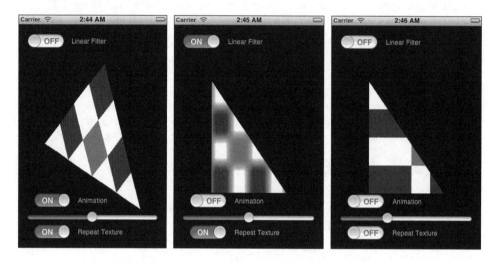

Figure 3.5   Screenshots of example OpenGLES_Ch3_3 show distortion, filter, and wrap modes.

The center screenshot in Figure 3.5 illustrates the effect of a GL_LINEAR filter magnifying a small texture to fill the entire triangle. The other two screenshots in the figure show the GL_NEAREST filter.

Example OpenGLES_Ch3_3 adds a method, -reinitWithAttribStride:numberOfVertices: data:, to the AGLKVertexAttribArrayBuffer class created in previous examples. Periodically reinitializing the vertex array buffer contents with changed vertex positions produces a simple animation intended to highlight texture distortions that naturally occur as part of texture mapping to geometry.

Texture sampling modes and texture wrapping modes are stored per texture identifier within OpenGL ES contexts. In other words, each texture buffer within the context has its own associated modes independent of any other texture buffers. The modes are configured by the glTexParameteri() function and typically don't change after a texture buffer has been initialized. However, example OpenGLES_Ch3_3 changes the modes in response to user input. The example extends GLKit's GLKEffectPropertyTexture class using a category as follows.

```
@implementation GLKEffectPropertyTexture (AGLKAdditions)

- (void)aglkSetParameter:(GLenum)parameterID
    value:(GLint)value;
{
   glBindTexture(self.target, self.name);

   glTexParameteri(
      self.target,
      parameterID,
      value);
}

@end
```

The -aglkSetParameter:value: method is named with the "aglk" prefix to avoid any possibility of method name conflicts in the future. If the added method was simply called -setParameter:value:, and Apple someday adds a method to GLKEffectPropertyTexture with the same name, the methods would conflict. The Objective-C runtime ends up picking one or the other of the implementations, but it might not be obvious to the programmer which implementation executes.

Opacity, Blending, and Multi-Texturing

OpenGL ES provides so many options for storing, mapping, and configuring textures that the whole subject often overwhelms programmers. An astronomical number of combinations and permutations exist for texel color formats, texture environment functions, sampling modes, and levels of detail. This section introduces even more options, so to keep the subject manageable, focusing on the most common modern use cases is necessary.

Use the GL_RGBA texture format containing Alpha components to specify the opacity of each texel. Figure 3.6 displays a texture with Alpha color element values so that a checkerboard pattern shows through the texels that are transparent. Typically, one or more texels are combined with lighting and vertex colors to determine the final color and opacity of each fragment. Chapter 4, "Shedding Some Light," introduces lighting. The resulting opacity of each fragment influences how the fragments are blended with the existing contents of a frame buffer.

Figure 3.6   Texture including Alpha color elements showing the pattern where texels are transparent.

When texture sampling calculates a fully opaque final fragment color, the fragment color simply replaces any corresponding pixel color that already exists in the frame buffer's pixel color render buffer. More interesting interactions are possible. If the calculated fragment color is partly or fully transparent, OpenGL ES uses a blend function to blend the fragment color and the corresponding pixel color render buffer pixel.

Enable blending by calling `glEnable(GL_BLEND)`. Then set the blending function by calling `glBlendFunc(sourceFactor, destinationFactor)`. The `sourceFactor` argument specifies how the final color components for each fragment influence blending. The `destinationFactor` argument specifies how the color components already in the destination frame buffer influence blending. The most common blending function configuration sets `sourceFactor` to `GL_SRC_ALPHA` and sets `destinationFactor` to `GL_ONE_MINUS_SRC_ALPHA` as follows:

```
glEnable(GL_BLEND);
glBlendFunc(GL_SRC_ALPHA, GL_ONE_MINUS_SRC_ALPHA);
```

Specifying `GL_SRC_ALPHA` multiplies the Alpha component of the source fragment with each of the other fragment color components. `GL_ONE_MINUS_SRC_ALPHA` multiplies (1.0—the Alpha component of the source fragment) with the color components of the pixel being updated in the frame buffer. As a result, if the fragment's Alpha value is zero, none of the fragment's color will appear in the frame buffer. If the fragment's Alpha value is 1.0, the fragment's color will completely replace the corresponding pixel color in the frame buffer. Alpha values between 0.0 and 1.0 mean that part of the fragment's color will be added to part of the corresponding pixel color in the frame buffer to produce a blended result. The final colors in the frame buffer are computed with the following equations when `glBlendFunc(GL_SRC_ALPHA, GL_ONE_MINUS_SRC_ALPHA)` is used:

$$Red_{final} = Alpha_{fragment} * Red_{fragment} + (1.0 - Alpha_{fragment}) * Red_{Frame\ Buffer}$$
$$Green_{final} = Alpha_{fragment} * Green_{fragment} + (1.0 - Alpha_{fragment}) * Green_{Frame\ Buffer}$$
$$Blue_{final} = Alpha_{fragment} * Blue_{fragment} + (1.0 - Alpha_{fragment}) * Blue_{Frame\ Buffer}$$
$$Alpha_{final} = Alpha_{fragment} + (1.0 - Alpha_{fragment}) * Alpha_{Frame\ Buffer}$$

Blending Fragment Colors in Example OpenGLES_Ch3_4

Using `glBlendFunc(GL_SRC_ALPHA, GL_ONE_MINUS_SRC_ALPHA)` produces the same result as the iOS Core Graphics "normal blend mode." Example OpenGLES_Ch3_4 produces the display shown in Figure 3.7. The leaves texture in Figure 3.7 blends with black pixels in the frame buffer's pixel color render buffer so that black pixels remain unmodified everywhere the leave's texture contains transparent texels. Then a second texture with the image of a bug blends with the pixel color render buffer. Wherever the bug texture's texels are transparent, the colors already in the frame buffer remain. The final rendered result shows a bug texture over the leaves texture over a black background.

Figure 3.7   A bug texture over a leaves texture over a black background.

Note

The layering effect shown in Figure 3.7 reveals the fundamental technique employed by iOS Core Animation technology. Each Core Animation layer uses a corresponding OpenGL ES pixel color render buffer to store pixel color data. The pixel color data for each layer is then used as an OpenGL ES texture buffer, and the texture buffers are blended together into the back frame buffer using the `glBlendFunc(GL_SRC_ALPHA, GL_ONE_MINUS_SRC_ALPHA)` function.

Example OpenGLES_Ch3_4 adds the following code in bold to the `−viewDidLoad` implementation from example OpenGLES_Ch3_3. The code loads a second texture and enables blending with the pixel color render buffer.

```
// Setup texture0
CGImageRef imageRef0 =
   [[UIImage imageNamed:@"leaves.gif"] CGImage];

self.textureInfo0 = [GLKTextureLoader
   textureWithCGImage:imageRef0
   options:[NSDictionary dictionaryWithObjectsAndKeys:
      [NSNumber numberWithBool:YES],
      GLKTextureLoaderOriginBottomLeft, nil]
   error:NULL];

// Setup texture1
CGImageRef imageRef1 =
   [[UIImage imageNamed:@"beetle.png"] CGImage];

self.textureInfo1 = [GLKTextureLoader
   textureWithCGImage:imageRef1
   options:[NSDictionary dictionaryWithObjectsAndKeys:
      [NSNumber numberWithBool:YES],
      GLKTextureLoaderOriginBottomLeft, nil]
   error:NULL];

// Enable fragment blending with Frame Buffer contents
glEnable(GL_BLEND);
glBlendFunc(GL_SRC_ALPHA, GL_ONE_MINUS_SRC_ALPHA);
```

In another slight change from previous examples, an NSDictionary object specifies
options applied when the textures are loaded from images. In this example, the
GLKTextureLoaderOriginBottomLeft key paired with the Boolean value, YES, instructs
GLKit's GLKTextureLoader class to flip the image data vertically. Flipping compensates for the
difference between the image origins and the OpenGL ES standard origin.

```
[NSDictionary dictionaryWithObjectsAndKeys:
   [NSNumber numberWithBool:YES],
    GLKTextureLoaderOriginBottomLeft, nil]
```

Example OpenGLES_Ch3_4 renders the same geometry twice: first with one texture and then
another. Blending happens each time a fragment colored by a texture is mixed with the pixel
color already in the pixel color render buffer. The following excerpt from OpenGLES_Ch3_4's
-glkView:drawInRect: implementation shows the relevant code.

```
self.baseEffect.texture2d0.name = self.textureInfo0.name;
self.baseEffect.texture2d0.target = self.textureInfo0.target;
[self.baseEffect prepareToDraw];

// Draw triangles using the first three vertices in the
// currently bound vertex buffer
[self.vertexBuffer drawArrayWithMode:GL_TRIANGLES
```

```
    startVertexIndex:0
    numberOfVertices:6];

self.baseEffect.texture2d0.name = self.textureInfo1.name;
self.baseEffect.texture2d0.target = self.textureInfo1.target;
[self.baseEffect prepareToDraw];

// Draw triangles using the first three vertices in the
// currently bound vertex buffer
[self.vertexBuffer drawArrayWithMode:GL_TRIANGLES
    startVertexIndex:0
    numberOfVertices:6];
```

The GLKit `baseEffect` is configured with the first texture, and `vertexBuffer` is drawn. Then the `baseEffect` is configured with the second texture, and `vertexBuffer` is drawn again. Blending with the pixel color render buffer occurs both times. The order of the drawing determines which texture appears on top of the other. In this case, the bug is above the leaves. Reversing the order the textures are drawn places the leaves visually above the bug.

Multi-Texturing in Example OpenGLES_Ch3_5

Many useful visual effects can be produced by blending fragment colors with the existing colors in a pixel color render buffer, but the technique has two fundamental downsides: the geometry must be rendered two or more times per display update, and the blending functions need to read color data out of the pixel color render buffer in order to blend the pixel colors with the fragment colors. Then the result is written back to the frame buffer. When multiple textures with Alpha data are overlapped as in Figure 3.7, the pixel color render buffer colors are read, blended, and written again for each texture. Reading and writing the pixel color render buffer multiple times to create one final rendered pixel as shown in example OpenGLES_Ch3_4 is called multi-pass rendering. As always, memory accesses limit performance, so multi-pass rendering is suboptimal. An alternative approach called *multi-texturing* avoids most downsides of multi-pass rendering.

All modern GPUs are capable of sampling texels from at least two texture buffers simultaneously. GLKit's `GLKBaseEffect` class supports two textures simultaneously. The hardware component that performs texel sampling and blending is called a texture unit or a sampler. If your application needs more than two texture units, use the following code sometime early in your program's execution to determine how many textures can be combined in a single pass:

```
GLint iUnits;
glGetIntegerv(GL_MAX_TEXTURE_UNITS, &iUnits);
```

The OpenGLES_Ch3_5 example produces output identical to OpenGLES_Ch3_4 except that the leaves and bug textures are mixed in one pass and the resulting fragment colors blend with the contents of the pixel color render buffer only once per display update.

Multi-texturing introduces another combinatorial group of configuration options. To help reduce the complexity, GLKit's `GLKEffectPropertyTexture` class in iOS 5 handles three common modes of multi-texturing: `GLKTextureEnvModeReplace`, `GLKTextureEnvMode Modulate`, and `GLKTextureEnvModeDecal`. `GLKEffectPropertyTexture` defaults to using `GLKTextureEnvModeModulate`, which almost always produces the best result. `GLKTextureEnvModeModulate` mixes any colors calculated for lighting and other effects with the colors sampled from a texture.

`GLKEffectPropertyTexture`'s `envMode` property configures the blending mode. OpenGLES_Ch3_5 loads the same two textures as OpenGLES_Ch3_4 but no longer needs to explicitly enable blending with the frame buffer's pixel color render buffer. Instead, `baseEffect`'s second texture property, `texture2D1`, is configured to use `GLKTextureEnvModeDecal`, which mixes the second texture with the first using an equation similar to `glBlendFunc(GL_SRC_ALPHA, GL_ONE_MINUS_SRC_ALPHA)`.

```
:self.baseEffect.texture2d1.envMode = GLKTextureEnvModeDecal;
```

Texture coordinates need to be provided for all texture units used. Multi-texturing supports use of separate texture coordinates for each texture. The `SceneVertex` data type in this book's examples could be expanded to store multiple sets of texture coordinates per vertex, but OpenGLES_Ch3_5 configures OpenGL ES 2.0 to use the same texture coordinates for both textures. The following complete implementation of the `-glkView:drawInRect:` method from example OpenGLES_Ch3_5 shows the steps. The bold code highlights the provision of texture coordinates to each texture unit:

```
- (void)glkView:(GLKView *)view drawInRect:(CGRect)rect
{
   // Clear back frame buffer (erase previous drawing)
   [(AGLKContext *)view.context clear:GL_COLOR_BUFFER_BIT];

   [self.vertexBuffer prepareToDrawWithAttrib:GLKVertexAttribPosition
      numberOfCoordinates:3
      attribOffset:offsetof(SceneVertex, positionCoords)
      shouldEnable:YES];

   [self.vertexBuffer prepareToDrawWithAttrib:GLKVertexAttribTexCoord0
      numberOfCoordinates:2
      attribOffset:offsetof(SceneVertex, textureCoords)
      shouldEnable:YES];

   [self.vertexBuffer prepareToDrawWithAttrib:GLKVertexAttribTexCoord1
      numberOfCoordinates:2
      attribOffset:offsetof(SceneVertex, textureCoords)
      shouldEnable:YES];

   [self.baseEffect prepareToDraw];

   // Draw triangles using the first three vertices in the
```

```
    // currently bound vertex buffer
    [self.vertexBuffer drawArrayWithMode:GL_TRIANGLES
        startVertexIndex:0
        numberOfVertices:6];
}
```

Custom Texturing in Example OpenGLES_Ch3_6

The power and flexibility of multi-texturing becomes even more apparent when using custom
OpenGL ES 2.0 fragment programs in OpenGL ES Shading Language. A bonus sample,
OpenGLES_Ch3_6, draws a cube using a Shading Language program created automatically
behind the scenes by GLKit's GLKBaseEffect and then draws a second cube using the
following custom vertex and fragment Shading Language programs. Don't worry about learning
Shading Language now, but if you're curious, play with OpenGLES_Ch3_6 to see how it works.

```
//
//  Shader.vsh
//  TestShaders
//
//

attribute vec4 aPosition;
attribute vec3 aNormal;
attribute vec2 aTextureCoord0;
attribute vec2 aTextureCoord1;

varying lowp vec4 vColor;
varying lowp vec2 vTextureCoord0;
varying lowp vec2 vTextureCoord1;

uniform mat4 uModelViewProjectionMatrix;
uniform mat3 uNormalMatrix;

void main()
{
    vec3 eyeNormal = normalize(uNormalMatrix * aNormal);
    vec3 lightPosition = vec3(0.0, 0.0, 1.0);
    vec4 diffuseColor = vec4(0.7, 0.7, 0.7, 1.0);

    float nDotVP = max(0.0, dot(eyeNormal, normalize(lightPosition)));

    vColor = vec4((diffuseColor * nDotVP).xyz, diffuseColor.a);
    vTextureCoord0 = aTextureCoord0.st;
    vTextureCoord1 = aTextureCoord1.st;

    gl_Position = uModelViewProjectionMatrix * aPosition;
}
```

A fragment shader is a short program executed by the GPU to perform operations needed to calculate the final color of every fragment in current render buffer. Files containing fragment shader programs typically use the .fsh file extension.

```
//
//   Shader.fsh
//   TestShaders
//

uniform sampler2D uSampler0;
uniform sampler2D uSampler1;
varying lowp vec4 vColor;
varying lowp vec2 vTextureCoord0;
varying lowp vec2 vTextureCoord1;

void main()
{
   // first texture Modulate, second texture Decal
   lowp vec4 color0 = texture2D(uSampler0, vTextureCoord0);
   lowp vec4 color1 = texture2D(uSampler1, vTextureCoord1);
   gl_FragColor = mix(color0, color1, color1.a) * vColor;
}
```

GL Shading Language programs tend to be both shorter and more self-documenting than other approaches for texture mixing configuration. However, OpenGL ES Shading Language is a complex topic worthy of an entire book such as *OpenGL Shading Language* (3rd Edition) by Randi J. Rost, Bill Licea-Kane, Dan Ginsburg, John M. Kessenich, Barthold Lichtenbelt, Hugh Malan, and Mike Weiblen. This book introduces the concepts gradually and shows examples in several chapters but is not a comprehensive reference.

Texture Compression

Apple recommends the use of texture compression with GPUs that support it. Texture compression minimizes the amount of memory required to store texture buffers while preserving relatively high texture level of detail. As of iOS 5, all iOS devices support the PowerVR Texture Compression (PVRTC) format. However, there is no guarantee that future Apple hardware will support the PVRTC format. Therefore, it is imperative that programs check for the existence of the non-standard OpenGL ES GL_IMG_texture_compression_pvrtc extension before using it. Apple recommends the following C function to check for extensions:

```
BOOL CheckForExtension(NSString *searchName)
{
   // For best results, extensionsNames should be stored so that it
   // does not need to be recreated on each invocation.
   NSString *extensionsString = [NSString
      stringWithCString:glGetString(GL_EXTENSIONS) encoding:
```

```
      NSASCIIStringEncoding];
   NSArray *extensionsNames = [extensionsString
      componentsSeparatedByString:@" "];

   return [extensionsNames containsObject:searchName];
}
```

A program can check whether compressed textures are supported with code using the following pattern:

```
if( CheckForExtension(@"GL_IMG_texture_compression_pvrtc") )
{
   // The extension is available.
}
```

Apple provides the command line `texturetool` utility program as part of the iOS SDK. The `texturetool` converts `.png` images into a format that can be directly loaded into compressed texture buffers as described at http://developer.apple.com/iphone/library/documentation/3DDrawing/Conceptual/OpenGLES_ProgrammingGuide/TextureTool/TextureTool.html. GLKit's `GLKTextureLoader` class also supports compressed textures.

Images used to initialize compressed textures need to have power of 2 dimensions, and they also need to be square. A 256 x 256 image can be used with a compressed texture buffer, but a 64 x 128 image cannot.

Apple provides sample code for using compressed textures at http://developer.apple.com/iphone/library/samplecode/PVRTextureLoader/.

Summary

The information in this chapter provides almost everything needed to implement a hardware-accelerated, 2D, sprite-based game. A sprite is a just moving image that includes transparent pixels, and the OpenGLES_Ch3_3 example even demonstrates one way to move textures around the display as a side effect of demonstrating distortion effects produced by texture sampling. Apple sample code at http://developer.apple.com/iphone/library/samplecode/GLImageProcessing shows how to use multi-texturing to implement powerful image processing effects such as brightness, contrast, saturation, hue, and sharpness adjustments to images. The sample hints at the implementation of Apple's hardware-accelerated Core Image technology that underlies commercial image processing applications.

So far, all the example programs have drawn simple triangles in 2D using 3D technology. Chapter 2 explained all the steps needed to display any OpenGL ES–based graphics on an iOS device. Chapter 3 extended the examples from Chapter 2 to display multiple textures on triangles. Chapter 4 dives into rendering in all three dimensions. Lighting is the key to presenting the illusion of three dimensions on a two-dimensional screen.

4

Shedding Some Light

3D computer graphics technologies convert mathematic descriptions of objects into convincing illusions. The human brain interprets pictures displayed on a flat screen and perceives non-existent depth based in part on geometric hints. For example, small objects are usually perceived to be further away than large objects. An object that partially covers another object is perceived to be in front. However, simulated lighting effects are also necessary to present the illusion of depth. Consider two renderings of the same geometric data in Figure 4.1. The image on the left is rendered without lighting. The image on the right is much more convincing with simulated lighting.

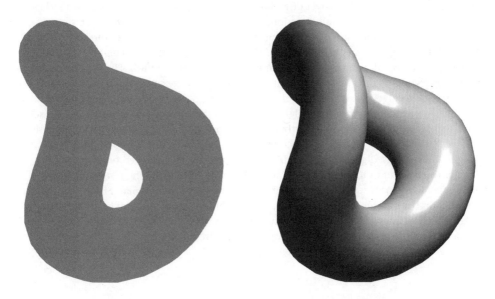

Figure 4.1   The same geometric data rendered without lighting and with simulated lighting.

This chapter introduces multiple techniques for simulating the interaction of light with 3D objects. OpenGL ES uses the graphics processing unit (GPU) to calculate the amount of simulated light that hits and scatters from geometry in a scene. Typically, the GPU performs lighting calculations for each vertex of each triangle and then interpolates the results between vertices to modify the final color for each rendered fragment. The quality and smoothness of simulated lighting therefore depends on the number of vertices that compose each 3D object. Alternative approaches for simulated lighting augment or replace the typical simulation. In many cases, lighting effects can be pre-calculated and "baked" into textures to produce realistic scenes without requiring GPU lighting calculation at all. Yet another approach leverages the capabilities of the GPUs to separately calculate and apply lighting effects to each individual fragment in the rendered scene.

This chapter introduces the concepts behind lighting simulation and takes advantage of GLKit to demonstrate lighting effects with relatively simple application code. GLKit replicates the traditional lighting capabilities of OpenGL ES 1.x and provides adequate built-in lighting simulation for most applications. After the basics of lighting are explained, this chapter describes some of the more advanced approaches made possible by OpenGL ES 2.0.

Ambient, Diffuse, and Specular Light

The OpenGL ES lighting simulation incorporates three distinct components of each light source: *ambient* light, *diffuse* light, and *specular* light. Programs separately configure the color of each component. The effect of each component of simulated light is shown in Figure 4.2. Ambient light comes from all directions and therefore illuminates all geometry equally. Programs specify the color and brightness of simulated ambient light to set the base level of background lighting in a scene. The color of the ambient light tints all geometry, so a red ambient light makes all geometric objects in a scene appear red or pink. The diffuse component of each light source is directional and lights each triangle in the scene based on the orientation of the triangle relative to the direction of the light. If the plane of a triangle is perpendicular to the direction of the light, the diffuse light directly hits the triangle and is scattered intensely, which makes the triangle appear brightly lit. If the plane of a triangle is parallel to the direction of the light or faces away from the direction of the light, hardly any diffuse light hits the triangle, so the diffuse light contributes little or nothing to the perceived brightness of the triangle. The color of diffuse light only tints triangles that are hit by the directional light. Finally, the light that is reflected from geometric objects is called specular. Shiny objects reflect a lot of light, but dull objects do not. The perceived brightness of specular light therefore depends on how much light hits each triangle and the shininess of the triangles. The color of the specular component determines the color of shiny highlights.

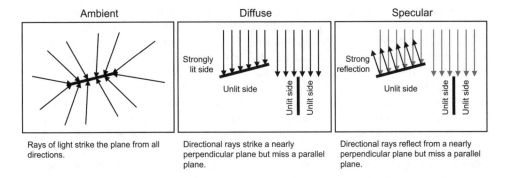

Ambient	Diffuse	Specular
Rays of light strike the plane from all directions.	Directional rays strike a nearly perpendicular plane but miss a parallel plane.	Directional rays reflect from a nearly perpendicular plane but miss a parallel plane.

Figure 4.2   Perception of simulated ambient, diffuse, and specular light components depends on the plane of each triangle struck by the light.

Figure 4.2 depicts light rays striking a plane. Arrows indicate the direction of the light. The figure also illustrates that each plane has two sides: a front side facing the light source and a back side facing away from the light source.

The effect of each light component on a rendered triangle depends upon three interrelated factors: configuration of the light, the orientation of the triangle relative to the direction of the light, and *material* properties of the triangle. OpenGL ES uses the term *material* to describe the properties of triangles that affect interaction with light components. Materials define how much of each light component is reflected or scattered. The more light that is reflected or scattered, the more intensely lit the triangle will seem. A high reflectance for specular light makes a triangle appear shiny like chrome or glass. Low specular reflectance presents the illusion of a dull material such as dirt or carpet.

Only the ambient component of each light source hits the backs of triangles. Some OpenGL ES implementations support optional two-sided lighting with separate materials on the front and back sides of triangles, but iOS version 5 does not support that option.

Note

Materials are important for rendering highly realistic scenes. Humans do not directly see light emitted from a light source unless looking at the source. We perceive objects around us because some amount of light reflects off each object in the environment before arriving at our eyes. As a result, we usually see light after it has been affected by interaction with materials. However, just like real objects are seldom composed of single color triangular facets, real objects seldom have just one material and real materials tend to be vastly more complicated than the OpenGL ES lighting simulation can replicate. The OpenGL ES lighting simulation is not sufficient on its own to render a shiny ball with scuff marks and dirt on it or a dull cement road with shiny oil stains. It's important to know that materials are supported by OpenGL ES for the occasions when a program needs to draw shiny crystal vases with animated dynamic lighting, but the vast majority of programs should leave the material settings at default values and use textures to produce desired effects.

The OpenGLES_Ch4_1 example program demonstrates how to enable and configure OpenGL ES 2.0 lighting via Apple's GLKit in iOS 5. Lighting is an area where OpenGL ES 1.x and OpenGL ES 2.0 differ radically. With the earlier standard, at least eight simultaneous lights are supported. Many more options and configuration possibilities exist in OpenGL ES 1.x than typical applications ever use. OpenGL ES 2.0 doesn't directly support any lights at all. Instead, custom Shading Language programs that run on the GPU are free to implement lighting calculations in any way that makes sense for the application. The GPU is able to quickly perform the lighting calculations explained in the next section, but lighting simulation still contributes computational overhead. GLKit's GLKBaseEffect class automatically generates Shading Language programs that replicate OpenGL ES 1.x lighting calculations for at least three lights. Using only one light source or even zero if possible is better. The "Bake Lighting into Textures" section explains one of the most commonly used techniques to render realistic lighting effects with minimal overhead.

Calculating How Much Light Hits Each Triangle

The interaction of light with 3D geometry plays a role in rendering whether the OpenGL ES 1.x lighting simulation or alternatives are used. The key to light interaction with geometry is calculating how much light hits and scatters from each geometric object, and to do that, calculating how close each triangle is to being perpendicular to the direction of the light is necessary. Linear algebra provides the solution. Triangles are defined by three vertices. Chapter 1, "Using Modern Mobile Graphics Hardware," showed how to compute the vector between any two vertices. Therefore, defining a triangle using one vertex and two vectors is also possible, as shown in Figure 4.3.

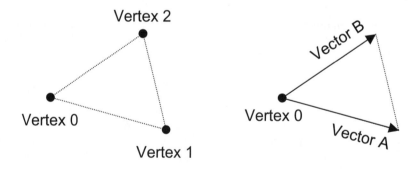

Figure 4.3   Two different ways to define the same triangle.

As mentioned in Chapter 1, many handy operations can be performed with vectors. One of the most important vector operations is the *cross product*: Given two vectors, the cross product of those two vectors defines a third vector that is perpendicular to the first two, as illustrated in Figure 4.4.

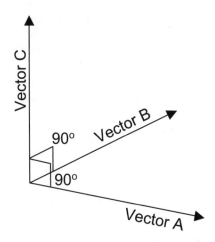

Figure 4.4   Vector C is the cross product of vector A and vector B.

The following equation calculates the cross product of two vectors using subtraction and multiplication instead of trigonometry; GPUs perform subtraction and multiplication very quickly:

```
VectorC.x = VectorA.y * VectorB.z — VectorA.z * VectorB.y;
VectorC.y = VectorA.z * VectorB.x — VectorA.x * VectorB.z;
VectorC.z = VectorA.x * VectorB.y — VectorA.y * VectorB.x;
```

> **Note**
>
> The cross product of VectorB x VectorA is the inverse of VectorA x VectorB. One common mistake is to unintentionally calculate the inverse cross product, which distorts lighting and makes the front side of each triangle into the back side. The easiest way to remember the order of the vectors is the "right-hand rule," which is nicely explained at http://en.wikipedia.org/wiki/Right-hand_rule. If you're looking down on a triangle, the vertices of the triangle are numbered in counterclockwise order. Using Figure 4.4 as an example and starting from the vertex where the vectors all join, the next vertex in counterclockwise order is the one at the end of vector A followed by the one at the end of vector B.

Lighting calculations depend on something called a *surface normal vector,* or *normal vector* for short. A normal vector can be calculated for any triangle: The direction of the normal vector is perpendicular to the plane of a triangle and is calculated using the cross product of any two vectors that define the triangle. Normal vectors are also *unit vectors,* which means that the magnitude, also known as the length, of a normal vector is always 1.0.

Any vector can be converted into a unit vector by dividing each component of the vector by the length of the vector. The result is a new vector that points in the same direction as the original and has a length equal to 1.0. Therefore, to calculate a normal vector, first calculate the cross product vector and then divide each component of the cross product vector by the length of the cross product vector. The operation is so common that converting vectors into unit vectors is commonly called the "normalize" operation. The OpenGLES_Ch4_1 example program uses the following code to calculate normal vectors:

```
/////////////////////////////////////////////////////////////////
// Returns a unit vector in the same direction as the cross
// product of vectorA and VectorB
GLKVector3 SceneVector3UnitNormal(
   const GLKVector3 vectorA,
   const GLKVector3 vectorB)
{
   return GLKVector3Normalize(
      GLKVector3CrossProduct(vectorA, vectorB));
}
```

The cross product is calculated by an inline function in GLKit's GLKVector3.h header file. The following implementation matches the actual GLKit implementation and has been formatted for presentation:

```
/////////////////////////////////////////////////////////////////
// Returns the Cross Product vectorA x vectorB
GLKVector3 GLKVector3CrossProduct(
   GLKVector3 vectorA,
   GLKVector3 vectorB)
{
   GLKVector3 result = {
      vectorA.y * vectorB.z - vectorA.z * vectorB.y,
      vectorA.z * vectorB.x - vectorA.x * vectorB.z,
      vectorA.x * vectorB.y - vectorA.y * vectorB.x
   };

   return result;
}
```

The GLKit GLKVector3Normalize(GLKVector3 vectorA) function requires a bit more explanation. The purpose of the function is to return a unit vector that has the same direction as vectorA but magnitude equal 1.0. The magnitude of a vector is the length of the vector, which can be calculated using the standard distance formula:

Length equals the square root of (vectorA.x2 + vectorA.y2 + vectorA.z2).

The following implementations of SceneVector3Length() and SceneVector3Normalize() are similar to the corresponding GLKVector3Length() and GLKVector3Normalize() functions. The GLKit functions should be used in production code to benefit from any maintenance or performance enhancements Apple provides in future framework versions. The SceneVector3 implementations format the code for presentation and show arithmetic error checking:

```
//////////////////////////////////////////////////////////////////
// Returns the length a.k.a. magnitude of vectorA
GLfloat SceneVector3Length(
   const GLKVector3 vectorA)
{
   GLfloat length = 0.0f;
   GLfloat lengthSquared =
      (vectorA.x * vectorA.x) +
      (vectorA.y * vectorA.y) +
      (vectorA.z * vectorA.z);


   if(FLT_EPSILON < lengthSquared)
   {  // avoid square root of zero error if lengthSquared
      // is too small
      length = sqrtf(lengthSquared);
   }

   return length;
 }
```

The FLT_EPSILON constant used in the preceding SceneVector3Length() function is defined in the standard float.h header file provided with the iOS SDK. The FLT_EPSILON constant is a very small positive number that will not be rounded to zero during floating-point math operations. It is important to make sure lengthSquared is not too close to zero and prevent inadvertently attempting to calculate the square root of zero.

After the length of a vector is known, the SceneVector3Normalize(GLKVector3 vectorA) function is implemented to scale vectorA into a unit vector as follows:

```
//////////////////////////////////////////////////////////////////
// Returns a Unit Vector with the same direction as vectorA
GLKVector3 SceneVector3Normalize(
   GLKVector3 vectorA)
{
   const GLfloat  length = SceneVector3Length(vectorA);
   float          oneOverLength = 0.0f;

   if(FLT_EPSILON < length)
   {  // avoid divide by zero if length too small
      oneOverLength = 1.0f / length;
   }

   GLKVector3 result = {
      vectorA.x * oneOverLength;
      vectorA.y * oneOverLength;
      vectorA.z * oneOverLength;
```

```
    };

    return result;
}
```

The amount of light that hits the triangle is readily calculated by determining the angle between the direction of the light and the normal vector. Once again, linear algebra provides a fast and convenient solution. The *dot product* of two unit vectors calculates the cosine of the angle between vectors, as shown in Figure 4.5. The cosine of the angle between a light direction unit vector and a triangle's surface normal vector determines the amount of light that hits the triangle. If the triangle is perpendicular to the light direction, the surface normal vector is parallel to the light direction so the angle between them is 0.0 degrees. The cosine of 0.0 degrees is 1.0, which means that the full intensity of the light hits the triangle. If the triangle is parallel to the direction of the light, the angle between the light and the surface normal vector is 90.0 degrees or –90 degrees, which both have cosine equal 0.0, so no light hits the triangle. Angles between 0.0 and 90.0 degrees have cosine values in the range 0.0 to 1.0 that determine how much light hits the triangle.

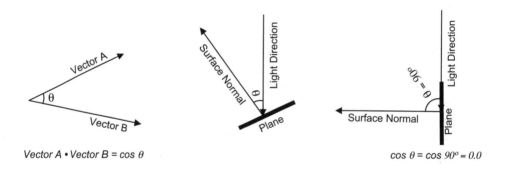

Figure 4.5 The dot product of unit vectors A and B equals cosine θ.

OpenGL ES programs specify separate normal vectors for every vertex. Normal vectors are typically calculated once and stored along with the positions and texture coordinates for vertices. The standard OpenGL ES 1.1 lighting simulation uses the GPU to calculate the dot product of the light direction and the normal vector for every vertex using the following equation:

```
DotProduct = (VectorA.x * VectorB.x) + (VectorA.y * VectorB.y) +
    (VectorA.z * VectorB.z);
```

If all three vertices of a triangle are given the same normal vector, called a *face normal*, the lighting simulation makes the triangle appear flat. If the normal vector of each vertex is an average of the normal vectors for all triangles that include the vertex, the lighting simulation creates the illusion that the triangles are slightly curved, as illustrated in Figure 4.6.

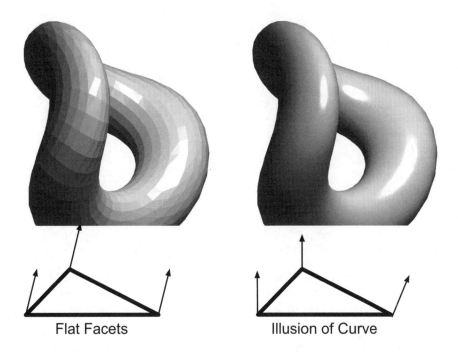

Flat Facets   **Illusion of Curve**

Figure 4.6   Two renderings of the same geometry showing the effect of normal vectors.

Using GLKit Lighting

GLKit for iOS 5 implements the standard lighting simulation equations for each light using Shading Language code similar to the following excerpt for diffuse lighting:

```
vec3 eyeNormal = normalize(uNormalMatrix * aNormal);
float nDotVP = max(0.0, dot(eyeNormal, ulightDirection));
vColor = vec4((uDiffuseColor * nDotVP).xyz, uDiffuseColor.a);
```

Don't worry about understanding the Shading Language excerpt for now. It's provided here only to show the flavor of the way GPUs implement lighting simulation. The code transforms each vertex's normal vector to match the orientation of the scene being rendered, calculates the dot product of the light direction and the new normal vector, and then uses the dot product to scale the contribution of the light's diffuse color. GLKit automatically generates Shading Language code similar to the excerpt to also mix in each light's specular and ambient colors.

GLKit's `GLKBaseEffect` class supports up to three simulated lights named `light0`, `light1`, and `light2`. Each light is represented by a `GLKBaseEffect` property with the same name. The properties are instances of the `GLKEffectPropertyLight` class, which in turn contains properties that configure each light. At a minimum, each light has a position, an ambient color, a diffuse color, and a specular color. Each light can be separately enabled or disabled.

The following code shows how to use GLKit lighting. The bold code configures light0:

```
// Create a base effect that provides standard OpenGL ES 2.0
// Shading Language programs and set constants to be used for
// all subsequent rendering
self.baseEffect = [[GLKBaseEffect alloc] init];
self.baseEffect.light0.enabled = GL_TRUE;
self.baseEffect.light0.diffuseColor = GLKVector4Make(
    0.7f, // Red
    0.7f, // Green
    0.7f, // Blue
    1.0f);// Alpha
self.baseEffect.light0.position = GLKVector4Make(
    1.0f,
    1.0f,
    0.5f,
    0.0f);
```

The light's diffuse color is set to an opaque medium gray. The light's specular and ambient colors are left with GLKit's default values of opaque white and opaque black, respectively. That means the ambient component of the light doesn't contribute to the scene and highly reflective objects appear very shiny.

The code sets the position of the light source using a GLKVector4 with four components. The first three components are either the X, Y, and Z position of the light source or the direction to an infinitely distant light source. The fourth component specifies whether the first three components are a position or a direction. If the fourth component is zero, the first three components are a direction. If the fourth component is non-zero, the light source projects light in all directions from its position. The light direction for each vertex therefore varies and must be calculated by the GPU using the direction from each vertex to the light source. Positional light sources can be configured as spot lights that shed light in a cone shape instead of all directions. The "Animating Colors and Lights" section of Chapter 6, "Animation," includes sample code for positional spot lights, and reference information is available at http://developer.apple.com/mac/library/documentation/Darwin/Reference/ManPages/man3/glLight.3.html.

Just enabling and configuring a light is not enough. Normal vectors must be provided for every vertex of every triangle that will be illuminated by a light. The OpenGLES_Ch4_1 example in the next section recalculates the normal vectors as needed, but most applications pre-calculate the normal vectors or load the normal vectors from a data file along with vertex position information.

After one or more of a base effect's lights are enabled, the lights determine the colors of rendered objects; the base effect's constant color and any vertex colors are ignored. The OpenGLES_Ch4_1 example draws the scene with a light enabled and then draws lines using a base effect's constantColor property instead of using a light. Two separate GLKBaseEffect instances are needed because with iOS 5, after a base effect's light is created, the constantColor property is ignored even if the base effect's light has been disabled. For example, baseEffect.light0.enabled = GL_FALSE;.

> **Note**
>
> GLKBaseEffect's constantColor property tells GLKBaseEffect what color to use for generated fragments as a last resort. Most OpenGL ES applications use some combination of lighting and textures to determine fragment colors. The constantColor property is only applicable when rendering flat unlit objects.

The OpenGLES_Ch4_1 Example

The OpenGLES_Ch4_1 example demonstrates GLKit-based lighting simulation and provides several options to explore the effects of normal vectors. Figure 4.7 shows screenshots of the OpenGLES_Ch4_1 application. A simple four-sided pyramid juts out of a flat plane. Directional light shining from behind and to the right of the pyramid lights some sides of the pyramid more intensely than others. Using face normal vectors produces a faceted look. Averaging the normal vectors makes the four-sided pyramid look almost like a smooth-sided cone. The third screenshot in Figure 4.7 depicts the calculated normal vectors and light direction using rendered lines.

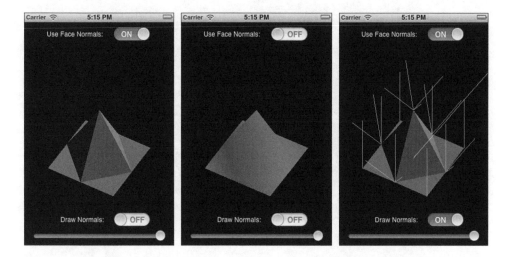

Figure 4.7   Screenshots of the OpenGLES_Ch4_1 example program.

Moving the slider in the OpenGLES_Ch4_1 application raises and lowers the apex of the pyramid, which changes the angles between the sides of the pyramid and the direction of the light. Each time the positions of vertices change, the normal vectors are recalculated.

Two different approaches are used calculate the normal vectors. When using face normal vectors, each vertex of each triangle has the same normal vector, so the triangles look flat. Otherwise, the normal vector for each vertex is an average of the normal vectors for all triangles that share the vertex. The example provides a user interface switch to enable drawing of the normal vectors and a line indicating the direction of the light. Examine the normal vectors as the slider is moved to visualize the shading produced as angles change between the normal vectors and the light direction.

Figure 4.8 illustrates the geometry used in the OpenGLES_Ch4_1 example. Nine vertices labeled A through I define eight triangles labeled 0 through 7. The user interface slider changes the Z coordinate of vertex E, which defines the pyramid's height. As vertex E moves up and down, triangles 2 through 5 change. Figure 4.8 identifies the same triangles shown in Figure 4.7. Example OpenGLES_Ch4_1 renders the triangles viewed from above and off to the side as shown in Figure 4.7. Figure 4.8 depicts the triangles as if viewed from directly above.

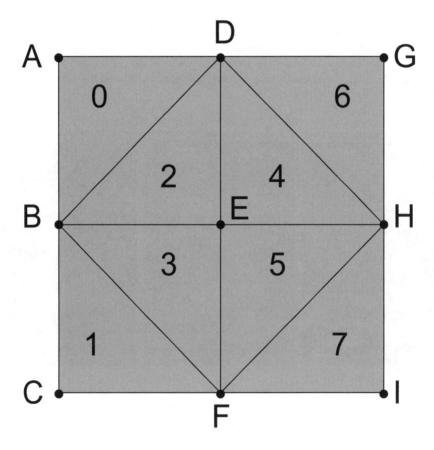

Figure 4.8   The relationships between vertices and triangles in Example OpenGLES_Ch4_1.

The variables, vertexA through vertexI, are defined and initialized in
OpenGLES_Ch4_1ViewController.m with the following code:

```
/////////////////////////////////////////////////////////////
// Define the positions and normal vectors of each vertex in the
// example.
SceneVertex vertexA = {{-0.5,  0.5, -0.5}, {0.0, 0.0, 1.0}};
SceneVertex vertexB = {{-0.5,  0.0, -0.5}, {0.0, 0.0, 1.0}};
SceneVertex vertexC = {{-0.5, -0.5, -0.5}, {0.0, 0.0, 1.0}};
SceneVertex vertexD = {{ 0.0,  0.5, -0.5}, {0.0, 0.0, 1.0}};
SceneVertex vertexE = {{ 0.0,  0.0,  0.0}, {0.0, 0.0, 1.0}};
SceneVertex vertexF = {{ 0.0, -0.5, -0.5}, {0.0, 0.0, 1.0}};
SceneVertex vertexG = {{ 0.5,  0.5, -0.5}, {0.0, 0.0, 1.0}};
SceneVertex vertexH = {{ 0.5,  0.0, -0.5}, {0.0, 0.0, 1.0}};
SceneVertex vertexI = {{ 0.5, -0.5, -0.5}, {0.0, 0.0, 1.0}};
```

A new data type, SceneTriangle, declares a structure that stores three vertices to define a
triangle. The example uses an array instance variable of the OpenGLES_Ch4_1ViewController
class to store the eight triangles depicted in Figure 4.8.

```
/////////////////////////////////////////////////////////////
// This data type is used to store information for triangles
typedef struct {
   SceneVertex vertices[3];
}
SceneTriangle;



/////////////////////////////////////////////////////////////
@interface OpenGLES_Ch4_1ViewController ()
{
   SceneTriangle triangles[8];
}

@end
```

OpenGLES_Ch4_1ViewController's -viewDidLoad method creates two GLKBaseEffect
instances called baseEffect and extraEffect as follows. Code in bold configures one of
baseEffect's lights:

```
// Create a base effect that provides standard OpenGL ES 2.0
// shading language programs and set constants to be used for
// all subsequent rendering
self.baseEffect = [[GLKBaseEffect alloc] init];
self.baseEffect.light0.enabled = GL_TRUE;
self.baseEffect.light0.diffuseColor = GLKVector4Make(
   0.7f, // Red
   0.7f, // Green
   0.7f, // Blue
```

```
   1.0f);// Alpha
self.baseEffect.light0.position = GLKVector4Make(
   1.0f,
   1.0f,
   0.5f,
   0.0f);

extraEffect = [[GLKBaseEffect alloc] init];
self.extraEffect.useConstantColor = GL_TRUE;
self.extraEffect.constantColor = GLKVector4Make(
   0.0f, // Red
   1.0f, // Green
   0.0f, // Blue
   1.0f);// Alpha
```

The next block of code in -viewDidLoad provides a preview of the techniques explained
in Chapter 5, "Changing Your Point of View." The entire scene in the OpenGLES_Ch4_1
example is rotated and positioned to make it easy to see changes to the height of the pyramid.
Comment out or delete the following block, and then rebuild and run the OpenGLES_Ch4_1
project to see the pyramid from the top down.

```
{  // Comment out this block to render the scene top down
   GLKMatrix4 modelViewMatrix = GLKMatrix4MakeRotation(
      GLKMathDegreesToRadians(-60.0f), 1.0f, 0.0f, 0.0f);
   modelViewMatrix = GLKMatrix4Rotate(
      modelViewMatrix,
      GLKMathDegreesToRadians(-30.0f), 0.0f, 0.0f, 1.0f);
   modelViewMatrix = GLKMatrix4Translate(
      modelViewMatrix,
      0.0f, 0.0f, 0.25f);

   self.baseEffect.transform.modelviewMatrix = modelViewMatrix;
   self.extraEffect.transform.modelviewMatrix = modelViewMatrix;
}
```

The eight triangles numbered 0 through 7 in Figure 4.8 are initialized using vertexA through
vertexI as follows. The triangles are then stored in a vertex attribute array buffer for use by
the GPU.

```
triangles[0] = SceneTriangleMake(vertexA, vertexB, vertexD);
triangles[1] = SceneTriangleMake(vertexB, vertexC, vertexF);
triangles[2] = SceneTriangleMake(vertexD, vertexB, vertexE);
triangles[3] = SceneTriangleMake(vertexE, vertexB, vertexF);
triangles[4] = SceneTriangleMake(vertexD, vertexE, vertexH);
triangles[5] = SceneTriangleMake(vertexE, vertexF, vertexH);
triangles[6] = SceneTriangleMake(vertexG, vertexD, vertexH);
triangles[7] = SceneTriangleMake(vertexH, vertexF, vertexI);
```

```
// Create vertex buffer containing vertices to draw
self.vertexBuffer = [[AGLKVertexAttribArrayBuffer alloc]
    initWithAttribStride:sizeof(SceneVertex)
    numberOfVertices:sizeof(triangles) / sizeof(SceneVertex)
    data:triangles
    usage:GL_DYNAMIC_DRAW];
```

The next block of code shows the entire implementation of
OpenGLES_Ch4_1View Controller's −glkView:drawInRect: method. The GLKit baseEffect
is prepared for drawing. The pixel color render buffer is cleared. The position and normal
attributes of each vertex are prepared for use by the GPU. The code in bold sends normal
vectors for each vertex to the GPU. The triangles rendered using baseEffect include light
simulation provided by the Shading Language programs GLKit automatically generates behind
the scenes. Finally, if OpenGLES_Ch4_1ViewController's shouldDrawNormals property value
is YES, the OpenGLES_Ch4_1ViewController's −drawNormals method is called.

```
/////////////////////////////////////////////////////////////////
// GLKView delegate method: Called by the view controller's view
// whenever Cocoa Touch asks the view controller's view to
// draw itself. (In this case, render into a frame buffer that
// shares memory with a Core Animation Layer)
- (void)glkView:(GLKView *)view drawInRect:(CGRect)rect
{
    [self.baseEffect prepareToDraw];

    // Clear back frame buffer (erase previous drawing)
    [(AGLKContext *)view.context clear:GL_COLOR_BUFFER_BIT];

    [self.vertexBuffer prepareToDrawWithAttrib:GLKVertexAttribPosition
        numberOfCoordinates:3
        attribOffset:offsetof(SceneVertex, position)
        shouldEnable:YES];
    [self.vertexBuffer prepareToDrawWithAttrib:GLKVertexAttribNormal
        numberOfCoordinates:3
        attribOffset:offsetof(SceneVertex, normal)
        shouldEnable:YES];

    // Draw triangles using vertices in the currently bound vertex
    // buffer
    [self.vertexBuffer drawArrayWithMode:GL_TRIANGLES
        startVertexIndex:0
        numberOfVertices:sizeof(triangles) / sizeof(SceneVertex)];

    if(self.shouldDrawNormals)
    {
        [self drawNormals];
    }
}
```

The `shouldDrawNormals` property is declared in `OpenGLES_Ch4_1ViewController.h` along with the `centerVertexHeight` and `shouldUseFaceNormals` properties. The code to update the values of properties resides in the `OpenGLES_Ch4_1ViewController` class implementation. `OpenGLES_Ch4_1ViewController` uses the Cocoa Touch *Target-Action* design pattern whenever a user interface object such as a slider or switch changes. The Target-Action design pattern is documented at http://developer.apple.com/iphone/library/documentation/General/Conceptual/Devpedia-CocoaApp/TargetAction.html. Essentially, methods that accept a single object argument are called by user interface objects to update application state. The specific object that changes state is the user interface object's target. The method called is the action. By convention, the argument to the action method is the user interface object that calls the action.

Many action methods are declared with the following form:

```
- (IBAction)takeShouldUseFaceNormalsFrom:(UISwitch *)sender;
- (IBAction)takeShouldDrawNormalsFrom:(UISwitch *)sender;
- (IBAction)takeCenterVertexHeightFrom:(UISlider *)sender;
```

Xcode's `.storyboard` editor enables visual user interface construction including specification of targets and actions. In example OpenGLES_Ch4_1, a user interface slider calls the `-takeCenterVertexHeightFrom:` action whenever the user moves the slider.

The implementation of `-takeCenterVertexHeightFrom:` is straightforward.

```
/////////////////////////////////////////////////////////////////
// This method sets the value of the center vertex height to the
// value obtained from sender
- (IBAction)takeCenterVertexHeightFrom:(UISlider *)sender;
{
   self.centerVertexHeight = sender.value;
}
```

As the `centerVertexHeight` property changes value, the triangles that include `vertexE` from Figure 4.8 also change. When the triangles change, the normal vectors for the triangles must be recalculated. That recalculation forms the key to example OpenGLES_Ch4_1.

`OpenGLES_Ch4_1ViewController` intercepts changes to properties by implementing custom accessor methods for the properties. Accessors are introduced in Chapter 2, "Making the Hardware Work for You." They are specially named methods called to change property values. The Objective-C compiler automatically generates calls to accessor methods when compiling dot notation syntax such as `self.centerVertexHeight = sender.value;`. The method that sets the value of the `centerVertexHeight` property is named `-setCenterVertexHeight:`.

```
/////////////////////////////////////////////////////////////////
// This method sets the value of centerVertexHeight and updates
// vertex normals
- (void)setCenterVertexHeight:(GLfloat)aValue
```

```
{
    centerVertexHeight = aValue;

    SceneVertex newVertexE = vertexE;
    newVertexE.position.z = self.centerVertexHeight;

    triangles[2] = SceneTriangleMake(vertexD, vertexB, newVertexE);
    triangles[3] = SceneTriangleMake(newVertexE, vertexB, vertexF);
    triangles[4] = SceneTriangleMake(vertexD, newVertexE, vertexH);
    triangles[5] = SceneTriangleMake(newVertexE, vertexF, vertexH);

    [self updateNormals];
}
```

Each time the —setCenterVertexHeight: method is called to change the value of the centerVertexHeight property, the height (Z component) of vertexE is changed and the four triangles that include vertexE are recreated. Then OpenGLES_Ch4_1ViewController's —updateNormals method is called to recalculate the affected normal vectors.

```
/////////////////////////////////////////////////////////////
// Called recalculate the normal vectors for the receiver's
// triangles using either face normals or averaged vertex normals.
- (void)updateNormals
{
    if(self.shouldUseFaceNormals)
    {  // Use face normal vectors to produce facets effect
       // Lighting Step 3
       SceneTrianglesUpdateFaceNormals(triangles);
    }
    else
    {  // Interpolate normal vectors for smooth rounded effect
       // Lighting Step 3
       SceneTrianglesUpdateVertexNormals(triangles);
    }

    // Reinitialize the vertex buffer containing vertices to draw
    [self.vertexBuffer
       reinitWithAttribStride:sizeof(SceneVertex)
       numberOfVertices:sizeof(triangles) / sizeof(SceneVertex)
       data:triangles];
}
```

The triangle vertex values including normal vectors are updated in the vertex attribute array buffer so they can be used by the GPU the next time the scene is rendered. If you are curious about the math to recalculate normal vectors, look at the `SceneTrianglesUpdateFaceNormals()` function in `OpenGLES_Ch4_1ViewController.m`. It uses the `SceneVector3UnitNormal()` function explained in the "Calculating How Much Light Hits Each Triangle" section of this chapter.

Experiment with the OpenGLES_Ch4_1 example to affect the rendered results. Try changing the position of the light. The example leaves default color values for the light source; try specifying colors for the ambient and specular light components. Try adding a second light source.

Bake Lighting into Textures

Using normal vectors requires storage for three floating-point values (12 bytes) in addition to the vertex position coordinates fore every lighted vertex. An extra 12 bytes per vertex adds up quickly when thousands or hundreds of thousands of vertices exist that define the geometry of a scene. Those extra 12 bytes not only consume scarce GPU-controlled memory, they also have to be read by the GPU every time the geometry is rendered.

If textures are being used anyway, one alternative to the OpenGL ES lighting simulation is to bake lighting into an existing texture. Textures are introduced in Chapter 3. In other words, apply textures that already contain the light and dark areas the lighting simulation would generate. Example OpenGLES_Ch4_2 uses a texture that includes lighting effects including shadows.

Baking light effects into textures only works well when neither the geometry nor the lights are dynamic. If lights move around or change colors, the baked-in lighting won't look right. If the geometry changes enough that a formerly dark area becomes exposed to light, the texture will look wrong. Chapter 6 explains how to create changing scenes without necessarily changing geometry.

Baked-in lighting effects present the illusion of more detail as shown in the OpenGLES_Ch4_2 example and Figure 4.9.

Figure 4.9   The illusion of detailed lighting and shadow provided by a texture.

Fragment Operations

As previously mentioned, the OpenGL ES 1.x lighting simulation replicated by GLKit calculates the dot product of the light direction vector and the vertex normal vector for every vertex. The dot product determines how much light hits the vertex. Then the calculated effect of lighting is interpolated between vertices to make the lighting seem smooth.

Textures enable control over the color of every rendered fragment for limited illusions of detailed lighting as in Figure 4.9. However, the GPU already performs complex calculations when determining the colors of fragments; why not use the GPU to recalculate the effect of lighting for every individual fragment instead of just for vertices? Of course, the GPU can be programmed to do just that.

The same lighting equation performed for vertices can be performed for every fragment. The lighting equation then requires a normal vector for every fragment. The solution is to encode the X, Y, Z components of normal vectors within each RGB texel of a texture. Such textures are called normal maps. The technique for per fragment lighting is often called *normal mapping*, *bump mapping*, or *DOT3 lighting* because all three terms essentially describe the effect.

A texture unit determines which normal map texel affects the fragment. A Shading Language program calculates the dot product of the vector represented by the selected texel and the light direction. The dot product is then used to scale the effect of the light color on the final fragment color.

Per-fragment lighting calculation works well even when the lights and geometry are dynamic. However, per fragment lighting is both computationally expensive for embedded GPUs and requires the use of normal maps that eat up GPU controlled memory. It can also be problematic to generate the normal maps. The PVRTextureTool that comes with the iPhone SDK is able to assist with normal map generation in some cases, but getting everything to look just right is tricky. As of iOS 5, available devices are not well suited for using per-fragment lighting because of the combination of primitive tool support, computational expense, and limited memory for textures. As embedded GPUs and tool support inevitably improve, advanced per-fragment lighting effects will become more practical.

Several excellent sources for more information about per fragment lighting are available at http://en.wikipedia.org/wiki/Normal_mapping. The *OpenGL ES 2.0 Programming Guide* by Aaftab Munshi, Dan Ginsburg, and Dave Shreiner contains a section on "per-pixel lighting with normal maps." Lighthouse3D is a site devoted mostly to 3D computer graphics and one of the best resources for exploring the subject of lighting more deeply. Lighthouse3D provides an excellent step-by-step tutorial for implementing the standard lighting equations per fragment at http://www.lighthouse3d.com/tutorials/glsl-tutorial/lighting/.

Summary

Real-world lighting effects are key to the way we perceive the environment around us, and simulated lighting effects add realism to 3D rendering. The traditional OpenGL ES vertex lighting simulation combined with materials offers wide-ranging configuration options but also suffers from limitations and relatively poor performance with embedded GPUs. Textures almost always produce higher quality rendered results than OpenGL ES materials. When textures are being used, it's possible to include some lighting effects in the textures and avoid the OpenGL ES lighting simulation entirely. Per-fragment lighting techniques are possible with all hardware that runs iOS and will become more common as memory, processor, and tools support improve.

So far, all the rendering examples have produced scenes that are frozen like a still photograph mounted on a wall. The next chapter shows how to render a scene from any point of view and fly around objects, viewing them from any angle.

5

Changing Your Point of View

This chapter explains and demonstrates techniques for rendering geometric objects from any point of view. 3D objects have fronts, sides, tops, and bottoms. Relatively simple mathematic operations called *transformations* determine which parts of the objects are visible in the rendered scene. Many people find mentally visualizing the effects that transformations have on rendering difficult. Even when the effects of transformations are correctly anticipated, relationships between the math and the end results might not be obvious. This chapter examines transformations with examples and then provides recipes for common transformations.

The Depth Render Buffer

Triangles, lines, and points are rendered in the order they are processed by the graphics processing unit (GPU). Without a *depth render buffer* or just *depth buffer* for short, fragments produced for the last object drawn always overwrite previously rendered overlapping fragments. The examples so far in this book have carefully controlled the order of drawing so that the correct final images are produced even without a depth buffer.

Transformations make rendering scenes from any point of view possible. The point of view determines which objects should be rendered in front of others in the scene. For example, when rendering the geometry of a human head from a point of view looking at the face, none of the triangles that compose the back of the head should be visible in the rendered scene. However, when relying on rendering order, if the triangles for the back of the head are the last ones processed by the GPU, they will be visible even when they shouldn't be.

In some cases, a program can sort objects into correct rendering order from back to front. The triangles in a human head object can be sorted so that the triangles of the face are the last ones processed by the GPU and therefore cover the triangles from the back of the head. Unfortunately, sorting the triangles often results in rewriting the contents of vertex buffers and defeats memory access optimizations provided by buffers. If the point of view changes to render the side of the head then some triangles from the face and some triangles from the back of the head should be visible in the rendered scene, and a different sort order is needed. A changing point of view makes recalculating the correct order for drawing objects necessary. Furthermore, sorting might not be sufficient. In some cases, triangles intersect each other and the correct rendering includes fragments from both triangles, but sorting forces all fragments from one of the triangles to cover fragments from the other.

A depth render buffer is an optional output buffer and is similar to a pixel color render buffer. Chapter 2, "Making the Hardware Work for You," introduced the concept of "other buffers" for use along with pixel color render buffers as illustrated in Figure 2.2. Almost every OpenGL ES application uses a depth buffer because almost every OpenGL ES application uses coordinate system transformations to change the rendering point of view. In most cases, a depth buffer eliminates the need to sort triangles, lines, and points.

> **Note**
>
> A depth buffer is also sometimes called a Z buffer because if the X and Y axes of the coordinate system correspond to the width and height of the screen, then the Z axis points in and out of the screen. The distance of a fragment from the point of view corresponds roughly to the fragment's position along a Z axis that points into the screen.

Each time a fragment is rendered, the depth of the fragment (distance of the fragment from the point of view) is calculated and compared to the value stored for that fragment position in the depth buffer. If the fragment has less depth (is closer to the point of view) then the fragment replaces any color already in the pixel color render buffer for that fragment position, and the depth buffer is updated with the depth of the fragment just rendered. If a fragment has greater depth than the value stored in the depth buffer, that means that some already-rendered fragment is closer to the point of view. In that case, the new fragment is discarded without updating the pixel color render buffer.

The GPU calculates the depth of every fragment as an intrinsic part of rendering. Using a depth buffer provides a place for the GPU to store the calculated depths that are then reused by the GPU to constrain fragment replacement in the pixel color render buffer.

Adding a Depth Buffer with GLKit

The `GLKView` class makes adding a depth buffer easy. Just set the view's `drawableDepthFormat` property to either `GLKViewDrawableDepthFormat16` or `GLKViewDrawableDepthFormat24` instead of the default value, `GLKViewDrawableDepthFormatNone:view.drawableDepthFormat = GLKViewDrawableDepthFormat16;`.

GLKit supports depth render buffers that use either 16 bits or 24 bits to store depth values. With 16 bits, only 65,536 different depths can be represented. If the depths of two fragments are very close, the depth buffer might not have enough precision to distinguish them. The final fragment color in the pixel color render buffer could come from either of the fragments that have close to the same depth. In fact, the result is sometimes called *Z-fighting* because the final fragment color often flickers back and forth between the possibilities and creates a visual distraction in the rendered scene.

Using 24 bits to store depth values distinguishes almost 17 million different depth values at the expense of consuming more of the GPU's scarce memory for the buffer. Even with 24 bits, Z-fighting remains a possibility when co-planar triangles overlap. It's just much less likely.

Optional steps for configuring OpenGL ES state allow programs to change the function used when the GPU performs depth tests. For example, calling the OpenGL ES `glDepthFunc( GL_ALWAYS)` function effectively disables depth testing because every rendered fragment replaces any prior color at the fragment's position in the pixel color buffer. The default depth testing function is `GL_LESS`, which means that each fragment's color only replaces pixel color buffer contents if the fragment's depth is less than the value stored for the fragment's position in the depth buffer. Smaller depth values mean that the fragment is closer to the view point. The complete set of depth testing functions than can be specified with `glDepthFunc()` are `GL_NEVER`, `GL_ALWAYS`, `GL_LESS`, `GL_LEQUAL`, `GL_EQUAL`, `GL_GEQUAL`, `GL_GREATER`, or `GL_NOTEQUAL`.

The `glClear()` function has already been used in examples from previous chapters; it clears the contents of buffers. For example, calling `glClear(GL_COLOR_BUFFER_BIT)` sets the value of every pixel in the current frame buffer's pixel color buffer to the color set by the `glClearColor()` function. Calling `glClear(GL_DEPTH_BUFFER_BIT)` sets every value in the current frame buffer's depth buffer the maximum depth value. Both buffers are commonly cleared in one line of code by combining arguments to `glClear()` via the C language bitwise OR operator as follows: `glClear(GL_COLOR_BUFFER_BIT | GL_DEPTH_BUFFER_BIT)`.

> **Note**
>
> The `AGLKContext` used in almost all of this book's examples includes `-setClearColor:` and `-clear:` methods to wrap the OpenGL ES `glClearColor()` and `glClear()` functions.

The OpenGLES_Ch5_1 and OpenGLES_Ch5_2 Examples

The OpenGLES_Ch5_1 and OpenGLES_Ch5_2 examples both render a sphere that represents the earth. Directional lighting simulates light from the sun hitting the earth. A texture mapped to the sphere shows the familiar continents, oceans, and weather. Figure 5.1 contains a screenshot from OpenGLES_Ch5_1 on the left and one from OpenGLES_Ch5_2 on the right.

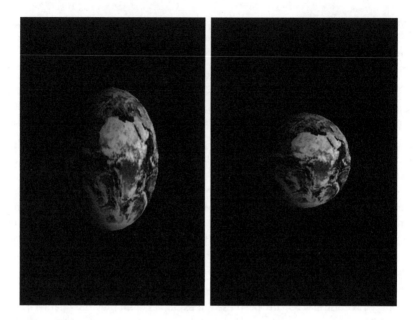

Figure 5.1   Two examples of a lit sphere with a texture of the earth.

The earth shown on the left of Figure 5.1 doesn't look like a sphere. It appears squashed or stretched into an egg shape. The stretched rendering effect was previously noted in examples from Chapter 2 and Chapter 3, "Textures." It happens because the default OpenGL ES coordinate system maps values from –1.0 to 1.0 along the X axis to the width of the screen and values from –1.0 to 1.0 along the Y axis to the height of the screen. However, the screen is not square; it's taller than it is wide. A sphere with radius 0.5 appears stretched on the screen because a distance of 0.5 along the Y axis covers more screen pixels than a distance of 0.5 along the X axis.

Examples OpenGLES_Ch5_1 and OpenGLES_Ch5_2 are nearly identical to each other, but OpenGLES_Ch5_2 uses a transformation to correct the stretched rendering effect.

The `OpenGLES_Ch5_1ViewController.m` file in OpenGLES_Ch5_1 includes `sphere.h`, which contains vertex positions, normal vectors, and texture coordinates for a sphere. The data in `sphere.h` was generated by a Perl language script that parses Wavefront `.obj` files and outputs corresponding C code. The `.obj` file format was developed and popularized by a company called Wavefront Technologies in the late 1980s. The file format remains popular because it's easy to parse with software. The `sphere.obj` data file used by examples in this chapter was created using a free open source 3D content creation tool called Blender available at http://www.blender.org/. The `sphere.obj` data file and the Perl script that parses it are both within the `Resources` directory inside the Chapter 5 examples available at http://opengles.cosmicthump.com/learning-opengl-es-sample-code/Examples.zip.

> **Note**
>
> Examples up to now have hard-coded vertex data. It's generally not a good idea to hard-code anything but the most straightforward constants like -1, 0, and 1. Examples provided vertex data definitions close to the code that used the data for simplicity of presentation, but Chapter 4, "Shedding Some Light," already pushed the practical limit of hard-coding by describing a pyramid with only eight vertices. The sphere used in examples OpenGLES_Ch5_1 and OpenGLES_Ch5_2 has 1,944 vertices. Imagine hard-coding that much data even if you didn't have to type it all. Some 3D scenes are composed of millions of vertices. In practice, external 3D editors such as Blender or the free Google SketchUp application (http://sketchup.google.com/), generate large quantities of vertex data in files that embedded applications later read. The sphere.h file is a compromise; it contains tool-generated data, but it's formatted as C code that can be directly compiled.

The following OpenGLES_Ch5_1ViewController.m file combines many of the OpenGL ES concepts introduced so far. The -viewDidLoad method adds code for using a depth buffer and multiple vertex buffers shown in bold:

```
/////////////////////////////////////////////////////////////////
// Called when the view controller's view is loaded
// Perform initialization before the view is asked to draw
- (void)viewDidLoad
{
   [super viewDidLoad];

   // Verify the type of view created automatically by the
   // Interface Builder storyboard
   GLKView *view = (GLKView *)self.view;
   NSAssert([view isKindOfClass:[GLKView class]],
      @"View controller's view is not a GLKView");

   view.drawableDepthFormat = GLKViewDrawableDepthFormat16;

   // Create an OpenGL ES 2.0 context and provide it to the
   // view
   view.context = [[AGLKContext alloc]
      initWithAPI:kEAGLRenderingAPIOpenGLES2];

   // Make the new context current
   [AGLKContext setCurrentContext:view.context];

   // Create a base effect that provides standard OpenGL ES 2.0
   // shading language programs and set constants to be used for
   // all subsequent rendering
   self.baseEffect = [[GLKBaseEffect alloc] init];

   // Configure a light to simulate the Sun
```

```
self.baseEffect.light0.enabled = GL_TRUE;
self.baseEffect.light0.diffuseColor = GLKVector4Make(
    0.7f, // Red
    0.7f, // Green
    0.7f, // Blue
    1.0f);// Alpha
self.baseEffect.light0.ambientColor = GLKVector4Make(
    0.2f, // Red
    0.2f, // Green
    0.2f, // Blue
    1.0f);// Alpha
self.baseEffect.light0.position = GLKVector4Make(
    1.0f, // Off to the right of the Earth
    0.0f,
   -0.8f, // A bit in front of the Earth
    0.0f);

// Setup texture
CGImageRef imageRef =
    [[UIImage imageNamed:@"Earth512x256.jpg"] CGImage];

GLKTextureInfo *textureInfo = [GLKTextureLoader
    textureWithCGImage:imageRef
    options:[NSDictionary dictionaryWithObjectsAndKeys:
        [NSNumber numberWithBool:YES],
        GLKTextureLoaderOriginBottomLeft, nil]
    error:NULL];

self.baseEffect.texture2d0.name = textureInfo.name;
self.baseEffect.texture2d0.target = textureInfo.target;

// Set the background color stored in the current context
((AGLKContext *)view.context).clearColor = GLKVector4Make(
    0.0f, // Red
    0.0f, // Green
    0.0f, // Blue
    1.0f);// Alpha

// Create vertex buffers containing vertices to draw
self.vertexPositionBuffer = [[AGLKVertexAttribArrayBuffer alloc]
    initWithAttribStride:(3 * sizeof(GLfloat))
    numberOfVertices:sizeof(sphereVerts) / (3 * sizeof(GLfloat))
    data:sphereVerts
    usage:GL_STATIC_DRAW];
self.vertexNormalBuffer = [[AGLKVertexAttribArrayBuffer alloc]
    initWithAttribStride:(3 * sizeof(GLfloat))
    numberOfVertices:sizeof(sphereNormals) / (3 * sizeof(GLfloat))
```

```
        data:sphereNormals
        usage:GL_STATIC_DRAW];
    self.vertexTextureCoordBuffer = [[AGLKVertexAttribArrayBuffer alloc]
        initWithAttribStride:(2 * sizeof(GLfloat))
        numberOfVertices:sizeof(sphereTexCoords) / (2 * sizeof(GLfloat))
        data:sphereTexCoords
        usage:GL_STATIC_DRAW];

    [((AGLKContext *)view.context) enable:GL_DEPTH_TEST];
}
```

Using multiple vertex attribute array buffers in example OpenGLES_Ch5_1 departs from the preceding examples, which stored all vertex components interleaved within a single buffer. Most GPUs perform optimally when all vertex attributes reside close together in memory. The GPU potentially reads all the needed values in a single memory operation. However, the script used to generate data declarations in sphere.h stores the vertex positions, normal vectors, and texture coordinates in separate arrays, so storing the data in separate buffers as shown in bold in the preceding –viewDidLoad implementation is easiest. Using separate buffers might sometimes provide a performance advantage when some vertex components change frequently and the rest remain static. For example, if texture coordinates never change but vertex positions change frequently, then storing the vertex positions in a buffer that uses the GL_DYNAMIC_DRAW hint but keeps the texture coordinates in a separate buffer that uses the GL_STATIC_DRAW hint might be optimal. Chapter 2 describes GL_DYNAMIC_DRAW and GL_STATIC_DRAW as part of the explanation of the glBufferData() function.

The implementation of –viewDidLoad concludes by enabling fragment depth testing. If you are curious to see what happens during rendering without a depth buffer, comment out the [((AGLKContext *)view.context) enable:GL_DEPTH_TEST]; line and rebuild.

Drawing with attributes provided by multiple vertex attribute array buffers differs a little from prior examples. Specifying GL_COLOR_BUFFER_BIT | GL_DEPTH_BUFFER_BIT to AGLKContext's –clear: method clears the depth buffer and the pixel color render buffer at the same time. AGLKContext's –clear: calls the glClear() function. Each of the AGLKVertexAttribArrayBuffer instances created in –viewDidLoad is prepared for drawing. Preparing calls glBindBuffer(), glEnableVertexAttribArray(), and glVertexAttribPointer(). Finally, a class method, +drawPreparedArraysWithMode:startVertexIndex:numberOfVertices:, added to AGLKVertexAttribArrayBuffer for this example calls glDrawArrays(), which draws vertices using data gathered from each of the prepared buffer pointers for attributes that have been enabled.

```
/////////////////////////////////////////////////////////////////
// GLKView delegate method: Called by the view controller's view
// whenever Cocoa Touch asks the view controller's view to
// draw itself. (In this case, render into a frame buffer that
// shares memory with a Core Animation Layer)
- (void)glkView:(GLKView *)view drawInRect:(CGRect)rect
```

```
{
   [self.baseEffect prepareToDraw];

   // Clear back frame buffer (erase previous drawing)
   [(AGLKContext *)view.context
      clear:GL_COLOR_BUFFER_BIT | GL_DEPTH_BUFFER_BIT];

   [self.vertexPositionBuffer
      prepareToDrawWithAttrib:GLKVertexAttribPosition
      numberOfCoordinates:3
      attribOffset:0
      shouldEnable:YES];
   [self.vertexNormalBuffer
      prepareToDrawWithAttrib:GLKVertexAttribNormal
      numberOfCoordinates:3
      attribOffset:0
      shouldEnable:YES];
   [self.vertexTextureCoordBuffer
      prepareToDrawWithAttrib:GLKVertexAttribTexCoord0
      numberOfCoordinates:2
      attribOffset:0
      shouldEnable:YES];

   // Draw triangles using vertices in the prepared vertex
   // buffers
   [AGLKVertexAttribArrayBuffer
      drawPreparedArraysWithMode:GL_TRIANGLES
      startVertexIndex:0
      numberOfVertices:sphereNumVerts];
}
```

OpenGLES_Ch5_2 modifies example OpenGLES_Ch5_1 with the following two bold code statements added near the end of the -glkView:drawInRect: method:

```
   // Scale the Y coordinate based on the aspect ratio of the
   // view's Layer which matches the screen aspect ratio for
   // this example
   const GLfloat  aspectRatio =
      (GLfloat)view.drawableWidth / (GLfloat)view.drawableHeight;

   self.baseEffect.transform.projectionMatrix =
      GLKMatrix4MakeScale(1.0f, aspectRatio, 1.0f);

   // Draw triangles using vertices in the prepared vertex
   // buffers
   [AGLKVertexAttribArrayBuffer
      drawPreparedArraysWithMode:GL_TRIANGLES
```

```
        startVertexIndex:0
        numberOfVertices:sphereNumVerts];
}
```

The GLKit `GLKMatrix4MakeScale()` function creates a basic *transformation matrix*. The function accepts three arguments that change the relative length of a unit along each of the three axes of the coordinate system. Specifying a value of `1.0` means no change. OpenGLES_Ch5_2 leaves the unit length along the X and Z axes unchanged but sets the unit length along the Y axis to the expression (`GLfloat`)`view.drawableWidth /` (`GLfloat`)`view.drawableHeight`, which calculates the *aspect ratio*. The `drawableWidth` property provides the width in pixels of the view's pixel color render buffer, which matches the view's full screen Core Animation layer. The `drawableHeight` property provides the height in pixels. The aspect ratio is the width divided by the height. Not as many pixels are available along the screen's X axis as along the Y axis. Scaling the Y axis by the aspect ratio counteracts the stretching effect seen with OpenGLES_Ch5_1.

> **Note**
>
> Scaling potentially has an effect on lighting. Scaling applies to all geometry, including normal vectors. After a normal vector has been scaled, it may no longer be a unit vector and therefore won't work correctly with the OpenGL ES lighting simulation. The Shading Language programs generated by GLKit's `GLKBaseEffect` class renormalize normal vectors as needed. For OpenGL ES 1.x, calling `glEnable(GL_NORMALIZE)` tells the GPU to make all normal vectors unit length after they have been scaled.

The "Transformations" section later in this chapter explains the role of transformation matrices when changing the point of view for rendering a scene. Along with the concepts of vertex attributes and vectors, matrices constitute the key to understanding 3D graphics.

Deep Dive: Adding a Depth Buffer Without GLKKit

Prior to the introduction of GLKit with iOS 5, developers needed to create a `UIView` subclass similar to `GLKView`. Recall the "Deep Dive: How Does GLKView Work?" section of Chapter 2. The OpenGLES_Ch2_2 example creates the `AGLKView` class to replicate many of the features of GLKit's `GLKView` class. Example OpenGLES_Ch5_3 similarly explores how `GLKView` works by replicating its depth buffer functionality. For almost every purpose, relying on Apple's optimized, tested, and future-proof implementation of `GLKView` rather than any application specific class is best. Feel free to skip this section if a continued deep dive into `GLKView` doesn't interest you.

The following steps are needed to manage an OpenGL ES depth buffer without the assistance of GLKit:

1. **Generate**—Ask OpenGL ES to generate a unique identifier for the depth buffer.

2. **Bind**—Tell OpenGL ES which buffer to use for subsequent operations.

3. **Configure Storage**—Specify the size of the depth buffer.

4. **Attach**—Attach the depth buffer to a frame buffer.

OpenGLES_Ch5_3 produces the same output as example OpenGLES_Ch5_2, but OpenGLES_Ch5_3 uses a version of `AGLKView` extended from example OpenGLES_Ch2_2 instead of GLKit's `GLKView`. A `drawableDepthFormat` property is added to the `AGLKView` as well as an instance variable to store an OpenGL ES depth buffer identifier. The following code added to `AGLKView`'s `-layoutSubviews` method creates and configures a depth buffer to match the size of the view's pixel color render buffer as needed:

```
if (0 != depthRenderBuffer)
{
   glDeleteRenderbuffers(1, &depthRenderBuffer);
   depthRenderBuffer = 0;
}

GLint currentDrawableWidth = self.drawableWidth;
GLint currentDrawableHeight = self.drawableHeight;

if(self.drawableDepthFormat !=
   AGLKViewDrawableDepthFormatNone &&
   0 < currentDrawableWidth &&
   0 < currentDrawableHeight)
{
   glGenRenderbuffers(1, &depthRenderBuffer);   // Step 1
   glBindRenderbuffer(GL_RENDERBUFFER,          // Step 2
      depthRenderBuffer);
   glRenderbufferStorage(GL_RENDERBUFFER,       // Step 3
      GL_DEPTH_COMPONENT16,
      currentDrawableWidth,
      currentDrawableHeight);
   glFramebufferRenderbuffer(GL_FRAMEBUFFER,    // Step 4
      GL_DEPTH_ATTACHMENT,
      GL_RENDERBUFFER,
      depthRenderBuffer);
}
```

The pixel color render buffer that shares memory with a Core Animation layer automatically resizes whenever the layer resizes. Extra buffers, such as the depth buffer, do not resize automatically. Whenever an `AGLKView` instance is resized, its associated layer resizes and the view's `-layoutSubviews` method is called. `AGLKView` implements `-layoutSubviews` to delete any existing depth buffer and create a new one that matches the new size of the pixel color render buffer.

Transformations

Transformations in mathematics convert vertex coordinates between coordinate systems. Each coordinate system is defined relative to some other reference coordinate system. With OpenGL ES, the ultimate reference coordinate system is the 2D array of pixel positions in a pixel color render buffer. The default 3D coordinate system is defined relative to the ultimate reference coordinate system and provides functions to convert positions in the range –1.0 to 1.0 along the default 3D X axis into corresponding pixel positions spread across the width of the pixel color render buffer. The default 3D coordinate system converts positions between –1.0 and 1.0 on the Y axis into corresponding pixel positions spread across the height of the pixel color render buffer. Positions along the Z axis of the default 3D coordinate system have no effect on the conversion to pixel coordinates except that vertices with Z values outside the range –1.0 and 1.0 are not drawn.

> **Note**
>
> During rendering, the GPU converts vertex data for points, lines, and triangles into colored fragments. The current coordinate system in effect when the GPU processes vertex data determines fragment positions in the pixel color render buffer and depth buffer. The current coordinate system therefore determines where each fragment appears onscreen and makes rendering scenes from any point of view possible.

Programs are able to define new coordinate systems relative to the default 3D coordinate system used as a reference. Any number of coordinate systems may be defined relative to other coordinate systems. In every case, vertex positions in a new coordinate system can be converted back into the reference coordinate system. As a result, it's possible to convert any vertex position in any coordinate system all the way back into a position in the pixel color render buffer.

It might seem like transformations require a lot of math to convert between coordinate systems, but linear algebra comes to the rescue again. Any number of basic transformations in any order can be captured and stored in a simple 4 by 4 *matrix* of floating-point values. *A matrix defines a coordinate system.* Chapter 11, "Math Cheat Sheet," contains the actual equations used by the GPU to convert vertices between coordinate systems.

Matrix math uses addition and multiplication almost exclusively and executes very quickly on modern GPUs. That's a good thing because the GPU transforms every vertex every time a scene is rendered, and having hundreds of thousands of vertices in a scene is common.

Basic Transformations

There are only four basic transformations: *translation, rotation, scale,* and *perspective.* The basic transformations combine to define how each vertex position in a new coordinate system converts into a position in a reference coordinate system. Translation, rotation, scale, and perspective are sufficient to produce an infinite variety of coordinate systems.

Each basic transformation corresponds to a simple change to a matrix. A matrix that defines a coordinates system identical to the reference coordinate system is called an *identity matrix.* Any two matrices can be combined in an operation called *concatenation* to produce a new matrix that contains all the transformations from both matrices. In reality, each basic transformation produces a simple matrix that is then concatenated with the current transformation matrix to form a new current matrix.

> **Note**
>
> Matrix concatenation is sometimes called matrix multiplication. The term *matrix multiplication* can also refer to the operation of transforming a vector or vertex from one coordinate system to another using a matrix. *Concatenation* is a more precise term that describes the combination of two matrices to form a third matrix that contains all the information in both of the source matrices.

Translation

Translation defines a new coordinate system by moving the origin of the new coordinate system relative to the origin of a reference coordinate system. Translation does not affect the length of a unit along the axes, and translation does not change the direction of the axes relative to the reference coordinate system. Figure 5.2 depicts a new coordinate system defined by translation relative to a reference coordinate system.

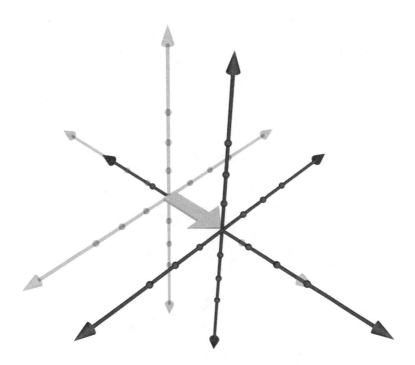

Figure 5.2   Translation.

GLKit provides the GLKMatrix4MakeTranslation(float x, float y, float z) function
to return a new matrix that defines a coordinate system by applying translation to an identity
matrix. The x, y, and z parameters specify the number of units to displace the new coordinate
system's origin along each axis of the current coordinate system used as a reference. The
GLKMatrix4Translate(GLKMatrix4 matrix, float x, float y, float z) function
returns a new matrix that defines a coordinate system by applying translation to the matrix
passed in as an argument. Conceptually, GLKMatrix4Translate() returns the concatenation
of the matrix argument and the new matrix produced by GLKMatrix4MakeTranslation().

```
GLKMatrix4 GLKMatrix4Translate(GLKMatrix4 matrix,
    float x, float y, float z)
{
    return GLKMatrix4Multiply(matrix,
      GLKMatrix4MakeTranslation(x, y, z));
}
```

Rotation

Rotation defines a new coordinate system by rotating the axes of the new coordinate system relative to the orientation of the axes in a reference coordinate system. The rotated coordinate shares the same origin as the reference coordinate system. Rotation does not affect the length of a unit along the axes. Only the direction of the axes changes. Figure 5.3 depicts a new coordinate system defined by rotation relative to a reference coordinate system.

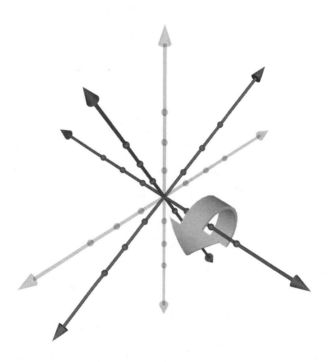

Figure 5.3   Rotation.

GLKit provides the GLKMatrix4MakeRotation(float angleRadians, float x, float y, float z) function to return a new matrix that defines a coordinate system by applying rotation to an identity matrix. The angleRadians argument specifies the number of radians to rotate. Degrees can be converted to radians with the GLKMathDegreesToRadians() function. The x, y, and z parameters specify which axis of the current coordinate system serves as the hub of rotation. For example, GLKMatrix4MakeRotation(GLKMathDegreesToRadians(30.0), 1.0, 0.0, 0.0); produces a new coordinate system by rotating an identity coordinate system's 30 degrees around the X axis. The GLKMatrix4Rotate(GLKMatrix4 matrix, float angleRadians, float x, float y, float z) function returns a new matrix that defines a coordinate system by applying rotation to the matrix passed in as an argument. Conceptually, `GLKMatrix4Rotate()` returns the concatenation of the `matrix` argument and the new matrix produced by `GLKMatrix4MakeRotation()`.

```
GLKMatrix4 GLKMatrix4Rotate(GLKMatrix4 matrix,
    float angleRadians, float x, float y, float z)
{
    return GLKMatrix4Multiply(matrix,
        GLKMatrix4MakeRotation(angleRadians, x, y, z));
}
```

Scaling

Scaling defines a new coordinate system by changing the length of a unit along each axis of the new coordinate system relative to the length of a unit along the axes in a reference coordinate system. The scaled coordinate systems shares the same origin as the reference coordinate system, and the direction of the axes usually does not change. However, scaling by a negative amount has the effect of flipping the direction of an axis. For example, if increasing values along an axis usually represent the direction up, then scaling that axis by a negative amount makes increasing values along the axis represent the direction down. Figure 5.4 depicts a new coordinate system defined by scaling relative to a reference coordinate system.

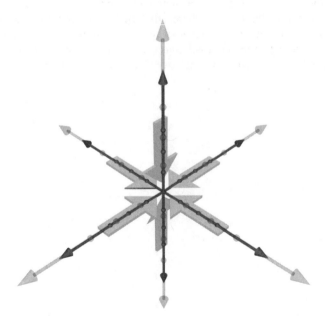

Figure 5.4   Scaling.

GLKit provides the GLKMatrix4MakeScale(float x, float y, float z) function to return a new matrix that defines a coordinate system by enlarging or reducing the unit length along any axis relative to an identity matrix. The x, y, and z parameters specify the factor used to enlarge or reduce the unit length along each axis. The GLKMatrix4Scale(GLKMatrix4 matrix, float x, float y, float z) function returns a new matrix that defines a coordinate system by applying scale factors to the matrix passed in as an argument. Conceptually, GLKMatrix4Scale() returns the concatenation of the matrix argument and the new matrix produced by GLKMatrix4MakeScale().

```
GLKMatrix4 GLKMatrix4Scale(GLKMatrix4 matrix,
    float x, float y, float z)
{
    return GLKMatrix4Multiply(matrix,
        GLKMatrix4MakeScale(x, y, z));
}
```

For example, GLKMatrix4Scale(matrix, 2.0, 1.0, 2.0) returns a new matrix that stretches the unit lengths along the X and Z axes of a coordinate system defined by the matrix argument.

Perspective

Perspective defines a new coordinate system by varying the length of a unit along each axis of the new coordinate system relative to the length of a unit along the axes in a reference coordinate system. Perspective does not change the origin or direction of axes, but each unit along the axes has smaller length the farther away it gets from the origin. This effect makes objects in the distance appear smaller than objects close to the origin. Figure 5.5 depicts a new coordinate system defined by perspective relative to a reference coordinate system.

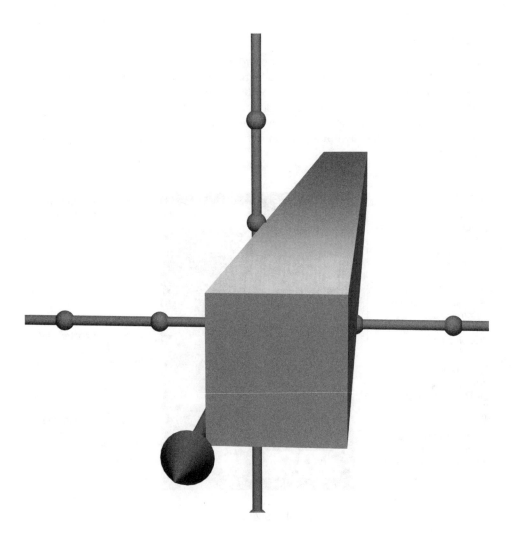

Figure 5.5   Perspective.

GLKit provides the GLKMatrix4MakeFrustum(float left, float right, float bottom, float top, float nearVal, float farVal) function to return a new matrix that defines a coordinate system with perspective relative to an identity matrix. Perspective coordinate systems are shaped like a pyramid called a frustum. The frustum is explained with more detail in the "Perspective and the Viewing Frustum" section of this chapter.

Order Matters

Basic transformations combine to define new coordinate systems, but the order of the transformations matters. Translation followed by rotation produces a different coordinate system than rotation followed by translation. Scaling followed by rotation produces a different coordinate system than rotation followed by scaling. Rotation followed by translation followed by scaling differs from translation followed by rotation followed by scaling, and so on. Example OpenGLES_Ch5_4 provides user interface controls, shown in Figure 5.6, to experiment with transformations.

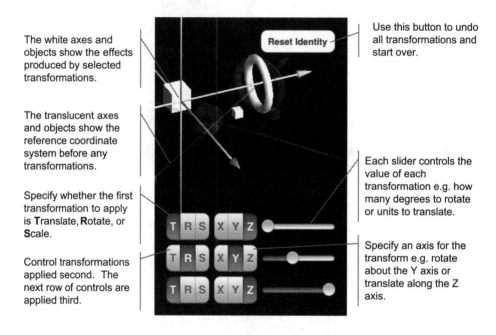

Figure 5.6   The OpenGLES_Ch5_4 example application.

The `projectionMatrix` and `modelviewMatrix`

GLKBaseEffect's transform property is an instance of GLKEffectPropertyTransform and stores three different matrices to support common operations. Two of the matrices, projectionMatrix and modelviewMatrix, respectively, define a coordinate system for the whole scene and a coordinate system used to control the apparent position of objects, also known as models within the scene. GLKBaseEffect concatenates the modelviewMatrix with the projectionMatrix to create a single modelviewProjectionMatrix that transforms object vertices all the way to the OpenGL ES default coordinate system. The default coordinate system maps directly into fragment positions in the pixel color render buffer. Figure 5.7 shows the conceptual sequence of transformations and the coordinate systems produced to transform vertices during rendering.

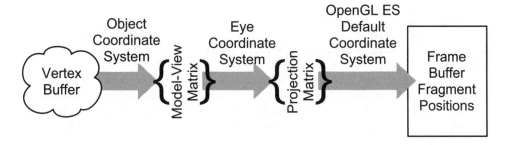

Figure 5.7   Vertex transformation matrices and resulting coordinate systems.

The OpenGLES_Ch5_4 application sets baseEffect's projectionMatrix to define an orthographic projection explained in the "Perspective and the Viewing Frustum" section of this chapter.

```
const GLfloat  aspectRatio =
     (GLfloat)view.drawableWidth / (GLfloat)view.drawableHeight;

  self.baseEffect.transform.projectionMatrix =
    GLKMatrix4MakeOrtho(
       -0.5 * aspectRatio,
       0.5 * aspectRatio,
       -0.5,
       0.5,
       -5.0,
       5.0);
```

The modelviewMatrix initialized in OpenGLES_Ch5_4ViewController's –viewDidLoad method produces a coordinate system that renders objects with an apparent point of view looking slightly down from above and to the right, as shown earlier in Figure 5.6.

```
GLKMatrix4 modelviewMatrix = GLKMatrix4MakeRotation(
   GLKMathDegreesToRadians(30.0f),
   1.0,  // Rotate about X axis
   0.0,
   0.0);
modelviewMatrix = GLKMatrix4Rotate(
   modelviewMatrix,
   GLKMathDegreesToRadians(-30.0f),
   0.0,
   1.0,  // Rotate about Y axis
   0.0);
```

```
modelviewMatrix = GLKMatrix4Translate(
   modelviewMatrix,
   -0.25,// Translate apparent position left and into the screen
   0.0,
   -0.20);
```

As the user moves the sliders shown in Figure 5.6, the values that control each of three user controlled transforms are updated. When example OpenGLES_Ch5_4 redraws, the modelviewMatrix is recalculated by the following code. First, the current value of the baseEffect's modelviewMatrix is saved so it can be restored later. The example creates a new matrix by concatenating the current modelviewMatrix with the three user-controlled transformation matrices in a specific order. Changing the order changes the final result of the transformations. Then, the baseEffect's modelviewMatrix is set to the new matrix.

```
// Save the current Modelview matrix
   GLKMatrix4 sevedModelviewMatrix =
      self.baseEffect.transform.modelviewMatrix;

   // Combine all of the user chosen transforms in order
   GLKMatrix4 newModelviewMatrix =
      GLKMatrix4Multiply(sevedModelviewMatrix,
      SceneMatrixForTransform(
         transform1Type,
         transform1Axis,
         transform1Value));
   newModelviewMatrix =
      GLKMatrix4Multiply(newModelviewMatrix,
      SceneMatrixForTransform(
         transform2Type,
         transform2Axis,
         transform2Value));
   newModelviewMatrix =
      GLKMatrix4Multiply(newModelviewMatrix,
      SceneMatrixForTransform(
         transform3Type,
         transform3Axis,
         transform3Value));

   // Set the Modelview matrix for drawing
   self.baseEffect.transform.modelviewMatrix = newModelviewMatrix;
```

After the user-controlled transformations are incorporated into the modelviewMatrix, the baseEffect is prepared for drawing and the objects in the scene are drawn with a white diffuse light.

```
// Make the light white
self.baseEffect.light0.diffuseColor = GLKVector4Make(
   1.0f, // Red
```

```
       1.0f, // Green
       1.0f, // Blue
       1.0f);// Alpha

[self.baseEffect prepareToDraw];

// Draw triangles using vertices in the prepared vertex
// buffers
[AGLKVertexAttribArrayBuffer
    drawPreparedArraysWithMode:GL_TRIANGLES
    startVertexIndex:0
    numberOfVertices:lowPolyAxesAndModels2NumVerts];
```

The modelviewMatrix is reset to the saved value, the light color is changed to yellow, and the same objects are drawn again. The yellow objects in the scene provide a reference so it's obvious how the user-controlled transformations affect where fragments from the white objects end up in the pixel color render buffer.

```
// Restore the saved Modelview matrix
self.baseEffect.transform.modelviewMatrix =
    sevedModelviewMatrix;

// Change the light color
self.baseEffect.light0.diffuseColor = GLKVector4Make(
       1.0f, // Red
       1.0f, // Green
       0.0f, // Blue
       0.3f);// Alpha

[self.baseEffect prepareToDraw];

// Draw triangles using vertices in the prepared vertex
// buffers
[AGLKVertexAttribArrayBuffer
    drawPreparedArraysWithMode:GL_TRIANGLES
    startVertexIndex:0
    numberOfVertices:lowPolyAxesAndModels2NumVerts];
```

Example OpenGLES_Ch5_4 saves and restores the modelviewMatrix by copying the matrix into a temporary variable. GLKit provides a convenient data type, GLKMatrixStack, and a set of functions for storing matrices in a stack data structure. A stack is a Last In First Out (LIFO) data structure very handy for storing matrices that a program might want to restore. GLKMatrixStack implements a stack of 4x4 matrices. The GLKMatrixStackPush() function copies the topmost matrix onto the top of the stack. GLKit provides a comprehensive set of functions for modifying the matrix on the top of the matrix stack, including the GLKMatrixStackMultiplyMatrix4() function with which all the other functions can be implemented. GLKMatrixStackGetMatrix4() returns the topmost matrix.

`GLKMatrixStackPop()` removes the topmost entry from the stack and restores the previous top matrix into the topmost position.

Applications push a new matrix on the top of the stack, manipulate it, use it to render geometry in OpenGL ES, and then pop it off the stack to restore the previous matrix to the top of the stack. Many of this book's examples use `GLKMatrixStack`, starting with OpenGLES_Ch5_5.

The `textureMatrix`

Desktop OpenGL and OpenGL ES 1.x incorporate three built-in matrix stacks. The first two store the projection matrix and the model-view matrix. The third, a texture matrix, applies transformations to the mapping of textures in the S and T coordinate system to the U and V coordinates of vertices. Texture mapping is explained in Chapter 3. At the time of this writing, `GLKBaseEffect`'s transform property does not use or provide a `textureMatrix`. Example OpenGLES_Ch5_5 therefore extends GLKit's `GLKBaseEffect` class with a new `AGLKTextureTransformBaseEffect` class to demonstrate some of the effects made possible using texture matrices. As with the other `AGLK` classes in this book, if and when GLKit adds a `textureMatrix` property, Apple's implementation should be used.

> ### Note
>
> The `AGLKTextureTransformBaseEffect` class in example OpenGLES_Ch5_5 uses custom OpenGL ES 2.0 Shading Language programs to implement texture matrix operations similar to the built-in support provided by OpenGL ES 1.x. Look at `AGLKTextureTransformBaseEffect`'s implementation to see how Shading Language programs are used in practice and a hint about how `GLKBaseEffect` may be implemented. GLKit exists so that you don't need to know all the details of Shading Language to produce 3D applications using common OpenGL ES features.

The following excerpt from OpenGLES_Ch5_5 shows relevant code in `OpenGLES_Ch5_5ViewController`'s `-glkView:drawInRect:` to demonstrate texture coordinate transformation using `AGLKTextureTransformBaseEffect`'s `textureMatrix2d1` property and a `GLKMatrixStack`. The `textureMatrix2d1` property stores the matrix used to transform texture coordinates for the second texture when multi-texturing. Multi-texture effects are explained in the "Opacity, Blending, and Multi-Texturing" section of Chapter 3. `AGLKTexture TransformBaseEffect` also provides a `textureMatrix2d0` property for separately transforming texture coordinates for the first texture when multi-texturing.

```
GLKMatrixStackPush(self.textureMatrixStack);

   // Scale and rotate about the center of the texture
   GLKMatrixStackTranslate(
      self.textureMatrixStack,
      0.5, 0.5, 0.0);
   GLKMatrixStackScale(
```

```
      self.textureMatrixStack,
      textureScaleFactor, textureScaleFactor, 1.0);
   GLKMatrixStackRotate(    // Rotate about Z axis
      self.textureMatrixStack,
      GLKMathDegreesToRadians(textureAngle),
      0.0, 0.0, 1.0);
   GLKMatrixStackTranslate(
      self.textureMatrixStack,
      -0.5, -0.5, 0.0);

   self.baseEffect.textureMatrix2d1 =
      GLKMatrixStackGetMatrix4(self.textureMatrixStack);

   [self.baseEffect prepareToDrawMultitextures];

   // Draw triangles using currently bound vertex buffer
   [self.vertexBuffer drawArrayWithMode:GL_TRIANGLES
      startVertexIndex:0
      numberOfVertices:sizeof(vertices) / sizeof(SceneVertex)];

GLKMatrixStackPop(self.textureMatrixStack);

self.baseEffect.textureMatrix2d1 =
      GLKMatrixStackGetMatrix4(self.textureMatrixStack);
```

The `textureScaleFactor` and `textureAngle` variables in the preceding code are controlled by sliders in the user interface. Run the example and experiment with slider settings to observe the resulting effects on textures. Change references to `self.baseEffect.textureMatrix2d1` to `self.baseEffect.textureMatrix2d0` to change the texture mapping that's transformed.

Transformation Cookbook

This section documents some common compound transformation sequences.

Skew

Skew is a compound transformation that produces axes that are no longer at right angles from each other. Cubes are deformed into boxes with trapezoidal sides.

1. Rotate about an axis.

2. Apply non-uniform scale such as scaling X but not Y or Z.

3. Rotate the opposite direction around the same axis used in step 1.

To see the skew effect in example OpenGLES_Ch5_4, first rotate about 45 degrees around the Y axis, and then scale the maximum amount along the X axis. Finally, rotate back around the Y axis. Experiment and try to align the white transformed axes with the translucent reference axes.

Rotate About a Point

Rotation and scaling always occur around the origin of the current coordinate system. Imagine that the sun is at the origin of the imaginary coordinate system for our solar system. The earth rotates around the sun, but the earth also rotates on its own axis. To rotate around a point other than the origin, the solution is simple:

1. Translate to the desired center of rotation.

2. Apply the desired rotation.

3. Translate back using the inverse of the translation values from step 1.

The previous section about the `textureMatrix` mode includes an example that rotates the texture coordinate system around the center of the texture instead of its lower-left corner. Try commenting out the lines that include translation in example OpenGLES_Ch5_5. Rebuild and re-run the example to see the result.

To rotate around the center of the doughnut shape in example OpenGLES_Ch5_4, set the first slider to translate along the Z axis and move the slider all the way to the left. Use the second slider to rotate around the Y axis. Set the third slider to translate along the Z axis and move the slider all the way to the right. Leaving the first and last sliders unchanged, experiment with different amounts of rotation with the middle slider.

Scale About a Point

Scaling about an arbitrary point is very similar to rotating about a point:

1. Translate to the desired center of the scaling.

2. Apply the desired scaling.

3. Translate back using the inverse of the translation values from step 1.

Perspective and the Viewing Frustum

OpenGL ES uses a geometric shape called a *viewing volume* to determine which of the generated fragments of a scene will be visible in the final rendered result. Geometry positioned outside the viewing volume is *clipped,* which just means it is discarded. The viewing volume is sometimes called a *projection.* Prior to this chapter, the viewing volume used in examples has been a cube that encompasses all vertices in the range –1.0 to 1.0 along the X axis, –1.0 to

1.0 along the Y axis, and –1.0 to 1.0 along the Z axis. That default projection results when the `projectionMatrix` is an identity matrix.

A cubic or rectangular viewing volume is called an *orthographic projection*. With an orthographic projection, the distance of each position from the viewpoint has no effect on the projection. The GLKit `GLKMatrix4MakeOrtho(GLfloat left, GLfloat right, GLfloat bottom, GLfloat top, GLfloat near, GLfloat far)` function returns a matrix that defines a rectangular viewing volume bounded by `left` and `right`, `bottom` and `top`, and `near` and `far`. The left side of Figure 5.8 depicts the viewing volume defined by the matrix returned from `GLKMatrix4MakeOrtho(-1.0, 1.0, -1.0, 1.0, 0.0, -6.0)`. The matrix returned from `GLKMatrix4MakeOrtho()` is normally concatenated with the current `projectionMatrix` to define a viewing volume.

When a *perspective projection* is used, the viewing volume is no longer rectangular. It becomes a truncated pyramid shape called a *frustum*, as depicted on the right side of Figure 5.8. Objects that are positioned far away from the view point are very small when projected into the 2D pixel color render buffer, but objects close to the viewpoint remain large. The GLKit `GLKMatrix4MakeFrustum()` function takes the same arguments as `GLKMatrix4MakeOrtho()` and creates a new transformation matrix that includes perspective. The new matrix is normally concatenated with the current `projectionMatrix` to define a viewing volume.

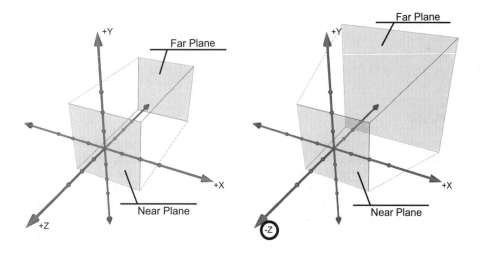

Figure 5.8   Orthographic and perspective viewing volumes.

The translucent shaded areas in Figure 5.8's two viewing volumes represent the near plane of each viewing volume. There are some constraints that apply to the near plane when using the `GLKMatrix4MakeFrustum()` function that do not apply to `GLKMatrix4MakeOrtho()`. Frustums cannot be defined with near plane Z position less than zero. Even small positive Z values for the near plane position are problematic. The range of positions from the near distance to the far distance are mapped into depth values in the depth buffer, and using either a large range or an excessively small near distance produces math rounding errors when the GPU calculates values to be stored in the depth buffer.

> **Note**
>
> The restrictions on `GLKMatrix4MakeFrustum()` produce a minor quirk: OpenGL ES defaults to a *negative* Z axis pointing into the screen, but `GLKMatrix4MakeFrustum()` always produces a viewing volume with the *positive* Z axis pointing into the screen. `GLKMatrix4MakeFrustum()` flips the sign of the Z axis.

Another key to using viewing volumes is to recognize that both orthographic and perspective projections produce the point of view of an observer standing at position {0, 0, 0} and looking straight down the Z axis. This chapter started by asserting that transformations enable any point of view, but in reality, the point of view is constant. Transformations apply to all the vertices in the scene and project those vertices onto the near plane of the viewing volume. Conceptually, OpenGL ES transforms all the geometry while the imaginary observer's viewpoint stands still. It only looks like the point of view changes while the whole world moves to provide the illusion.

Example OpenGLES_Ch5_6 demonstrates the use of `GLKMatrix4MakeFrustum()` to produce perspective transformation. The example simulates the earth rotating on its axis while the moon orbits the Earth. When the moon is close to the viewpoint, it appears large but gets smaller and smaller as it travels away from the viewpoint. Example OpenGLES_Ch5_6 also demonstrates each of the common compound transformations with the exception of skew.

Summary

This chapter introduced depth buffers, transformations, GLKit's matrices, GLKit's matrix stack, and viewing volumes. None of the examples in this chapter actually change the components of vertices stored in vertex buffers. The vertex positions remain constant. Instead, transformations change the way that the vertices are projected into the 2D pixel color render buffer. Example OpenGLES_Ch5_6 produces some simple animations by dynamically changing the current `modelviewMatrix`. Chapter 6, "Animation," further explores the possibilities for animation based on transformations and introduces several other approaches for achieving animation and special effects.

6

Animation

Changing visible aspects of a rendered scene over time produces graphical animation. Modifications to the coordinate system create the illusion of motion within a scene. Changes to vertex data generate effects such as rippling water and waving flags. Variation of colors and lighting provide cinematic atmosphere in many simulations. Changing the texture coordinate system animates texture mapping over geometry, and changing texture data produces effects that look like movies.

The keys to animation are managing time and performing application logic in response to the passage of time. GLKit's GLKViewController class includes flexible timing support. The controller's —update method is called automatically at configurable periodic rates. Immediately after —update, the controller's view redraws. Most importantly, GLKViewController synchronizes update and view drawing with display refresh.

The display refresh rate typically depends on the hardware of embedded devices and establishes the maximum number times per second pixels onscreen can change color. Therefore, GLKViewController's —update, GLKView's —drawInRect:, and GLKView's delegate method, -glkView:drawInRect:, provide the ideal triggers for applications to implement animation. There's no advantage to changing visible aspects of a rendered scene faster than the display refresh rate; the user only sees the last update prior to display refresh.

GLKViewController's properties, timeSinceLastUpdate, timeSinceLastDraw, timeSinceLastResume, and timeSinceFirstResume store time intervals measured in seconds and fractions of seconds. Timing information controls animation. For example, if a geometric object moves a simulated five centimeters every second, multiplying timeSinceLastUpdate times five centimeters determines how far the object moved since the last time its position was updated. GLKViewController's paused property controls whether updates are paused or not, and framesDisplayed stores the total number of times the display has updated since the application launched.

All the examples for this chapter use GLKViewController for both timing and integration with iOS features such as automatic display orientation changes. If you're curious how GLKViewController works, the custom AGLKViewController class included in examples OpenGLES_Ch2_2 and OpenGLES_Ch5_3 partially reimplements GLKViewController's timing features using Apple's Core Animation class, CADisplayLink. As Chapter 2, "Making the Hardware Work for You," explains, Core Animation ultimately controls the display of rendered scenes by swapping the OpenGL ES front frame buffer and back frame buffer during hardware display refresh. Core Animation's CADisplayLink calculates the timing information used by GLKViewController.

Motion Within a Scene: The OpenGLES_Ch6_1 Example

Animation often includes objects moving relative to the user's point of view or the user's point of view changing relative to object positions. Example OpenGLES_Ch5_6 from Chapter 5, "Changing Your Point of View," demonstrates one way to change the point of view depicted in a rendered scene. The example swaps between an orthographic projection and a perspective projection. The point of view, like so many 3D graphics concepts, exists in an abstract mathematic realm. In reality, the current OpenGL ES point of view never changes. Matrices define how geometric objects such as triangles map to fragment positions in the pixel color render buffer. Changing the matrices changes the mapping to create the illusion that the point of view changed. In essence, the viewer didn't move; the calculated location of every visible object changed relative to the viewer.

This chapter's first example, OpenGLES_Ch6_1, simulates a bumper car amusement park ride. Cars bounce around between walls and collide with each other. Figure 6.1 shows two screenshots illustrating different points of view for the scene. The first screenshot creates the illusion that the viewer is above the cars looking slightly down. The second screenshot shows the scene from a point of view inside one of the cars in action.

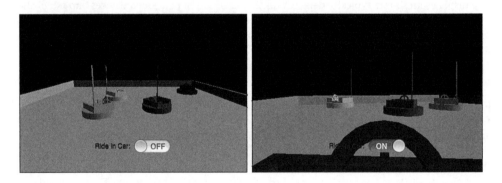

Figure 6.1   Screenshots showing different points of view.

None of the vertex attributes such as position or normal vectors in OpenGLES_Ch6_1 change while the application runs. Animation of cars bouncing around the rink results entirely from time-based changes to the coordinate systems represented by a matrices. If fact, each car is drawn at position {0, 0, 0} in its own local coordinate system. The cars appear to move around the scene as their local coordinate systems change relative to the coordinate systems used to render the other cars and the rink.

Example OpenGLES_Ch6_1 builds on several concepts introduced in previous chapters. Animation results when cars appear to move relative to each other and the viewer. The point of view itself animates when the user toggles "Ride in Car" mode.

Looking at a Specific 3D Position

OpenGLES_Ch6_1 uses GLKit's `GLKMatrix4MakeLookAt()` function to calculate a transformation matrix representing almost any desired point of view. `GLKMatrix4MakeLookAt()` is similar to the `gluLookAt()` utility function from desktop OpenGL but not part of OpenGL ES. Handy functions such as `GLKMatrix4MakeLookAt()` recreate many features missing from OpenGL ES and provide one of the best reasons to use GLKit in iOS applications.

`GLKMatrix4MakeLookAt()` has six arguments, as shown in the following function declaration. The first three arguments specify the {x, y, z} location of the observer's eye. The second three parameters specify the {x, y, z} position at which the observer is looking. `GLKMatrix4MakeLookAt()` calculates and returns a model-view matrix that aligns a vector from the `eye` position to the `lookat` position with the center line of the current viewing volume. The `GLKMatrix4MakeLookAt()` function doesn't produce useful results if the eye location and look-at position are the same. Chapter 5 explains viewing volumes and the model-view matrix.

```
GLKMatrix4 GLKMatrix4MakeLookAt(
    float eyeX, float eyeY, float eyeZ,
    float lookatX, float lookatY, float lookatZ,
    float upX, float upY, float upZ);
```

The final three arguments to `GLKMatrix4MakeLookAt()` are the {x, y, z} components of a vector that defines the direction, "up." Changing the "up" direction produces the same effect as tilting the observer's head.

Note

The "up" direction can be any vector, but the math used by the implementation of `GLKMatrix4MakeLookAt()` cannot produce a useful point of view that looks directly along the "up" vector. The limitation exists because when looking directly "up" or "down," the math used by `GLKMatrix4MakeLookAt()` attempts to calculate the tangent of 90 degrees, which is mathematically undefined. This "undefined" phenomenon also occurs in the real world when mechanical gyroscopes encounter "gimble lock" and produce wobbling unreliable data. However, a clever mathematic solution exists called *quaternions,* briefly described in Chapter 11, "Math Cheat Sheet," and at http://en.wikipedia.org/wiki/Quaternion. GLKit includes a `GLKQuaternion` data type and functions to manipulate it. Wikipedia recounts the story of Sir William Rowan Hamilton's discovery of quaternions in 1843 as one of the most famous and interesting in mathematics.

OpenGLES_Ch6_1's `OpenGLES_Ch6_1ViewController` stores the current eye position and look-at position in properties named `eyePosition` and `lookAtPosition`. The controller's `-glkView:drawInRect:` method sets the current model-view matrix with the following code:

```
// Set the modelview matrix to match current eye and look-at
// positions
self.baseEffect.transform.modelviewMatrix =
   GLKMatrix4MakeLookAt(
      self.eyePosition.x,
      self.eyePosition.y,
      self.eyePosition.z,
      self.lookAtPosition.x,
      self.lookAtPosition.y,
      self.lookAtPosition.z,
      0, 1, 0);
```

In 3D applications, a point of view within the action is called a "first person" point of view (POV) because it presents the scene a viewer would have by standing inside the application environment. An alternative point of view, "third person," simulates a view looking down from a vantage outside the action. A new method, `-updatePointOfView`, added to the example's `OpenGLES_Ch6_1ViewController` sets the "target" eye position and look-at position as follows. The target positions play a role in animation as explained in the next section of this chapter.

```
- (void)updatePointOfView
{
   if(!self.shouldUseFirstPersonPOV)
   { // Set the target point of view to arbitrary "third person"
     // perspective
     self.targetEyePosition = GLKVector3Make(6.00, 1.75, 0.0);
     self.targetLookAtPosition = GLKVector3Make(0, 0.5, 0);
   }
   else
   { // Set the target point of view to a position within the
     // last car and facing the direction of the car's motion.
     SceneCar *viewerCar = [cars lastObject];

     // Set the new target position up a bit from center of
     // car
     self.targetEyePosition = GLKVector3Make(
        viewerCar.position.x,
        viewerCar.position.y + 0.45f,  // up an arbitrary amount
        viewerCar.position.z);

     // Look from eye position in direction of motion
     self.targetLookAtPosition = GLKVector3Add(
        eyePosition,
```

```
        viewerCar.velocity);
    }
}
```

The third person point of view places the viewer's eye to the side above the rink and looks at a position slightly above the center of the rink. The third person eye and look-at positions are arbitrary and don't change. In contrast, the first person point of view changes as the car the viewer rides within moves and turns. The eye position is set just above the car's current position and the look-at position is a spot in front of the car in the direction the car is traveling. In the preceding code, `viewerCar.velocity` is a vector with direction that specifies the direction the car travels and magnitude that specifies how fast the car moves. Adding `viewerCar.velocity` to `eyePosition` calculates a position in front of the car.

Working with Time

Jarring visual changes such as instantaneously swapping from third person to first person point of view disorient users. `OpenGLES_Ch6_1ViewController`'s –update method provides smooth transition animation when the user changes the point of view for rendering. The animation results from using a *low pass filter* to gradually reduce the difference between the current point of view and the user's chosen point of view. A low pass filter makes repetitive gradual changes to a calculated value and must be called many times to produce significant effects. It's called "low pass" because low-frequency, long-term changes to the value being filtered have dramatic effects but high-frequency changes have little lasting impact. The following code from example OpenGLES_Ch6_1's `SceneCar.m` implements the low pass filter:

```
/////////////////////////////////////////////////////////////////
// This function returns a value between target and current. Call
// this function repeatedly to asymptotically return values closer
// to target: "ease in" to the target value.
GLfloat SceneScalarSlowLowPassFilter(
    NSTimeInterval elapsed,     // seconds elapsed since last call
    GLfloat target,             // target value to approach
    GLfloat current)            // current value
{   // Constant 4.0 is an arbitrarily "small" factor
    return current + (4.0 * elapsed * (target - current));
}


/////////////////////////////////////////////////////////////////
// This function returns a vector between target and current.
// Call repeatedly to asymptotically return vectors closer
// to target: "ease in" to the target value.
GLKVector3 SceneVector3SlowLowPassFilter(
    NSTimeInterval elapsed,     // seconds elapsed since last call
    GLKVector3 target,          // target value to approach
    GLKVector3 current)         // current value
{
```

```
    return GLKVector3Make(
        SceneScalarSlowLowPassFilter(elapsed, target.x, current.x),
        SceneScalarSlowLowPassFilter(elapsed, target.y, current.y),
        SceneScalarSlowLowPassFilter(elapsed, target.z, current.z));
}
```

The low pass filter works because it's called repeatedly, and each time it returns a new current value that's closer to the "target" value. Each time OpenGLES_Ch6_1ViewController's –update is called, the low pass filter functions are called again and the current point of view becomes closer to the target point of view until eventually the current point of view matches the target point of view.

Functions such as low pass filters smooth animation. OpenGLES_Ch6_1 applies filters when changing the orientation of cars, too. As a car rebounds off a wall and reverses direction, the car doesn't spin to face the new direction instantaneously. Instead, the target orientation changes to the new direction and the car's current orientation gradually updates until it matches the target. Almost every 3D simulation benefits from filtering of one sort or another.

OpenGLES_Ch6_1 adds five new classes to the group of classes developed over the preceding chapters: SceneMesh, SceneModel, SceneCar, SceneCarModel, and SceneRinkModel. The SceneMesh class exists to manage large quantities of vertex data and coordinate transfer of the data to GPU-controlled memory. A *mesh* is a collection of triangles that share vertices or sides and define 3D shapes. The SceneModel class draws all or parts of meshes. A single *model* may be composed of multiple meshes, and many models may share the same mesh. Models represent 3D objects such as cars, mountains, or human figures that have shapes defined by meshes. Models group all the meshes needed for the represented 3D object. The SceneCar class encapsulates each bumper car's current position, velocity, color, yaw angle, and model. *Yaw* is a term from ships and aerospace that refers to rotation abut the vertical axis, in this case the Y axis. Yaw defines the orientation of the car and changes over time to make the car face its direction of motion. The SceneCarModel subclass of SceneModel encapsulates a mesh in the shape of a single car. Each SceneCar instance uses the same SceneCarModel instance. If the bumper cars had different shapes so that one looked like a truck and another like an airplane, then the SceneCar instances would each use a different model. Finally, the SceneRinkModel subclass of SceneModel encapsulates a mesh for the rink's walls and floor.

SceneCar implements a –drawWithBaseEffect: method to set the current material color to match the car's color, translate the model-view coordinate system to the car's current position, rotate the coordinate system to match the car's current yaw angle, and draw the bumper car model. Translation and rotation are explained in Chapter 5.

```
/////////////////////////////////////////////////////////////////
// Draw the receiver: This method sets anEffect's current
// material color to the receiver's color, translates to the
// receiver's position, rotates to match the receiver's yaw
// angle, draws the receiver's model. This method restores the
// values of anEffect's properties to values in place when the
// method was called.
```

```
- (void)drawWithBaseEffect:(GLKBaseEffect *)anEffect;
{
   // Save effect attributes that will be changed
   GLKMatrix4  savedModelviewMatrix =
      anEffect.transform.modelviewMatrix;
   GLKVector4  savedDiffuseColor =
      anEffect.material.diffuseColor;
   GLKVector4  savedAmbientColor =
      anEffect.material.ambientColor;

   // Translate to the model's position
   anEffect.transform.modelviewMatrix =
      GLKMatrix4Translate(savedModelviewMatrix,
         position.x, position.y, position.z);

   // Rotate to match model's yaw angle (rotation about Y)
   anEffect.transform.modelviewMatrix =
      GLKMatrix4Rotate(anEffect.transform.modelviewMatrix,
         self.yawRadians,
         0.0, 1.0, 0.0);

   // Set the model's material color
   anEffect.material.diffuseColor = self.color;
   anEffect.material.ambientColor = self.color;

   [anEffect prepareToDraw];

   // Draw the model
   [model draw];

   // Restore saved attributes
   anEffect.transform.modelviewMatrix = savedModelviewMatrix;
   anEffect.material.diffuseColor = savedDiffuseColor;
   anEffect.material.ambientColor = savedAmbientColor;
}
```

All the examples in this chapter reuse the SceneMesh class, and all but one use the SceneModel class. The view controller in each example allocates and initializes SceneMesh and SceneModel instances. The controller's –update method is called automatically at the display refresh rate and updates variables to indirectly control the coordinate systems for drawing. Then, the controller's –glkView:drawInRect: sends messages to draw the models and meshes.

Animating Vertex Data

Example OpenGLES_Ch6_2 modifies the vertex attributes within a mesh over time to simulate a flag waving in the wind. Figure 6.2 shows the result. *Mesh animation* produces dramatic effects that are sometimes indispensable, but mesh animation is not very common in 3D graphics because it requires frequent copies of vertex data between central processing unit (CPU)-controlled memory and graphics processing unit (GPU)-controlled memory. Coordinate system changes produce many of the same effects as vertex attribute changes without all the data copying. For example, animated 3D human figures are frequently constructed from complex non-rectangular meshes that define the shapes of the figures. As the figures walk, run, or jump, the vertices within the meshes remain constant and transformation matrices make it seem like limbs move and skin stretches over the character's joints and muscles. Chapter 7, "Loading and Using Models," explains models in more detail.

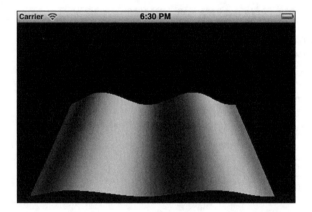

Figure 6.2   A screenshot of the flag waving in example OpenGLES_Ch6_2.

When using mesh animation, optimizations to reduce the amount of data copied often provide large benefits. The simplest way to supply a GPU with geometric data for triangles is to specify all three vertices of each and every triangle. However, a significant optimization called a *triangle strip* is available when drawing triangles that share sides. A triangle strip combines a series of two or more connected triangles. The first triangle in the strip is defined by the first three vertices, and each subsequent triangle shares two vertices with the preceding triangle in the strip. Figure 6.3 shows how to draw a square with two triangles labeled A and B but only four vertices labeled 0, 1, 2, and 3. The two triangles in Figure 6.3 share the vertices numbered 1 and 2.

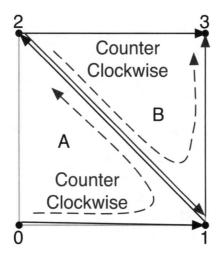

Figure 6.3   Four vertices are needed to draw a four-sided shape composed of two triangles.

Sharing vertices reduces the amount of memory required to store geometric information and reduces the total number of vertices that the GPU must process. Individually specifying three vertices for every triangle in a scene requires (3 * N) vertices where N is the number of triangles. Drawing the same scene with triangle strips only requires (2 + N) vertices.

The order of the vertices in triangles and triangle strips makes a difference. OpenGL ES uses vertex order to determine which face of each triangle is the *front face*. In a 3D scene, every triangle has a front and a back. Most of the time, it doesn't matter which face you can see, but OpenGL ES can be configured to skip rendering one side or the other with a mode called *back face culling* as described in Chapter 7. By convention, normal vectors point out of the front face due to the *right-hand rule* first mentioned in Chapter 4, "Shedding Some Light." For triangle A in Figure 6.3, the normal vector is calculated using vertices (0, 1, 2) in counterclockwise order. If the vertices were processed in the opposite order, (0, 2, 1), the resulting normal vector would point in the opposite direction.

If the square in Figure 6.3 is drawn as two separate triangles, the correct order of vertices is triangle(0, 1, 2) followed by triangle(2, 1, 3). That way, both triangles process vertices in counterclockwise order. However, if the square in Figure 6.3 is drawn as a single triangle strip with four vertices, triangleStrip(0, 1, 2, 3), OpenGL ES interprets the triangle strip vertices in a very significant order: the first triangle rendered is triangle(0, 1, 2), but the second triangle is not triangle(1, 2, 3); instead, the second triangle rendered is triangle(2, 1, 3). Figure 6.4 shows a more complex triangle strip that draws five connected triangles. The vertices in Figure 6.4 are submitted to OpenGL ES in the order triangleStrip(0, 1, 2, 3, 4, 5, 6), but those vertices are processed in the order (0, 1, 2), (2, 1, 3), (2, 3, 4), (4, 3, 5), (4, 5, 6), giving all five triangles a counterclockwise sequence of vertices.

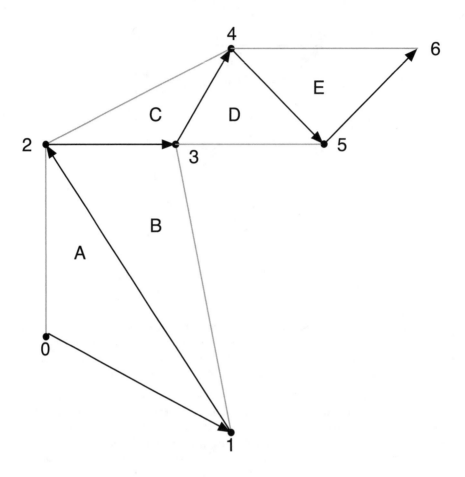

Figure 6.4   A triangle strip that forms a complex shape.

The numbers in Figure 6.4 indicate the order that the vertices are stored in a vertex buffer. Drawing the triangle strip illustrated in Figure 6.4 is as easy as binding the vertex attribute array buffer into the current OpenGL ES context and calling glDrawArrays(GL_TRIANGLE_STRIP, 0, 7).

Using Indexed Vertices

There's a trick to drawing meshes like the one illustrated in Figure 6.5. When a mesh has multiple columns, drawing the entire mesh with a single call to glDrawArrays(GL_TRIANGLE_STRIP, ...) without duplicating vertices is not possible. Drawing each column as a separate triangle strip is necessary. However, each column in the mesh shares half of its vertex data with the preceding column. For example, the vertex labeled 5 in Figure 6.5 is part of the triangles labeled A, B, and C in the first column and also part of the triangles labeled D,

E, and F in the second column. Drawing each column with a separate triangle strip requires duplication in memory of vertices shared between columns. In other words, the same vertex data has to be stored in the vertex buffer used to draw the first column and the vertex buffer used to draw the second column.

Indexed vertices provide an optimization that eliminates wasteful duplication of vertex data. When using indexed vertices, store each vertex exactly once in memory no matter how many triangles use the vertex.

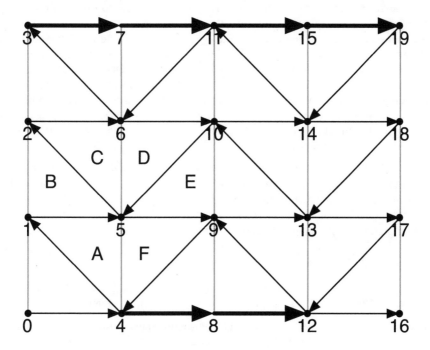

Figure 6.5   Geometric relationships of mesh vertices and indices.

To apply indexed vertices, create a new buffer called an *element array buffer* to store vertex indices. Each value in the element array buffer identifies a vertex by the vertex's position in a separate vertex attribute array buffer. Index 0 identifies the first vertex in the vertex attribute array buffer. Index 5 identifies the sixth (counting from zero) vertex in the vertex attribute array buffer, and so on. Element array buffers are created much like other buffers, as shown in the following pseudo code.

```
glGenBuffers(1, &indexBuffer);
glBindBuffer(GL_ELEMENT_ARRAY_BUFFER, indexBuffer);
glBufferData(GL_ELEMENT_ARRAY_BUFFER, <size>,
      <address>, <usage_hint>);
```

Store vertex index values within the element array buffer in the order that the referenced vertices are used to draw the triangle strip. The same index value can be used any number of times by repeating the value in the element array buffer.

Drawing with an element array buffer is similar to drawing with the `glDrawArrays()` function but uses the `glDrawElements(GLenum mode, GLsizei count, GLenum type, const GLvoid *indices)` function instead. The supported values of the mode argument to `glDrawElements()` are GL_POINTS, GL_LINE_STRIP, GL_LINE_LOOP, GL_LINES, GL_TRIANGLE_STRIP, GL_TRIANGLE_FAN, and GL_TRIANGLES. Example OpenGLES_Ch6_2 uses the GL_TRIANGLE_STRIP mode. All the modes are documented at http://www.khronos.org/opengles/documentation/opengles1_0/html/glDrawElements.html. The second argument to `glDrawElements()` specifies the number of indices to use. For triangle strips, the number of indices equals the number of triangles to draw plus 2. The third argument specifies the type of the index values and must either be GL_UNSIGNED_BYTE or GL_UNSIGNED_SHORT. Note: At most 65,536 unique indices can be referenced when using the GL_UNSIGNED_SHORT type, and only 256 unique indices are available when using GL_UNSIGNED_BYTE. The last argument to `glDrawElements()` is a pointer to the memory containing the indices. When using an element array buffer, the fourth argument is actually a byte offset into the element array buffer and should be NULL when starting with the first index.

There is a trick for drawing meshes with `glDrawElements()`: To draw multiple mesh rows with one call to `glDrawElements()`, empty triangles are inserted at the end of each column. Figure 6.5 shows the empty triangles with thick lines. The following list contains vertex indices in the order they must be stored in the element array buffer to draw the mesh. The list highlights indices that produce empty triangles in bold.

{0, 4, 1, 5, 2, 6, **3, 7, 11,** 6, 10, 5, 9, **4, 8, 12,** 9, 13, 10, 14, **11, 15, 19,** 14, 18, 13, 17, 12, 16}

The triangle with vertices (3, 7, 11), the triangle with vertices (4, 8, 12), and the triangle with vertices (11, 15, 19) have no area and produce no fragments when rendered.

This mesh drawing pattern with empty triangles efficiently draws meshes with up to 65,536 separate vertices using just one call to `glDrawElements()`. The wasted GPU processing time to process an empty triangle per column is much lower than the extra processing time needed for separate calls to `glDrawElements()` that would otherwise be needed for each column.

The OpenGLES_Ch6_2 Example

Example OpenGLES_Ch6_2 subclasses the SceneMesh class from OpenGLES_Ch6_1 to create the SceneAnimatedMesh class. The following code is an excerpt from SceneMesh and is similar to code from all the –glkView:drawInRect: implementations in the view controllers of previous examples. An AGLKVertexAttribArrayBuffer instance is created if necessary to store mesh vertex attributes. A new element array buffer is created, initialized with indices, and bound into the OpenGL ES context as shown in bold.

```
/////////////////////////////////////////////////////////////////
// This method prepares the current OpenGL ES 2.0 context for
// drawing with the receiver's vertex attributes and indices.
- (void)prepareToDraw;
{
   if(nil == self.vertexAttributeBuffer &&
      0 < [self.vertexData length])
   { // vertex attiributes haven't been sent to GPU yet
      self.vertexAttributeBuffer =
         [[AGLKVertexAttribArrayBuffer alloc]
         initWithAttribStride:sizeof(SceneMeshVertex)
         numberOfVertices:[self.vertexData length] /
            sizeof(SceneMeshVertex)
         data:[self.vertexData bytes]
         usage:GL_STATIC_DRAW];

      // No longer need local data storage
      self.vertexData = nil;
   }

   if(0 == indexBufferID && 0 < [self.indexData length])
   { // Indices haven't been sent to GPU yet
      // Create an element array buffer for mesh indices
      glGenBuffers(1, &indexBufferID);
      NSAssert(0 != self.indexBufferID,
         @"Failed to generate element array buffer");

      glBindBuffer(GL_ELEMENT_ARRAY_BUFFER, self.indexBufferID);
      glBufferData(GL_ELEMENT_ARRAY_BUFFER,
         [self.indexData length],
         [self.indexData bytes],
         GL_STATIC_DRAW);

      // No longer need local index storage
      self.indexData = nil;
   }

   // Prepare vertex buffer for drawing
   [self.vertexAttributeBuffer
      prepareToDrawWithAttrib:GLKVertexAttribPosition
      numberOfCoordinates:3
      attribOffset:offsetof(SceneMeshVertex, position)
      shouldEnable:YES];

   [self.vertexAttributeBuffer
      prepareToDrawWithAttrib:GLKVertexAttribNormal
      numberOfCoordinates:3
```

```
        attribOffset:offsetof(SceneMeshVertex, normal)
        shouldEnable:YES];

    [self.vertexAttributeBuffer
        prepareToDrawWithAttrib:GLKVertexAttribTexCoord0
        numberOfCoordinates:2
        attribOffset:offsetof(SceneMeshVertex, texCoords0)
        shouldEnable:YES];

    // Bind the element array buffer (indices)
    glBindBuffer(GL_ELEMENT_ARRAY_BUFFER, indexBufferID);
}
```

The SceneAnimatedMesh class provides the following —drawEntireMesh method that calls glDrawElements() instead of the glDrawArrays() function used in prior examples:

```
///////////////////////////////////////////////////////////////
// Draw the entire mesh after it has been prepared for drawing
- (void)drawEntireMesh;
{
    // Draw triangles using vertices in the prepared vertex
    // buffers and indices from the bound element array buffer
    glDrawElements(GL_TRIANGLE_STRIP,
        NUM_MESH_INDICES,
        GL_UNSIGNED_SHORT,
        NULL);
}
```

The example animates the mesh by changing the Y coordinates of the mesh's vertices over time. The rippling wave effect is produced by calling the following SceneAnimatedMesh method at a regular rate from the view controller's —update method.

```
///////////////////////////////////////////////////////////////
// This method modifies vertex positions and recalculates
// normals. The vertex attribute array is reinitialized with the
// modified vertex data in this class' -draw method.
- (void)updateMeshWithElapsedTime:(NSTimeInterval)anInterval;
{
    int     currentRow;
    int     currentColumn;

    // For each position along +X axis of mesh
    for(currentColumn = 0; currentColumn < NUM_MESH_COLUMNS;
        currentColumn++)
    {
        const GLfloat   phaseOffset = 2.0f * anInterval;
        const GLfloat   phase = 4.0 * currentColumn /
            (float)NUM_MESH_COLUMNS;
```

```
   const GLfloat   yOffset = 2.0 *
      sinf(M_PI * (phase + phaseOffset));

   // For each position along -Z axis of mesh
   for(currentRow = 0; currentRow < NUM_MESH_ROWS; currentRow++)
   {
      mesh[currentColumn][currentRow].position.y =
         yOffset;
   }
}


SceneMeshUpdateNormals(mesh);

[self makeDynamicAndUpdateWithVertices:&mesh[0][0]
   numberOfVertices:sizeof(mesh) / sizeof(SceneMeshVertex)];
}
```

The bold code in the preceding method sets the Y coordinate of each vertex to the value of a sine trigonometry function based on the current column of vertices being modified and a time interval. The time interval changes each time the values are recalculated producing a moving wave effect. Sine is only used because it produces a visually interesting repeating pattern. Other functions besides sine will work. Try different equations such as yOffset = 2.0 * cosf(phase * phase + phaseOffset) or yOffset = 2.0 * sinf(M_PI * (sinf(phase) + phaseOffset)) to experiment with different waves.

Each time the vertex positions change, the vertex normal vectors must be recalculated as well. The call to SceneMeshUpdateNormals() accomplishes that using an algorithm similar to the one introduced in Chapter 4. The face normal of each triangle in the mesh is calculated, and the normal vector for each vertex is set to an average of the face normal vectors for all triangles that include the vertex. Averaging the face normal vectors produces a smooth lighting effect instead of facets.

Finally, calling makeDynamicAndUpdateWithVertices: numberOfVertices: sends the updated vertex attributes to GPU-controlled memory and sets the mesh's usage hint to GL_DYNAMIC_DRAW indicating that the vertex attributes are prone to frequent updates.

Note

Mesh animation consumes memory bandwidth to copy the updated vertex data from CPU-controlled memory to GPU-controlled memory. Minimizing the overall amount of copying that takes place is important because memory bandwidth is the number one bottleneck in embedded systems. One approach that avoids copying uses an OpenGL ES 2.0 Shading Language program running on the GPU to calculate new vertex positions directly in GPU-controlled memory. Chapter 7 includes such a program in the "Advanced Models" section.

Animating Colors and Lights: The OpenGLES_Ch6_3 Example

Figure 6.6 is a screenshot produced from example OpenGLES_Ch6_3. OpenGL ES lights can be repositioned or aimed at different locations over time to produce visual effects. The color and intensity of each light can be varied. The OpenGLES_Ch6_3 example adds lighting animation to the waving flag produced by example OpenGLES_Ch6_2.

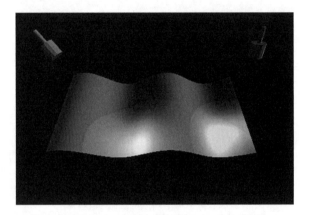

Figure 6.6   Animated spotlights illuminate a waving flag.

Example OpenGLES_Ch6_3 uses "spotlights" that were briefly mentioned in Chapter 4. Spotlights are positional light sources configured to shed light in a cone shape instead of all directions. In addition to a position, each spotlight has a spotDirection, a spotCutoff angle, and a spotExponent, as illustrated in Figure 6.7. The spotDirection is a vector that defines the direction the cone of light shines. The spotCutoff angle is the angle in degrees that determines how wide the cone of light will be. The spotExponent determines how quickly the light fades from the center of the spot to the edges.

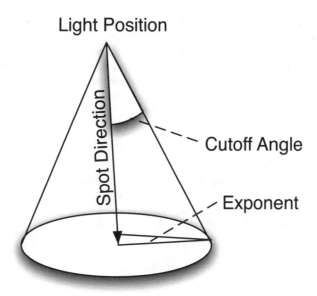

Figure 6.7   Spotlight properties.

GLKit's GLKBaseEffect and GLKEffectPropertyLight classes work together to implement spotlights. GLKit provides two different implementations of OpenGL ES lighting. Setting GLKBaseEffect's lightingType property to GLKLightingTypePerVertex tells GLKit to calculate light values for each vertex in the geometry and interpolate between vertices. Setting lightingType to GLKLightingTypePerPixel produces higher quality rendering by recalculating light effects for each fragment at the cost of greater computational workload for the GPU than per-vertex calculations. Without fragment calculations for spotlights, the edges of the lit areas appear jagged. Set the lightingType to GLKLightingTypePerVertex in OpenGLES_Ch6_3ViewController's —viewDidLoad method to see the jagged appearance.

Example OpenGLES_Ch6_3 and the subsequent examples in this chapter use the custom AGLKTextureTransformBaseEffect subclass of GLKit's GLKBaseEffect class. The two classes produce identical rendered results in OpenGLES_Ch6_3. The implementation of AGLKTextureTransformBaseEffect highlights coordinate system transformations that apply to light positions and directions as explained later in this section. In addition, later examples use texture effects that GLKBaseEffect doesn't support at the time of this writing. Using AGLKTextureTransformBaseEffect now minimizes the number of changes needed between example OpenGLES_Ch6_3 and subsequent examples.

> **Note**
>
> The implementation of `AGLKTextureTransformBaseEffect` reproduces a subset of
> GLKit's `GLKBaseEffect` class including spotlights and directional lights. The Shading
> Language program used by `AGLKTextureTransformBaseEffect` is elaborate and still
> doesn't provide every lighting feature of `GLKBaseEffect`. As with all the "AGLK" classes,
> using the Apple-supported versions when possible is better. Explore the implementation of
> `AGLKTextureTransformBaseEffect` for a flavor of the way GLKit may be implemented with
> OpenGL ES 2.0 and the potential extent of Shading Language programs.

Spotlights are configured in `OpenGLES_Ch6_3ViewController`'s `-viewDidLoad` method. First,
the method sets the overall lighting model.

```
// Use high quality lighting (important for spot lights)
self.baseEffect.lightingType = GLKLightingTypePerPixel;
self.baseEffect.lightModelTwoSided = GL_FALSE;
self.baseEffect.lightModelAmbientColor = GLKVector4Make(
    0.6f, // Red
    0.6f, // Green
    0.6f, // Blue
    1.0f);// Alpha
```

Two-sided lighting enables the use of separate materials for "front" and "back" sides of
geometric objects. The front side is whichever side has a normal vector pointing away
from the side. The interaction of lights with materials determines fragment colors, so using
separate materials has the potential to produce dramatic effects. At the time of this writing,
`GLKBaseEffect` only supports one material at a time, so enabling two-sided lighting just
determines whether "back" sides are lit at all.

Two spotlights are defined. The code for `light1` is similar to the following code for `light0`
except that `light0` has a yellow color (equal parts red and green) and `light1` has a cyan color
(equal parts green and blue).

```
//Light 0 is a spot light
self.baseEffect.light0.enabled = GL_TRUE;
self.baseEffect.light0.spotExponent = 20.0f;
self.baseEffect.light0.spotCutoff = 30.0f;
self.baseEffect.light0.diffuseColor = GLKVector4Make(
    1.0f, // Red
    1.0f, // Green
    0.0f, // Blue
    1.0f);// Alpha
self.baseEffect.light0.specularColor = GLKVector4Make(
    0.0f, // Red
    0.0f, // Green
    0.0f, // Blue
    1.0f);// Alpha
```

A third light, `light2`, is configured as a simple directional light. Recall from Chapter 4 that the position of a directional light is a four-component vector with the last component set to `0.0`. The `spotLight2Position` variable is initialized to the vector, `{0.0f, 0.5f, 1.0f, 0.0f}`. The position is interpreted as the direction light shines from an infinitely distant source.

```
// Light 2 is directional
self.baseEffect.light2.enabled = GL_TRUE;
self.baseEffect.light2Position = spotLight2Position;
self.baseEffect.light2.diffuseColor = GLKVector4Make(
   0.5f, // Red
   0.5f, // Green
   0.5f, // Blue
   1.0f);// Alpha
```

The –viewDidLoad method configures most properties of the spotlights, and the properties never change again. However, unlike the directional light, the spotlights' positions and directions are not specified up-front. By convention, OpenGL transforms the position and direction of positional lights using the current model-view matrix in effect when the position and direction are set. The positions and directions therefore must be reset every time the coordinate systems for the lights change.

Example OpenGLES_Ch6_3 rotates the spotlights to move the light beams as they interact with the changing geometry of the waving flag. OpenGLES_Ch6_3ViewController uses four new properties, spotLight0TiltAboutXAngleDeg, spotLight0TiltAboutZAngleDeg, spotLight1TiltAboutXAngleDeg, and spotLight1TiltAboutZAngleDeg, to animate light directions. As with other animations, functions based on time determine the changing property values.

```
- (void)updateSpotLightDirections
{
   // Tilt the spot lights using periodic functions for simple
   // smooth animation (constants are arbitrary and chosen for
   // visually interesting spot light directions)
   spotLight0TiltAboutXAngleDeg = -20.0f + 30.0f * sinf(
      self.timeSinceLastResume);
   spotLight0TiltAboutZAngleDeg = 30.0f * cosf(
      self.timeSinceLastResume);
   spotLight1TiltAboutXAngleDeg = 20.0f + 30.0f * cosf(
      self.timeSinceLastResume);
   spotLight1TiltAboutZAngleDeg = 30.0f * sinf(
      self.timeSinceLastResume);
}
```

Two methods of OpenGLES_Ch6_3ViewController, -drawLight0 and -drawLight1, each transform the model-view coordinate system based on spotlight tilt angle properties, set a spotlight's position and direction, and then draw a simple model of a "can light" to mark the position and orientation of the light. The following bold code configures the spotlight as a positional light at the origin, and the spot direction always points down the negative Y axis.

The "can light" model correspondingly uses a mesh of vertices near the origin and appears to point down the negative Y axis. The local coordinate system created each time a light and model draw produces the moving light effect seen in the example.

```
- (void)drawLight0
{
   // Save effect attributes that will be changed
   GLKMatrix4  savedModelviewMatrix =
      self.baseEffect.transform.modelviewMatrix;

   // Translate to the model's position
   self.baseEffect.transform.modelviewMatrix =
      GLKMatrix4Translate(savedModelviewMatrix,
          spotLight0Position.x,
          spotLight0Position.y,
          spotLight0Position.z);
   self.baseEffect.transform.modelviewMatrix =
      GLKMatrix4Rotate(
          self.baseEffect.transform.modelviewMatrix,
          GLKMathDegreesToRadians(self.spotLight0TiltAboutXAngleDeg),
          1,
          0,
          0);
   self.baseEffect.transform.modelviewMatrix =
      GLKMatrix4Rotate(
          self.baseEffect.transform.modelviewMatrix,
          GLKMathDegreesToRadians(self.spotLight0TiltAboutZAngleDeg),
          0,
          0,
          1);

   // Configure light in current coordinate system
   self.baseEffect.light0Position = GLKVector4Make(0, 0, 0, 1);
   self.baseEffect.light0SpotDirection = GLKVector3Make(0, -1, 0);

   [self.baseEffect prepareToDraw];
   [self.canLightModel draw];

   // Restore saved attributes
   self.baseEffect.transform.modelviewMatrix =
      savedModelviewMatrix;
}
```

Animating Textures

Transforming the model-view coordinate system over time makes rendered objects appear to move relative to the point of view or vice versa. Changing the texture coordinate system over time animates the way textures map to geometry. The next example, OpenGLES_Ch6_4, loads and maps a translucent texture to the waving flag from example OpenGLES_Ch6_3. The example rotates the texture coordinate system based on elapsed time to produce the screenshot in Figure 6.8.

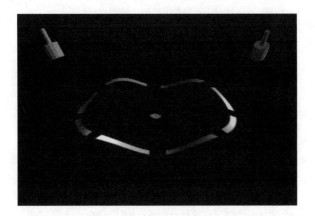

Figure 6.8   An animated texture mapped to the waving flag geometry.

The OpenGLES_Ch6_4 Example

OpenGLES_Ch6_4ViewController's -viewDidLoad method loads and configures at texture with the following code that's nearly identical to texture loading in previous examples going all the way back to OpenGLES_Ch3_1:

```
// Setup texture0
CGImageRef imageRef0 =
   [[UIImage imageNamed:@"RadiusSelectionTool.png"] CGImage];

GLKTextureInfo *textureInfo0 = [GLKTextureLoader
   textureWithCGImage:imageRef0
   options:nil
   error:NULL];

self.baseEffect.texture2d0.name = textureInfo0.name;
self.baseEffect.texture2d0.target = textureInfo0.target;
```

A new method, -updateTextureTransform, added to OpenGLES_Ch6_4ViewController rotates the texture coordinate system. Recall from Chapter 3, "Textures," that the texture coordinate system spans from 0.0 to 1.0 along each of the S and T axes. The following code rotates about the center of the texture by translating to {0.5, 0.5}, rotating, and then translating back {-0.5, -0.5}. The texture matrix and the recipe for rotating about a point are explained in Chapter 5.

```
- (void)updateTextureTransform
{
   // Rotate the texture
   // Translate to center of texture coordinate system
   self.baseEffect.textureMatrix2d0 =
      GLKMatrix4MakeTranslation(
         0.5,
         0.5,
         0.0);
   // Rotate
   self.baseEffect.textureMatrix2d0 =
      GLKMatrix4Rotate(
         self.baseEffect.textureMatrix2d0,
         self.timeSinceLastResume, // use interval as num radians
         0,
         0,
         1);
   // Translate back to texture coordinate system origin
   self.baseEffect.textureMatrix2d0 =
      GLKMatrix4Translate(
         self.baseEffect.textureMatrix2d0,
         -0.5,
         -0.5,
         0);
}
```

OpenGLES_Ch6_4ViewController's –update method updates the texture matrix and spotlight directions as follows:

```
/////////////////////////////////////////////////////////////
// This method is called automatically at the update rate of the
// receiver (default 30 Hz).
- (void)update
{
   [self updateSpotLightDirections];
   [self updateTextureTransform];
}
```

That's all it takes to implement the rotating texture. The combination of changing vertex positions in the waving flag mesh and a changing texture matrix produces a visually complex animation. The AGLKTextureTransformBaseEffect class is needed in example

OpenGLES_Ch6_4 because at the time of this writing, GLKit's built-in `GLKBaseEffect` doesn't implement the texture matrix.

The OpenGLES_Ch6_5 Example

Example OpenGLES_Ch6_5 stores several 2D images within a single OpenGL ES texture called a *texture atlas*. Each image is slightly different from the others and serves as a frame in short movie. When the frames are shown in rapid succession, they present the illusion of motion. Example OpenGLES_Ch6_5 uses the same basic technique as OpenGLES_Ch6_4 for loading and mapping a texture to geometry, but OpenGLES_Ch6_5 uses a texture atlas.

OpenGLES_Ch6_5's texture atlas image is 1024 pixels wide and 1024 pixels long. It's divided into 8 rows that are 128 pixels tall and 8 columns that are 128 pixels wide, as shown in Figure 6.9. There is space for 64 sub-images in the texture atlas, but only 51 sub-images are needed in the example. As a result, the last row and part of the second to last row in Figure 6.9 remain unused.

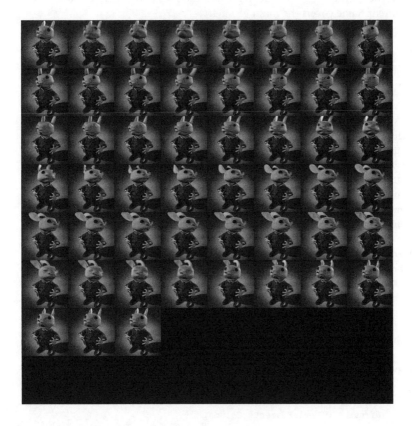

Figure 6.9   A texture atlas that stores still images in a grid.

The following constants help calculate the position within the texture atlas of each movie frame.

```
///////////////////////////////////////////////////////////////
// Constants used to calculate the texture position of each
// sub-image in a texture atlas that contains still frames from
// a movie
static const int numberOfMovieFrames = 51;
static const int numberOfMovieFramesPerRow = 8;
static const int numberOfMovieFramesPerColumn = 8;
static const int numberOfFramesPerSecond = 15;
```

Example OpenGLES_Ch6_5 distributes S and T texture coordinates in the range 0.0 to 1.0 across the mesh vertices just like example OpenGLES_Ch6_4. Without any modifications to the texture matrix, the whole atlas would be mapped to the mesh geometry. However, the example needs to render the mesh covered by only one movie frame at a time. The following code first translates the texture coordinate system so that the origin, {0.0, 0.0}, corresponds to the lower-left corner of the current movie frame and then scales the texture coordinate system so that the current frame covers the mesh geometry:

```
- (void)updateTextureTransform
{
   // Calculate which sub-image of the texture atlas to use
   int      movieFrameNumber =
      (int)floor(self.timeSinceLastResume * numberOfFramesPerSecond) %
         numberOfMovieFrames;

   // Calculate the position of the current sub-image
   GLfloat   currentRowPosition =
      (movieFrameNumber % numberOfMovieFramesPerRow) *
      1.0f / numberOfMovieFramesPerRow;
   GLfloat   currentColumnPosition =
      (movieFrameNumber / numberOfMovieFramesPerColumn) *
      1.0f / numberOfMovieFramesPerColumn;

   // Translate to origin of current frame
   self.baseEffect.textureMatrix2d0 =
      GLKMatrix4MakeTranslation(
         currentRowPosition,
         currentColumnPosition,
         0.0f);
   // Scale to make current frame fill coordinate space
   self.baseEffect.textureMatrix2d0 =
      GLKMatrix4Scale(
         self.baseEffect.textureMatrix2d0,
         1.0f/numberOfMovieFramesPerRow,
         1.0f/numberOfMovieFramesPerColumn,
         1.0f);
}
```

Run example OpenGLES_Ch6_5 to see the combination of animated vertex data, animated lights, and animated textures in one application. Try modifying the examples to change the point of view over time as well. For example, vary the arguments to `GLKMatrix4MakeLookAt()` using a filter or a periodic function such as `sinf()`. Add spotlights to example OpenGLES_Ch6_1 for a more dramatic bumper car simulation.

Summary

Animation provides a fourth dimension, time, in addition to the three dimensions of X, Y, and Z coordinates. Animation approaches presented in this chapter underlay applications of many types including games, scientific visualization, and the user interface effects of Cocoa Touch. Almost all animations result from changing coordinate systems over time. That's true whether moving objects around in a scene, pointing spotlights, spinning textures, or walking around a dungeon maze with a first-person point of view. Changing vertex attributes produces animation such as the waving flag examples in this chapter, but frequently changing vertex data should be avoided for optimal performance.

Chapter 7 and Chapter 8, "Special Effects," extend the `SceneModel` and `SceneAnimatedMesh` classes introduced in this chapter. Models are essential for most 3D applications because the alternative, hard-coded vertex data rapidly becomes unwieldy. Chapter 7 explores more sophisticated models than the bumper car, rink, and can light used in this chapter. Chapter 8 demonstrates several techniques that produce compelling visual illusions with minimal run-time processing.

7

Loading and Using Models

So far, the geometric vertex attributes used in each example have been compiled right into the applications. The very first example, OpenGLES_Ch2_1, hard codes the locations of three vertices to define a triangle. By Chapter 5, "Changing Your Point of View," generated C language header files contain more complex definitions for geometry. Compiling vertex data directly into an application has the advantage of fast loading but also has constraints.

Loading vertex attributes and other data at runtime provides a more flexible and dynamic alternative to compiling the data right into the application. This chapter introduces runtime data loading. Many tools exist to create the data. Many incompatible file formats exist to store the data. Several techniques may be used to interpret the data in files and ultimately convert loaded data into vertex attributes, textures, and effects that OpenGL ES requires.

Before jumping into code, it's worth examining the reasons for loading data at runtime. A focus on end goals helps select a technical approach from the myriad available options. The following goals are assumed:

- Provide acceptable loading and runtime performance.
- Reduce the amount of scarce memory consumed at runtime.
- Update or add data to applications without recompiling.
- Simplify application development with multiple team members.

Reading data from the iOS file system during application launch will never be as fast as using data compiled into the application. However, reading from the file system can provide acceptable performance if used with care. The key is to store data in a way that requires minimal processing while loading. Another approach is to delay loading data until the last possible moment or loading data asynchronously in a separate thread from the main application user interface. The paramount goal is to make the application respond to the user as quickly as possible.

Data compiled into an application resides in central processor unit (CPU)-controlled memory as long as the application runs. A second copy of at least some of the data must be stored in graphics processing unit (GPU)-controlled memory as well to enable rendering. Keeping multiple copies of the same data might not present a problem with small data sets, but memory is scarce in embedded systems. When there are many complex scenes, the extra storage for two copies might not be acceptable. Worse, simultaneously storing many scenes in CPU-controlled memory becomes wasteful when only one scene can be seen at a time anyway. Loading only the data currently needed, passing it to GPU-controlled memory, and then freeing the CPU-controlled memory reduces overall memory requirements dramatically.

Applications intended to interact with user created data obviously can't contain the data compiled into the application itself. Some applications download data over network interfaces at runtime. A game might ship with limited levels and receive additional levels via the Internet through subscriptions or via in-app purchases. Ideally, runtime loading enables all of these scenarios.

Finally, runtime loading often simplifies application development. It's particularly important with large development teams when data generation happens on a different schedule than software development. Artists like to see their creations in the application promptly and need a process to enable rapid iterative improvements. The ideal approach loads the artists' new data without even restarting the application let alone recompiling it.

Modeling Tools and Formats

Creating vertex attribute data with a text editor or in code is difficult, error prone, and tedious. Many "modeling" tools exist for creating 3D data ranging from vertex attributes to animation, physics, lighting, and other effects. *Modeling* is the term used by 3D content creators to describe the process of developing 3D data called *models*. Table 7.1 compares popular modeling tools.

Table 7.1   **Popular 3D Modeling Tools Compared**

Tool	Where to Go	Strength	Weakness
Autodesk 3ds Max Products	usa.autodesk.com/ 3ds-max	Animated figure models, low polygon models, texture management; extensibility with third-party plug-ins.	Not available for Mac OS X; expensive; free trial version available.
Autodesk Maya	usa.autodesk.com/ maya	Cinematic scenes with high level of detail and lighting; available for Mac OS X.	Expensive; free trial version available.

Tool	Where to Go	Strength	Weakness
Blender	www.blender.org	Free, open source, strong user community.	Complex user interface disdains any semblance of any platform's conventions.
Google SketchUp	sketchup.google.com	Free basic version adequate for many needs; pro version relatively inexpensive; simple elegant user interface.	Little animation capability; few advanced modeling tools for special effects.

Table 7.1 lists a tiny subset of available tools. A tool not listed might meet specific needs. Wikipedia explores the comparison more comprehensively at http://en.wikipedia.org/wiki/Comparison_of_3D_computer_graphics_software.

The models in this book were produced with SketchUp or Blender and sometimes a combination of the two. Examples need to be accessible to the widest possible audience; SketchUp and Blender are both free and available for Mac OS X.

Each 3D modeling tool stores data describing the created models in different and often proprietary file formats. Most tools import or export model data from other tools. Sometimes, third-party plug-ins enable model import and export. A reliable documented file format for 3D data interchange between tools was desperately needed for decades. The Wavefront .OBJ format became popular for data interchange because it's easy to parse, but it's very limited. The format is unable to store critical information produced by modern applications. Using .OBJ format to exchange models between tools entails the danger of inadvertently discarding useful information.

The solution today is the *COLLADA* format controlled by the Khronos Group, the same organization that controls OpenGL standards. COLLADA uses Extensible Markup Language (XML) to store model data in otherwise ordinary text files. It's free to use with no royalties or other fees, and the specification is available at www.khronos.org/collada. Almost all modern modeling tools export models in COLLADA format and most import the format as well.

COLLADA stores geometry, materials, textures, lights, animations, and more in files with the .dae extension. Vertex data is typically organized in a compact representation with instancing, which means the same vertex data may be used in more than one model or mesh. Chapter 6, "Animation," introduces meshes, and this chapter elaborates on the concept.

COLLADA enables information exchange between modeling tools and 3D applications. The format usually transfers data without loss. However, COLLADA is not well-suited for storing the data to be loaded directly by iOS applications. The complexity needed for complete interoperability between tools makes the format difficult to parse. The best practice uses an off-line tool to read COLLADA files and output a subset of the data specifically suited for the iOS application.

The Asset Pipeline

Asset pipeline describes the sequence of tools used to create 3D data, convert data between formats, optimize, test for problems, and output data suitable for efficient loading in an application. This book uses a simple asset pipeline that starts with SketchUp or Blender, as shown in Figure 7.1.

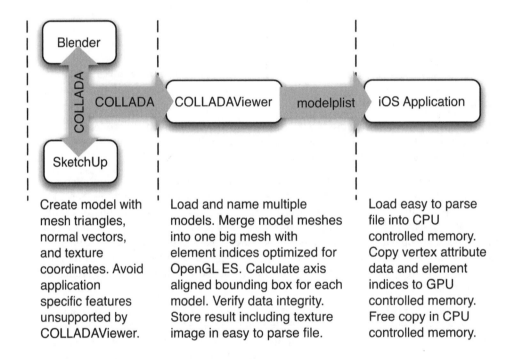

Figure 7.1   COLLADAViewer-based asset pipeline.

The COLLADAViewer application runs on Mac OS X and is included with this chapter's examples at http://opengles.cosmicthump.com/learning-opengl-es-sample-code/. COLLADAViewer.app leverages Mac OS X's NSXMLDocument and related NSXML classes to parse .dae files. A relatively small amount of Objective-C code, only five classes, extracts the raw data of interest from the NSXMLDocument and converts it into meshes and models.

Alternative tools for parsing .dae files exist. The OpenCOLLADA (http://opencollada.org/) Open Source Software Development Kit (SDK) parses .dae files and provides a foundation for interpreting the data or converting it to other formats.

Many modeling tools apply OpenCOLLADA to implement import and export. Versions of the COLLADAViewer application have been built using OpenCOLLADA, but frankly, OpenCOLLADA is huge and has many library dependencies that are not common on Mac OS X. For some rough numbers, OpenCOLLADA implements thousands of C++ classes scattered through more than 1,200 separate source files. When dependencies such as the popular C++ "boost" library are included in the total, building OpenCOLLADA for Mac OS X requires compilation of more than 20,000 C++ files comprising more than 4.2 million lines of code. For the needs of COLLADAViewer, using Mac OS X's built-in libraries and Objective-C makes more sense.

Other options for parsing .dae files include the official but outdated COLLADA Document Object Model (DOM) available at http://sourceforge.net/projects/collada-dom/ and a commercial library called FCollada. One of the most interesting projects, Open Asset Import Library, available at http://assimp.sourceforge.net/, strives to load a long list of 3D model formats including COLLADA. New projects should consider Open Asset Import Library in part because it loads models into a straightforward data structure and supports various post-processing steps for general optimization.

COLLADAViewer.app suffices for converting COLLADA documents into data easily imported into iOS applications, but COLLADAViewer has a long list of limitations. For example, COLLADAViewer assumes each .dae file contains exactly one model. No COLLADA library/ instance objects are supported. Blender automatically exports models with suitable meshes, but you must "explode" all "Components" in SketchUp before exporting to COLLADA. There's an "Explode" context menu available by right-clicking models in SketchUp. COLLADAViewer only uses one texture image at a time; you must combine all the texture images needed into one large texture atlas shared by models. The texture image from the last imported model supercedes all others in COLLADAViewer. The best practice creates the texture atlas before mapping it to any models with the various modeling tools. When all models use the same texture image, it doesn't matter which order they are imported into COLLADAViewer. Finally, COLLADAViewer assumes that models have positions near the coordinate system origin.

> **Note**
>
> This book's example models were built in units of meters, but SketchUp always exports COLLADA files in inches by converting the user's chosen unit into equivalent inches. COLLADAViewer automatically converts models to "+Y axis up" orientation and scales models back into meters regardless of the units and orientation used in modeling tools. Models with dimensions larger than a few tens of meters or smaller than a few centimeters are difficult to see in COLLADAViewer. Similarly, models positioned more than a few meters away from the coordinate system origin cannot be seen in COLLADAViewer.

Figure 7.2 shows a screenshot of the COLLADAViewer application after three separate COLLADA files have been imported and combined. The mouse scroll wheel and two-finger-drag on a track pad zooms in and out. Options toggle display of normal vectors and the –Z axis for reference. Example OpenGLES_Ch7_1 revisits the bumper car simulation from Chapter 6 and loads the models shown in Figure 7.2.

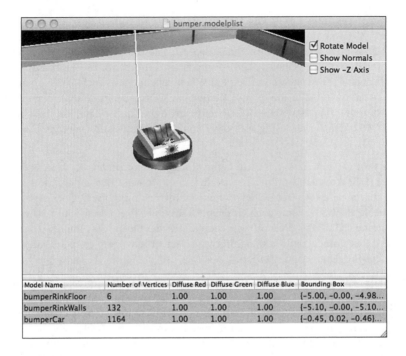

Figure 7.2   COLLADAViewer screenshot.

Even with its limitations, COLLADAViewer.app provides a starting point for building a comprehensive COLLADA model viewer for Mac OS X. Another example, XRay, at http://www.hfink.eu/collada/xray, uses OpenCOLLADA, provides source code, and includes an Xcode project for building on Mac OS X.

COLLADAViewer saves imported models in files with the extension .modelplist. Property lists, or *plists,* define a native Mac OS X and iOS file format documented at http://developer.apple.com/library/ios/documentation/Cocoa/Conceptual/PropertyLists. Property lists organize data into a structured format that remains very efficient. Applications frequently use property lists on both Mac OS X and iOS. For example, system and application user defaults are stored as plist format files. In a nutshell, plist files store hierarchies of serialized Cocoa/Cocoa Touch NSData, NSArray, NSDictionary, NSString, NSDate, and NSNumber objects. Plist files are compatible between Mac OS X and iOS, so modelplist files written by COLLADAViewer.app on Mac OS X can be directly read by iOS applications as compact binary files. The next section explains the specific hierarchy of Cocoa Touch objects used in modelplist files.

Reading modelplist Files

Regardless of model file formats, the GPU ultimately processes vertex attribute buffers and index buffers resident in GPU-controlled memory. Good application performance depends on the efficiency of sending data to the GPU in the right format. Fast loading by iOS applications remains the primary goal for combining and converting COLLADA files into modelplist files. In the interest of runtime speed, all meshes from all models are combined into a single buffer of vertex attributes that can be sent to the GPU in one operation. Similarly, another buffer contains all index data. Modelplist files store the texture image data to be sent to the GPU directly in a single texture buffer operation.

The following code sample shows the steps for loading modelplist files. The bold line of code uses the Cocoa Touch NSKeyedUnarchiver class to deserialize objects from modelplist data with one statement. The code then extracts a textureInfo object, a consolidated mesh, and a dictionary that maps model names to ranges of mesh data.

```
- (BOOL)readFromData:(NSData *)data
   ofType:(NSString *)typeName
   error:(NSError **)outError
{
   NSDictionary *documentDictionary =
      [NSKeyedUnarchiver unarchiveObjectWithData:data];

   self.textureInfo = [GLKTextureInfo
      textureInfoFromUtilityPlistRepresentation:
         [documentDictionary objectForKey:
         UtilityModelManagerTextureImageInfo]];

   self.consolidatedMesh = [[UtilityMesh alloc]
      initWithPlistRepresentation:[documentDictionary
      objectForKey:UtilityModelManagerMesh]];

   self.modelsDictionary =
      [self modelsFromPlistRepresentation:[documentDictionary
      objectForKey:UtilityModelManagerModels]
      mesh:self.consolidatedMesh];

   return YES;
}
```

Plists may contain any combination of supported Cocoa Touch objects. It's common for plists to store dictionaries of arrays of dictionaries and similar nested hierarchies. The modelplist format stores a specific hierarchy, but plists are inherently extensible. Additional data may be stored in modelplist files as long as required elements are present.

> **Note**
>
> Apple defines the standard for the general plist format. The specific hierarchy of objects in modelplist files supports examples in this book. Different applications could certainly store different information or forego the plist format entirely. Load model data in whatever format makes sense for each application as long as the format is fast, compact, and supported by the asset pipeline you use.

Modelplist files must contain certain objects. First and foremost, the "root" object is an `NSDictionary`. The root object is the object returned from `NSKeyedUnarchiver`'s `-unarchiveObjectWithData:` method. The root object contains all other objects in the plist. Dictionaries store a collection of key-value pairs optimized for fast lookup by key. Dictionaries created in code may use almost any objects as keys, but dictionaries in plists always use strings for keys. The root dictionary in modelplist files must contain at least three keys: `textureImageInfo`, `models`, and `mesh`.

```
///////////////////////////////////////////////////////////////
// Constants used to access model properties from a plist
// dictionary.
NSString *const UtilityModelManagerTextureImageInfo =
    @"textureImageInfo";
NSString *const UtilityModelManagerMesh =
    @"mesh";
NSString *const UtilityModelManagerModels =
    @"models";
```

In modelplist files, the objects paired with each root dictionary key are also dictionaries. Figure 7.3 illustrates the format. The objects shown in gray are the same in every modelplist file. The white objects contain unique data to be extracted from files. The keys in the "models" dictionary are the names of the contained models. Each model must have a unique name because each key may only occur once in a dictionary.

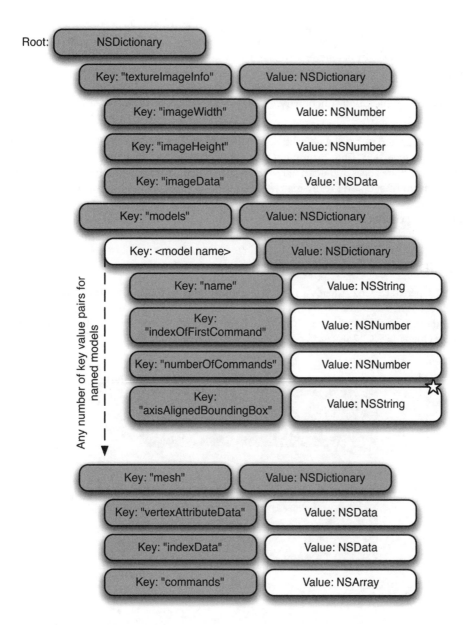

Figure 7.3   The structure of the modelplist format.

Example OpenGLES_Ch7_1 provides `UtilityTextureInfo`, `UtilityModelManager`, `UtilityModel`, and `UtilityMesh` classes that each extract the relevant information from modelplist files. `UtilityTextureInfo` uses the "textureImageInfo" dictionary. `UtilityModelManager` uses the "models" dictionary and creates a new dictionary of `UtilityModel` instances that each read a <model name> dictionary. The `UtilityMesh` class grabs data out of the "mesh" dictionary.

The next section contains code to use `UtilityTextureInfo`, `UtilityModelManager`, `UtilityModel`, and `UtilityMesh` classes. Meshes and models work in much the same way as in examples OpenGLES_Ch6_2 through OpenGLES_Ch6_5 from Chapter 6. A mesh is a grid of triangles that share edges and define 3D shapes. The original source of mesh data (hard coded or loaded from files) doesn't really matter. GPUs excel at rendering meshes with optimizations such as indexed vertices. The efficiency of sending static/unchanging mesh data to the GPU enables high-performance rendering.

The OpenGLES_Ch7_1 Example

Example OpenGLES_Ch7_1 loads a single modelplist file at runtime. The file contains a mesh with all the vertex attributes and indices for all the models needed by the example. The file also contains a single texture image used for all the models. Figure 7.4 shows the output from example OpenGLES_Ch7_1.

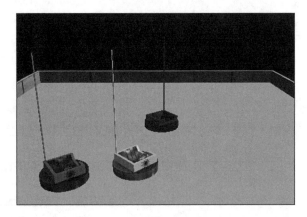

Figure 7.4   Output from example OpenGLES_Ch7_1.

Conceptually, models are composed of one or more meshes. Models may draw each component mesh with different coordinate system transformations and material attributes. Imagine the head of a human figure model turning without the shoulders turning. The head and shoulders might be separate meshes used by the same model.

However, the most efficient way to draw with OpenGL ES uses a single large unchanging mesh resident in GPU-controlled memory. A good compromise is for each model to draw different subsets of a single large mesh by specifying the range of vertex indices corresponding to the parts used by the model. That's exactly how the UtilityModel and UtilityMesh classes interact in OpenGLES_Ch7_1. All the UtilityModel instances share the same UtilityMesh instance. Models reference an array of drawing commands stored by the mesh. Different commands draw different subsets of the mesh using different OpenGL ES modes such as GL_TRIANGLES or GL_TRIANGLE_STRIP. Triangle strips are explained in Chapter 6.

The bumper car simulation in OpenGLES_Ch7_1 uses the same basic simulation logic from OpenGLES_Ch6_1. The SceneCar class is almost identical in both examples. Where the example in Chapter 6 uses compiled-in model data, OpenGLES_Ch7_1 adds the UtilityModelManager class to load model data at runtime.

```
self.modelManager =
   [[UtilityModelManager alloc] initWithModelPath:modelsPath];
```

The UtilityModelManager – initWithModelPath: method initializes an NSData object with the contents of the file at the specified path and then invokes the -readFromData:ofType:error: method shown in the "Reading Modelplist Files" section to extract model, mesh, and texture objects from data.

```
NSData *data = [NSData dataWithContentsOfFile:aPath
   options:0
   error:&modelLoadingError];

if(nil != data)
{
   [self readFromData:data
      ofType:[aPath pathExtension]
      error:&modelLoadingError];
}
```

The UtilityMesh class in example OpenGLES_Ch7_1 is a more general version of the SceneMesh class from Chapter 6. UtilityMesh adds a property to store an array of commands. The UtilityModel class has properties to identify the range of mesh drawing commands applicable to each model.

```
@property (assign, nonatomic, readwrite) NSUInteger
   indexOfFirstCommand;
@property (assign, nonatomic, readwrite) NSUInteger
   numberOfCommands;
@property (assign, nonatomic, readonly)
   AGLKAxisAlignedBoundingBox axisAlignedBoundingBox;
```

UtilityModels also have an axisAlignedBoundingBox property pre-calculated by COLLADAViewer and stored with the model in the modelplist file. An *axis-aligned bounding box* spatially contains every vertex in a model. It stores the minimum and maximum x, y, z values found in the model's mesh. The axis-aligned bounding box defines the volume of 3D space occupied by a model and comes in handy for many purposes. The `SceneCar` class in this example and example OpenGLES_Ch6_1 back in Chapter 6 uses the axis-aligned bounding box property to detect collisions between cars.

The `UtilityModel` `-draw` method sends a message to the mesh to draw using commands within the model's command range.

```
- (void)draw
{
   [self.mesh drawCommandsInRange:NSMakeRange(
      indexOfFirstCommand_, numberOfCommands_)];
}
```

The `UtilityMesh` `-drawCommandsInRange:` method loops calling `glDrawElements()` with the commands in the model's range as follows:

```
- (void)drawCommandsInRange:(NSRange)aRange;
{
   if(0 < aRange.length)
   {
      const NSUInteger lastCommandIndex =
         (aRange.location + aRange.length) - 1;

      NSParameterAssert(aRange.location < [self.commands count]);
      NSParameterAssert(lastCommandIndex < [self.commands count]);

      for(NSUInteger i = aRange.location;
         i <= lastCommandIndex; i++)
      {
         NSDictionary *currentCommand =
            [self.commands objectAtIndex:i];
         const GLsizei  numberOfIndices = (GLsizei)[[currentCommand
            objectForKey:@"numberOfIndices"]
            unsignedIntegerValue];
         const GLsizei  firstIndex = (GLsizei)[[currentCommand
            objectForKey:@"firstIndex"] unsignedIntegerValue];
         GLenum mode = (GLenum)[[currentCommand
            objectForKey:@"command"] unsignedIntegerValue];

         glDrawElements(mode,
            (GLsizei)numberOfIndices,
            GL_UNSIGNED_SHORT,
            ((GLushort *)NULL + firstIndex));
      }
   }
}
```

Comparing example OpenGLES_Ch7_1 to example OpenGLES_Ch6_1 highlights two different implementations of the central concepts embodied by meshes and models. Even with the different implementations, the capabilities of the mesh and model classes in the two projects are similar enough that the SceneCar class can use either implementation interchangeably. The same vertex attributes end up in GPU-controlled memory even though they come from different sources. The concepts enable almost any asset pipeline using almost any tools as long as the key relationships between meshes and models exist.

Back Face Culling

Example OpenGLES_Ch7_1 employs a new mode, GL_CULL_FACE, within the OpenGL ES state machine. As mentioned in Chapter 6, every triangle has a front side and a back side defined by the order OpenGL ES receives the triangle's vertices. Culling refers to an optional optimization used by OpenGL ES to discard vertex attributes early before much processing has been performed. Back face culling discards triangles that face away from the viewer. When viewing a simulated solid object, back faces usually face inside the object, so discarding back facing triangles doesn't degrade the scene; even without culling, seeing the back faces would only be possible if your point of view was inside a solid object.

OpenGLES_Ch7_1ViewController doesn't enable GL_CULL_FACE just for optimization: Models loaded from SketchUp are often "two sided." In SketchUp terminology, that means the front and back sides of triangles have different materials, different colors, and different textures. Without back face culling, OpenGL ES tries to render both sides of "two sided" triangles, but the two sides are effectively co-planar primitives that produce Z-fighting.

Chapter 5 described Z-fighting. In example OpenGLES_Ch7_1, Z-fighting makes it random whether the final fragment color in the frame buffer's pixel color render buffer originates from the front face or the back face of "two-sided" triangles. In practice, half the fragments come from each side and the triangles twinkle as the fragments flip back and forth between colors.

Back face culling avoids Z-fighting by only rendering front sides. The following code in bold from OpenGLES_Ch7_1ViewController enables back face culling:

```
- (void)glkView:(GLKView *)view drawInRect:(CGRect)rect
{
   // Clear back frame buffer (erase previous drawing)
   // and depth buffer
   [((AGLKContext *)view.context)
      clear:GL_COLOR_BUFFER_BIT|GL_DEPTH_BUFFER_BIT];

   // Cull back faces: Important! many Sketchup models have back
   // faces that cause Z fighting if back faces are not culled.
   [((AGLKContext *)view.context) enable:GL_CULL_FACE];

   // Calculate the aspect ratio for the scene and setup a
   // perspective projection
   const GLfloat  aspectRatio =
      (GLfloat)view.drawableWidth / (GLfloat)view.drawableHeight;
```

```
self.baseEffect.transform.projectionMatrix =
  GLKMatrix4MakePerspective(
    GLKMathDegreesToRadians(35.0f),// Standard field of view
    aspectRatio,
    4.0f,    // Don't make near plane too close
    20.0f); // Far arbitrarily far enough to contain scene

[self.modelManager prepareToDraw];
[self.baseEffect prepareToDraw];

// Draw the rink
[self.rinkModelFloor draw];
[self.rinkModelWalls draw];

// Draw the cars
[cars makeObjectsPerformSelector:
  @selector(drawWithBaseEffect:)
  withObject:self.baseEffect];
}
```

Advanced Models

A thorough exploration of advanced modeling falls outside the scope of this book, but several concepts and terms deserve mention if only to provide a foundation for further study. This section describes fairly complicated subjects that mostly interest programmers who want to animate models of human figures and certain types of meshes. Skip this section if you're itching to move on to the next major topic, but there are some fun examples to explore here.

Skeletal Animation

Skeletal animation describes a technique for posing and animating models. A mesh provides the visible portion of the model like in preceding examples, but in addition, an invisible hierarchy of interconnected "joints" and "bones," also known as an *armature* or rig, deforms the mesh. By animating the armature, the mesh vertices follow along. For example, a mesh representing the leg and foot of a human figure appears to lift and swing with the pivot of armature joints representing ankle, knee, and hip. The term *skeletal animation* suggests its primary use animating models that simulate humans or other animals, but the approach applies to almost any mesh animation, including the flag waving effect in Chapter 6.

Skeletal animation provides a huge optimization when animating models that use complex meshes. Sending new orientations for relatively few armature joints to the GPU is faster than recalculating and sending every vertex position in a mesh. As explained in this section and the next, each armature joint is controlled with a transformation matrix. The GPU already transforms every vertex position with the model view and projection matrices as explained in Chapter 5. Using an armature adds very little extra calculation per vertex. Artists who create models typically find skeletal animation intuitive. Moving a joint to pose an arm is easier than manually moving every vertex in the corresponding mesh. Almost all modeling tools that support animation apply skeletal animation.

Armature joints consist of a position and a transformation matrix. The position is actually a displacement from an optional "parent" joint. The displacement from one joint to the next represents an invisible bone. The joints form a hierarchy so that changes to a parent joint influence all the connected "child" joints. For example, when an elbow changes position, the connected wrist also moves to keep the displacement (distance) between the elbow and the wrist constant. The position of any joint can be calculated using the concatenation of its parent joint's transformation matrix and the joint's own transformation matrix. The following code returns the cumulative transformations for a joint. It uses a variant of the recipes from the "Transformation Cookbook" section of Chapter 5:

```
//////////////////////////////////////////////////////////////////
// Returns the cumulative matrix that includes parent transforms
- (GLKMatrix4)cumulativeTransforms;
{
    GLKMatrix4 result = GLKMatrix4Identity;

    if(nil != parent)
    {
        result = [parent cumulativeTransforms];
    }

    GLKVector3 d = self.cumulativeDisplacement;

    // Use the classic recipe for transform about a point:
    // translate to the location of the joint, rotate, and
    // translate back.
    result = GLKMatrix4Translate(result, d.x, d.y, d.z);
    result = GLKMatrix4Multiply(result, self.matrix);
    result = GLKMatrix4Translate(result, -d.x, -d.y, -d.z);

    return result;
}
```

Example OpenGLES_Ch7_2 helps to visualize joints. Three simple models are loaded from a modelplist file. To keep the example simple, the lengths of the models also determine the displacements of the joints. User interface sliders shown in Figure 7.5 let you experiment with rotating joints to see the effect on the models. The first joint, the one with no parent, is at the bottom.

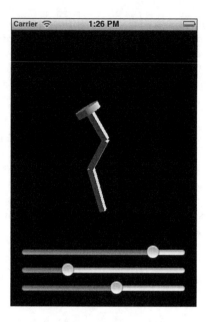

Figure 7.5   Models used to visualize an armature.

Example OpenGLES_Ch7_2 uses the GPU to implement armature-based animation. A new subclass of GLKBaseEffect, UtilityArmatureBaseEffect, creates and uses a custom OpenGL ES Shading Language program. Use UtilityArmatureBaseEffect's –prepareToDrawArmature method to apply armature-based animation. The inherited –prepareToDraw method still works and uses the standard GLKit Shading Language programs. UtilityArmatureBaseEffect has a jointsArray property to store UtilityJoint instances. Updating joint properties at runtime and then calling –prepareToDrawArmature sends all the needed information for the Shading Language program to recalculate vertices and normal vectors right in GPU memory.

The OpenGLES_Ch7_2ViewController class contains the following code to create three joints and add them to the example's UtilityArmatureBaseEffect instance. The joint positions are initialized from the axis-aligned bounding boxes of loaded models. Joint positions and orientations are usually loaded directly from model files rather than calculated; the example uses the model dimensions for convenience and simplicity only.

```
// Create collection of joints
UtilityJoint *bone0Joint = [[UtilityJoint alloc]
   initWithDisplacement:GLKVector3Make(0, 0, 0)
   parent:nil];
float bone0Length = self.bone0.axisAlignedBoundingBox.max.y -
   self.bone0.axisAlignedBoundingBox.min.y;

UtilityJoint *bone1Joint = [[UtilityJoint alloc]
   initWithDisplacement:GLKVector3Make(0, bone0Length, 0)
```

```
    parent:bone0Joint];
float bone1Length = self.bone1.axisAlignedBoundingBox.max.y -
    self.bone1.axisAlignedBoundingBox.min.y;

UtilityJoint *bone2Joint = [[UtilityJoint alloc]
    initWithDisplacement:GLKVector3Make(0, bone1Length, 0)
    parent:bone1Joint];

baseEffect.jointsArray = [NSArray arrayWithObjects:
    bone0Joint,
    bone1Joint,
    bone2Joint,
    nil];
```

Each model is assigned a single joint index with an expression like [self.bone0
assignJoint:0]. The index ends up stored along with other attributes for each vertex in the
model's mesh. The Shading Language program uses the index to look up which joint matrix
transforms each vertex. Within the Shading Language program, each joint matrix has already
been concatenated with the projection matrix, the model-view matrix, and its parent joint's
matrix, so each vertex is transformed using the cumulative influence of each joint in the
hierarchy: its own joint, the joint's parent joint, its grandparent joint, and so on.

Adding extra attributes to vertices requires the definition of new constants. OpenGL ES 2.0
doesn't apply any intrinsic meaning to attribute constants. It's up to Shading Language
programs to interpret the data. The Shading Language programs generated by Apple's
GLKBaseEffect class apply meaning to the constants GLKVertexAttribPosition,
GLKVertexAttribNormal, GLKVertexAttribColor, GLKVertexAttribTexCoord0, and
GLKVertexAttribTexCoord1. All except the GLKVertexAttribColor attribute have been used
in prior examples.

```
typedef enum {
    UtilityArmatureVertexAttribPosition =
        GLKVertexAttribPosition,
    UtilityArmatureVertexAttribNormal =
        GLKVertexAttribNormal,
    UtilityArmatureVertexAttribTexCoord0 =
        GLKVertexAttribTexCoord0,
    UtilityArmatureVertexAttribTexCoord1 =
        GLKVertexAttribTexCoord1,
    UtilityArmatureVertexAttribJointMatrixIndices,
    UtilityArmatureVertexAttribJointNormalizedWeights,
} UtilityArmatureVertexAttrib;
```

UtilityArmatureBaseEffect redefines the GLKit attributes and adds two
new ones, UtilityArmatureVertexAttribJointMatrixIndices and
UtilityArmatureVertexAttribJointNormalizedWeights. The example's UtilityMesh class
stores joint information in a buffer and sends the extra values to the GPU in much the same
way as other per-vertex attributes.

```
glEnableVertexAttribArray(
   UtilityArmatureVertexAttribJointMatrixIndices);
glVertexAttribPointer(
   UtilityArmatureVertexAttribJointMatrixIndices,
   4,                       // number of coordinates
   GL_FLOAT,                // data is floating point
   GL_FALSE,                // no fixed point scaling
   sizeof(UtilityMeshJointInfluence),// bytes per vert
   (GLubyte *)NULL +
      offsetof(UtilityMeshJointInfluence, jointIndices));

glEnableVertexAttribArray(
   UtilityArmatureVertexAttribJointNormalizedWeights);
glVertexAttribPointer(
   UtilityArmatureVertexAttribJointNormalizedWeights,
   4,                       // number of coordinates
   GL_FLOAT,                // data is floating point
   GL_FALSE,                // no fixed point scaling
   sizeof(UtilityMeshJointInfluence),// bytes per vert
   (GLubyte *)NULL +
      offsetof(UtilityMeshJointInfluence, jointWeights));
```

The code for managing extra vertex attributes uses the `UtilityMeshJointInfluence` data structure, which is similar to the `UtilityMeshVertex` structure. The next section, "Skinning," explains `UtilityMeshJointInfluence` and joint weights.

The `OpenGLES_Ch7_2ViewController` class also contains code to update joints when you move a slider. The following method accepts the floating-point value of a slider and uses it to rotate the joint at index zero in `jointsArray`. Multiplying the slider's value by `M_PI` and `0.5` just scales the range of values to plus or minus `M_PI/2` radians (+/– 90 degrees). Similar methods update the other two joints.

```
- (void)setJoint0AngleRadians:(float)value
{
   joint0AngleRadians = value;

   GLKMatrix4  rotateZMatrix = GLKMatrix4MakeRotation(
      value * M_PI * 0.5, 0, 0, 1);

   [(UtilityJoint *)[baseEffect.jointsArray objectAtIndex:0]
      setMatrix:rotateZMatrix];
}
```

Almost any transformation can be set for a joint. Rotating about the Z axis keeps things simple for the example. Try changing the code to rotate around the X axis or translate. Scale works, too, but when scale factors are non-uniform (scale more in one direction than another), the lighting equations in the Shading Language program produce lower-quality results.

As with the `UtilityTextureTransformBaseEffect` class in some of Chapter 5's examples, the source code for `UtilityArmatureBaseEffect` and its Shading Language program are included with the relevant examples. `UtilityArmatureBaseEffect` takes joint matrices containing cumulative transformations from the joint hierarchy and concatenates them with the model-view and projection matrices. At the same time, it calculates new matrices for transforming normal vectors. `UtilityArmatureBaseEffect` sends an array of resulting matrices to the GPU. The `UtilityArmatureVertexAttribJointMatrixIndices` attribute for each vertex determines which matrices in the array provided by `UtilityArmatureBaseEffect` apply to each vertex.

Note

A normal vector transformation matrix is the transpose of the inverse of the cumulative model-view transformations. Don't worry if that makes little sense to you right now. It's a minor detail that seldom requires direct attention. `GLKBaseEffect` automatically calculates the "normal matrix" as needed. The `UtilityArmatureBaseEffect` class similarly calculates an array of "normal matrices" as needed.

Figure 7.6 illustrates the relationship between joint matrices and the `UtilityArmatureVertexAttribJointMatrixIndices` attribute of each vertex. There can be many joint matrices supplied by `UtilityArmatureBaseEffect` at one time, but not every joint matrix is referenced by every vertex.

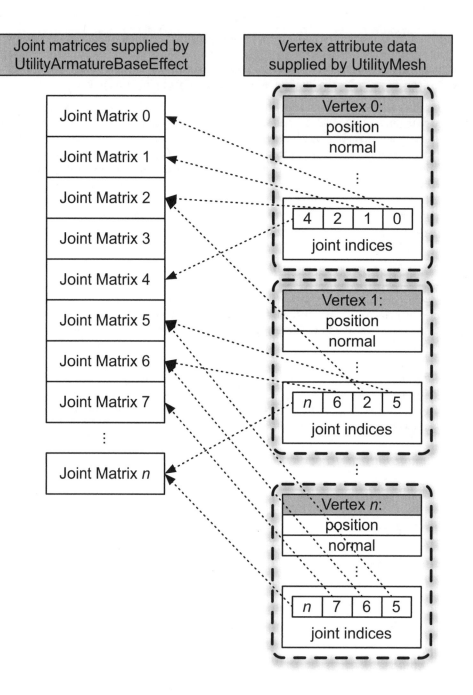

Figure 7.6   Per-vertex indices select joint matrices.

Skinning

As shown in Figure 7.5, gaps open between models when joint orientations change. The effect occurs in example OpenGLES_Ch7_2 because only one joint influences each vertex, and the separate "bones" are drawn with separate models. More organic and smoother mesh animations are possible when the vertices within a single mesh are directly influenced by multiple joints. To accomplish that, more than one joint index is stored with each vertex. The Shading Language program looks up all the joints referenced by each vertex. Each joint's influence on a vertex's final position depends on scale factors known as *weights*. One joint might impart 50% of the influence, another joint imparts 30%, and two more joints each contribute 10%. The ratios don't matter as long as the total influence adds up to 100%.

Figure 7.7 contains screenshots from example OpenGLES_Ch7_3 and shows the effects of combining multiple joint influences. The process of assigning joints indices and weights to each vertex is called *skinning*. Proportionally blending the influence of multiple joints on each mesh vertex deforms the mesh, like stretching skin over bones.

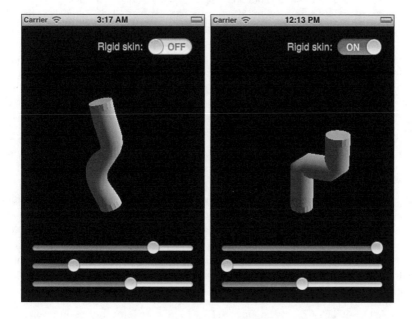

Figure 7.7   The effects of multiple joint influences on vertex position.

OpenGLES_Ch7_3 uses the same joints as OpenGLES_Ch7_2 but draws a single large mesh named "tube" instead of the separate bone models. Play with example OpenGLES_Ch7_3 to get a sense of the mesh deformations produced by moving the sliders.

Smooth mesh deformation works by calculating the transformed position of each mesh vertex multiple times: once for each indexed joint. If the multiple resulting transformed positions are averaged, the calculated position corresponds to skinning with each indexed joint imparting equal influence. The weights provide additional control. Using weights, one joint might have a large influence while another has a very small influence.

The "Rigid skin:" user interface switch provided by example OpenGLES_Ch7_3 toggles between two different "skins." The left one in Figure 7.7 weights the contribution of each joint proportionally to the distance of the joint from each vertex. Joints far away have less influence than joints nearby. With the "Rigid skin:" switch in the "ON" position, weights are set so that each vertex is influenced solely by the closest joint below the vertex, but remember, each joint already contains the influence of its parent joint.

Skinning enables creation of complex models such as human figures with "skin" that deforms realistically as joints move. As a knee bends, the skin near the knee stretches, but skin by the thigh remains unaffected.

> ### Note
>
> COLLADA files are able to store joints and weights. An explanation for parsing and applying COLLADA joints and weights exists at http://www.wazim.com/Collada_Tutorial_1.htm. COLLADA files also store multiple sets of joint orientations to add yet another dimension to skeletal animation. Each set of orientations is analogous to the positions of sliders in OpenGLES_Ch7_3. Each set creates a different "pose." One set might position a figure with arms at its sides and head turned to look over a shoulder. Another set might position the figure with arms in the air and head bowed. Interpolating between the orientation sets produces smooth animation from one pose to another over time.

Example OpenGLES_Ch7_3 implements the two different algorithms for automatically assigning joints and weights in the `UtilityModel` class. The specific code isn't very important because automatically skinned models are seldom used in real applications. Instead of calculating joint influences at runtime, loading the joint indices and weights from a file while loading the rest of the model works much better. Artists specify the weights within offline modeling tools to exert fine control over skinning. Example OpenGLES_Ch7_3's two methods, `-automaticallySkinSmoothWithJoints:` and `-automaticallySkinRigidWithJoints:`, also suffer the disadvantage that they need access to mesh vertex data to work. Ideally, the copy of mesh vertices in CPU-controlled memory is discarded as soon as the data has been sent to the GPU, but to support dynamic calculations for re-skinning, the mesh data must be retained in CPU-controlled memory.

Both example OpenGLES_Ch7_2 and OpenGLES_Ch7_3 store joint indices and weights using the following data structure for each vertex:

```
/////////////////////////////////////////////////////////////
// Type used to store vertex attributes
typedef struct
{
   GLKVector4 jointIndices; // encoded float for Shading Language
   GLKVector4 jointWeights; // weight factor for each joint index
}
UtilityMeshJointInfluence;
```

There are some quirks and limitations inherent to `UtilityMeshJointInfluences`. Only four joint indices and four joint weights may be stored per vertex. Four joints are usually enough to provide realistic skinning. Remember that lots of joints may be used to deform a single mesh. Any of those joints can potentially influence an individual vertex in the mesh. Each vertex selects which four joints. Joint indices are stored as four floating-point values in a `GLKVector4` even though indices are naturally integers or bytes. OpenGL ES 2.0 Shading Language cannot accept integer or byte attributes per vertex. It's a limitation of most current embedded GPUs. OpenGL ES 2.0 Shading Language reserves the type names, `short` and `byte`, for future implementations.

Inverse Kinematics and Physics Simulation

The ancient Greek term *kinematics* refers generally to the motion of objects. In a modern context, kinematics refers to the sequence of joint orientation changes needed to pose a figure with skeletal animation. Forward kinematics define a sequence of joint orientation changes: rotate shoulder 15 degrees, then rotate elbow 45 degrees, then rotate wrist 70 degrees, and then rotate finger joint to scratch head. *Inverse kinematics* present a much more interesting and avant-garde approach. Start with the goal, touching finger to top of head, and work backward to find all the joint orientation changes necessary to make that happen.

With a GPU-optimized system of inverse kinematics, the amount of information sent to and from the CPU to the GPU can be minimized. Instead of sending updated orientations for every joint, simply send the final position of end joints or the tips of imaginary "bones." All the other joint orientations are derived from the requested final position.

Inverse kinematics gets very complex. To work correctly, model-specific constraints must be observed. For example, a hand is not permitted to travel through the head on the way to scratching the top. An elbow is not permitted to bend backward.

Real-time physics simulations and inverse kinematics in particular are hot research topics. Robotics companies, modeling tool makers, and 3D simulator developers are racing to provide general-purpose solutions. In the mean time, the popular open source "Bullet Physics" engine provides many of the pieces. Bullet detects collisions between armature components to at least prevent an arm from traveling through a torso or an elbow from bending backwards. That barely scratches the capabilities of Bullet Physics. It can be integrated with both Blender and SketchUp and exports to COLLADA. Find Bullet Physics and Xcode projects for building demos on Mac OS X and iOS at http://bulletphysics.org/.

Summary

Models represent 3D objects with shapes defined by one or more meshes. Loading models at runtime provides flexibility essential to many 3D applications. Avoid complex parsing or data conversions when loading models in embedded systems by preprocessing the data offline and storing data in native formats. Models can be very complex, but they're composed of simple geometric attributes. There's nothing special about the model data format used in this chapter.

The concepts of models and meshes enable almost any asset pipeline using almost any tools and any formats.

Model armatures, skeletal animation, and skinning use the GPU to deform meshes at runtime. Updating a relatively small number of joint matrices avoids the need to update large amounts of vertex data and repeatedly resend that data to the GPU. Artists specify the joints and weights that provide fine control over skeletal animation and skinning. COLLADA files store the artist-supplied data. Armatures also supply information used with physics simulations to detect when a model collides with other objects or part of a model collides with itself.

The next chapter introduces special effects. They are 3D gimmicks and illusions that enhance the appearance of rendered scenes. Special effects give viewers the impression that scenes contain much more detail than actually exists.

8

Special Effects

This chapter introduces three techniques for adding apparent detail to 3D applications without dramatically increasing the number of vertices processed. Each technique uses 2D images designed to fool the eye even when moving and panning within a 3D scene. The first, a *skybox*, encloses the rendered scene in a cube with textures on all six sides. The textures make it seem like geometry extends all the way to an imaginary horizon. The second effect, *particles*, efficiently simulates explosions, water flowing, or smoke billowing. Finally, *billboards* take advantage of textured triangles aligned with the point of view to conceal the absence of depth.

Skybox

Figure 8.1 shows a partially unfolded skybox and a screenshot of a scene rendered from inside the skybox. The skybox texture provides the illusion of a panoramic vista all the way to a horizon no matter how the point of view changes within the box.

Figure 8.1   Skybox illusion.

A skybox only uses 12 triangles, two for each of the six sides of the cube. OpenGL ES provides a special texture mapping mode called *cube mapping* to make effects like the skybox work. Each of the six cube sides has a mapped 2D texture. When rendering, OpenGL ES calculates each fragment color based on the 3D direction vector from the point of view to a location on the surface of the cube. The location on the surface of the cube then corresponds to S and T texel coordinates within a texture for one of the six sides. Chapter 3, "Textures," explains S and T texel coordinates.

Figure 8.2 illustrates the volume rendered by an imaginary camera placed within the skybox. For the represented camera orientation, a vector extended from the center of the lens to any point within the volume hits one of three sides, North, West, or Bottom. The side hit determines which of the six textures to sample. The S and T coordinates within the sampled texture depend on where the vector hits the side. For example, in Figure 8.2, a vector pointing to the upper-right corner of the rendered scene hits in approximately the center of the North side, resulting in S and T coordinates of approximately {0.5, 0.5} within the North side's texture. In contrast, a vector pointing to the lower-left corner of the scene hits the Bottom side's texture.

Figure 8.2   Texel color sampling with cube texture.

As the imaginary camera changes orientation, vectors from the camera hit different sides of the cube. A camera pointed straight up might sample exclusively from the cube's Top texture. A camera turned 90 degrees clockwise from the orientation in Figure 8.2 would produce vectors that sample from the North, East, and Bottom textures.

Apple's GLKit provides the `GLKSkyboxEffect` class specifically for rendering skyboxes in iOS 5 applications. Example OpenGLES_Ch8_1 uses `GLKSkyboxEffect` to produce the screenshot in Figure 8.1. The example animates the point of view around a model of a sailboat within the skybox to show off the effect.

The following code excerpt from the `OpenGLES_Ch8_1ViewController` class identifies the steps for allocating, initializing, and configuring a skybox:

```
// Create and configure skybox
self.skyboxEffect = [[GLKSkyboxEffect alloc] init];
self.skyboxEffect.textureCubeMap.name = self.textureInfo.name;
self.skyboxEffect.textureCubeMap.target =
   self.textureInfo.target;
self.skyboxEffect.xSize = 6.0f;
self.skyboxEffect.ySize = 6.0f;
self.skyboxEffect.zSize = 6.0f;
```

The size of the skybox is arbitrary. It needs to be large enough to contain the scene to be rendered, and it needs to be a cube (all sides have equal size) to avoid texture distortion when rendering. The center of the skybox is set just before drawing and must be kept close to the eye position used when setting the point of view. If the eye position gets too close to an edge of the skybox cube, texture stretching spoils the illusion.

`GLKTextureLoader` provides methods to work with cube mapped textures required by `GLKSkyboxEffect`. The following bold code initializes `self.textureInfo` with an image named skybox0.png loaded as a cube mapped texture:

```
// Load cubeMap texture
NSString *path = [[NSBundle bundleForClass:[self class]]
   pathForResource:@"skybox0" ofType:@"png"];
NSAssert(nil != path, @"Path to skybox image not found");
NSError *error = nil;
self.textureInfo = [GLKTextureLoader
   cubeMapWithContentsOfFile:path
   options:nil
   error:&error];
```

To draw the skybox, set the `GLKSkyboxEffect` instance's center equal to the eye position and set the `projectionMatrix` and `modelViewMatrix` to match the transformations used to render other parts of the scene. Call the skybox's −prepareToDraw method, and then call the skybox's −draw method. Example OpenGLES_Ch8_1ViewController does it as follows:

```
// Draw skybox centered on eye position
self.skyboxEffect.center = self.eyePosition;
```

```
self.skyboxEffect.transform.projectionMatrix =
    self.baseEffect.transform.projectionMatrix;
self.skyboxEffect.transform.modelviewMatrix =
    self.baseEffect.transform.modelviewMatrix;
[self.skyboxEffect prepareToDraw];
[self.skyboxEffect draw];
```

> **Note**
>
> Similar to skyboxes, another effect, the *environment map* (also called reflection map), makes
> it easy to simulate mirrors and other reflective surfaces such as water. GLKit includes the
> `GLKReflectionMapEffect` class. Your application configures the properties on the reflec-
> tion map just like a `GLKBaseEffect` instance and sets one more property, `textureCubeMap`.
> Rendering a reflection is the same operation as rendering a skybox. In both cases, textures are
> sampled based on a direction. With the skybox, the direction is from the viewer to the sides of
> an enclosing cube. For an environment map, the direction is from the reflective surface to the
> sides of an enclosing cube.

Deep Dive: How Does GLKSkyboxEffect Work?

The `AGLKSkyboxEffect` class in example OpenGLES_Ch8_2 reimplements GLKit's
`GLKSkyboxEffect` and shows how to build a skybox effect with OpenGL ES 2.0. Example
OpenGLES_Ch8_2 uses `AGLKSkyboxEffect` instead of `GLKSkyboxEffect` but is otherwise the
same as example OpenGLES_Ch8_1.

`AGLKSkyboxEffect` has the following interface similar to `GLKSkyboxEffect`:

```
//
//  AGLKSkyboxEffect.h
//
//

#import <GLKit/GLKit.h>

@interface AGLKSkyboxEffect : NSObject <GLKNamedEffect>

@property (nonatomic, assign) GLKVector3 center;
@property (nonatomic, assign) GLfloat xSize;
@property (nonatomic, assign) GLfloat ySize;
@property (nonatomic, assign) GLfloat zSize;
@property (strong, nonatomic, readonly) GLKEffectPropertyTexture
    *textureCubeMap;
@property (strong, nonatomic, readonly) GLKEffectPropertyTransform
    *transform;

- (void) prepareToDraw;
```

```
- (void) draw;

@end
```

The implementation of AGLKSkyboxEffect draws the skybox cube as a single triangle strip with the following vertices. Each side of the cube has length 1.0, (–0.5 to 0.5). Those dimensions are convenient when scaling the skybox to any desired size.

```
// The 8 corners of a cube
const float vertices[AGLKSkyboxNumCoords] = {
    -0.5, -0.5,  0.5,
     0.5, -0.5,  0.5,
    -0.5,  0.5,  0.5,
     0.5,  0.5,  0.5,
    -0.5, -0.5, -0.5,
     0.5, -0.5, -0.5,
    -0.5,  0.5, -0.5,
     0.5,  0.5, -0.5,
};

glGenBuffers(1, &vertexBufferID);
glBindBuffer(GL_ARRAY_BUFFER, vertexBufferID);
glBufferData(GL_ARRAY_BUFFER,
    sizeof(vertices),
    vertices,
    GL_STATIC_DRAW);

// Indices of triangle strip to draw cube
// Order is critical to make "front" faces be on inside
// of cube.
const GLubyte indices[AGLKSkyboxNumVertexIndices] = {
    1, 2, 3, 7, 1, 5, 4, 7, 6, 2, 4, 0, 1, 2
};
glGenBuffers(1, &indexBufferID);
glBindBuffer(GL_ELEMENT_ARRAY_BUFFER, indexBufferID);
glBufferData(GL_ELEMENT_ARRAY_BUFFER,
    sizeof(indices),
    indices,
    GL_STATIC_DRAW);
```

AGLKSkyboxEffect uses a vertex attribute array buffer and an element array buffer to draw the cube using code similar to previous examples. The trick to drawing a skybox is to make sure the "front" face of each triangle is inside the box. Otherwise, rendering a scene from within the box produces incorrect results. The order of vertices in each triangle defines the front face as explained in the "Back Face Culling" section of Chapter 7, "Loading and Using Models."

To prepare for drawing, the skybox's texture is bound. The skybox then translates its coordinate system to position the box with its center at the location specified by the center property and scales the coordinate system to the size specified by the `xSize`, `ySize`, and `zSize` properties. The transformations apply to the skybox's `modelviewMatrix`, which already includes transformations for the point of view by the time the skybox is prepared for drawing.

```
GLKMatrix4 skyboxModelView = GLKMatrix4Translate(
   self.transform.modelviewMatrix,
   self.center.x, self.center.y, self.center.z);
skyboxModelView = GLKMatrix4Scale(
   skyboxModelView,
   self.xSize, self.ySize, self.zSize);
```

Next, the skybox's vertex attribute array buffer and element array buffer are bound and configured:

```
glEnableVertexAttribArray(GLKVertexAttribPosition);
glBindBuffer(GL_ARRAY_BUFFER, vertexBufferID);
glVertexAttribPointer(GLKVertexAttribPosition,
   3,
   GL_FLOAT,
   GL_FALSE,
   0,
   NULL);
glBindBuffer(GL_ELEMENT_ARRAY_BUFFER, indexBufferID);
```

`AGLKSkyboxEffect`'s —draw method sends the vertex data to the graphics processing unit (GPU) with a single call to `glDrawElements()`, as follows:

```
- (void)draw
{
   glDrawElements(GL_TRIANGLE_STRIP,
      AGLKSkyboxNumVertexIndices,
      GL_UNSIGNED_BYTE,
      NULL);
}
```

The Skybox Shading Language Program

GLKit generates Shading Language programs automatically, so you usually don't need to write your own. Nevertheless, several custom OpenGL ES Shading Language programs have been used in prior examples. The bonus example, OpenGLES_Ch3_6, back in Chapter 3, "Textures," adapted one of Apple's sample programs to render and animate two similar cubes: One cube is drawn using GLKit's `GLKBaseEffect` and the other is drawn using a custom Shading Language program that duplicates the relevant parts of the Shading Language program generated by `GLKBaseEffect`.

Example OpenGLES_Ch5_5 from Chapter 5, "Changing Your Point of View," creates the `AGLKTextureTransformBaseEffect` class and related Shading Language program to demonstrate texture coordinate transformations not yet supported by GLKit in iOS 5.

Examples in Chapter 6, "Animation," expand `AGLKTextureTransformBaseEffect` to simulate spotlights similar to OpenGL ES 1.1 built-in capabilities that GLKit also reproduces. In fact, the custom Shading Language program used by `AGLKTextureTransformBaseEffect` pushes the practical limits of Shading Language program complexity in iOS 5. Chapter 7 introduces the `AGLKArmatureBaseEffect` class and its accompanying comparatively simple Shading Language program.

This section offers a whirlwind tour to partially demystify custom Shading Language programs. The topic is large and complex and more thoroughly explained by other books such as *OpenGL ES 2.0 Programming Guide* by Aaftab Munshi, Dan Ginsburg, and Dave Shreiner. Apple's GLKit reduces and often eliminates the Shading Language code otherwise needed to use OpenGL ES 2.0, but Apple can't realistically provide every Shading Language program you might ever want. In the process of recreating `GLKSkyboxEffect`, the `AGLKSkyboxEffect` class in example OpenGLES_Ch8_2 uses a Shading Language program simple enough to provide a gentle introduction.

OpenGL ES 2.0 Shading Language programs always include two *shader* subprograms. One, the *vertex shader*, executes once for every vertex processed when rendering a scene. The other, a *fragment shader*, executes once for every fragment that may be written to the pixel color render buffer. Scenes routinely contain tens or hundreds of thousands of vertices. The GPU calculates a million or more fragment colors each time it renders a scene. Recall that duplicate fragments occur when geometric objects overlap. The depth buffer can determine which of the overlapping fragments produces the final value in the pixel color render buffer. Otherwise, the last fragment color calculated for each position replaces previously calculated values.

Modern GPUs are very fast and highly parallel. Nevertheless, simple Shading Language programs usually execute faster than complex ones. Simplicity becomes crucially important when executing a program 60 million or more times per second. Using rough numbers, a fragment shader containing 100 instructions to calculate 1 million fragment colors requires a GPU that executes 6 billion instructions per second to produce 60 rendered frames per second.

The Vertex Shader

The vertex shader runs once for each vertex submitted to the GPU, and each time a vertex shader runs, it must set the value of a built-in variable named `gl_Position`. The value assigned to `gl_Position` specifies a position in the pixel color render buffer's coordinate system sometimes called *clip space* because values outside the render buffer's coordinate system can't be seen and are therefore "clipped out" of rendered results. The vertex shader is free to calculate `gl_Position` using any desired logic, but typically, the incoming vertex position attribute is transformed by the model-view and projection matrices to calculate the corresponding position in the pixel color render buffer as described in Chapter 5. Example OpenGLES_Ch8_2 uses the following vertex shader. The bold code shows assignment of the `gl_Position` variable.

```
//
// AGLKSkyboxShader.vsh
//
```

```
//

/////////////////////////////////////////////////////////////////
// VERTEX ATTRIBUTES
/////////////////////////////////////////////////////////////////
attribute vec3 a_position;

/////////////////////////////////////////////////////////////////
// UNIFORMS
/////////////////////////////////////////////////////////////////
uniform highp mat4      u_mvpMatrix;
uniform sampler2D       u_unitCube[1];

/////////////////////////////////////////////////////////////////
// Varyings
/////////////////////////////////////////////////////////////////
varying lowp vec3       v_texCoord[1];


void main()
{
   v_texCoord[0] = a_position;
   gl_Position = u_mvpMatrix * vec4(a_position, 1.0);
}
```

Breaking the entire vertex shader down, first, the attributes required for every vertex are declared. This shader only uses one attribute, position, per vertex. The OpenGL ES Shading Language keyword, attribute, declares an attribute and is followed by the data type of the attribute. In this case, attribute vec3 a_position; declares an attribute named a_position that is a vector composed of three floating-point components. The names of attributes are completely arbitrary. Attributes may be used in any way by vertex programs. It's up to the programmer who supplies a vertex attribute array buffer to the GPU to know that a position attribute is required by the current Shading Language program. There's little or no compiler support or runtime checking. A misguided programmer could supply vertex color attributes instead of positions, and the GPU would consequently render garbage without detecting or reporting any errors. OpenGL ES Shading Language might look a bit like C, but it's really a form of standardized GPU assembly language, and you are programming very close to "the metal" as some programmers say. Vertex attributes are only available in vertex shaders. Fragment shaders can't access them.

Uniform variables are stored in GPU-controlled memory. Their values must be set prior to submitting vertex attributes to the GPU, and the values may not change until all submitted vertices have been processed. The uniform keyword declares uniform variables and is usually followed by a precision specification and a data type. The uniform highp mat4 u_mvpMatrix; statement declares a uniform variable named u_mvpMatrix that is a four-by-four matrix of high-precision floating-point values. High-precision values correspond to the

`GLfloat` C data type. In addition to *highp*, two other precisions, *mediump* and *lowp*, are also available. The OpenGL ES 2.0 standard doesn't specify the exact precisions implied by `mediump` and `lowp` except that `lowp` variables must be able to store color component values and `mediump` must support some precision between `lowp` and `highp`. For iOS devices, `lowp` variables store floating-point values in the range –1.0 to 1.0 and are sufficient for storing normalized vectors and color component vectors.

In many cases, the GPU can operate on `lowp` variables more efficiently than `highp` variables, so it pays to use the lowest precision that meets each program's needs. Transformation matrices such as the `u_mvpMatrix` variable used in this example require storage for values outside the range –1.0 to 1.0 and consequently must be declared `highp`.

The other uniform variable used in the example stores the identifier for a texture sampler unit, also known as a texture unit.

```
uniform samplerCube     u_unitCube[1];
```

The `samplerCube` data type is another bit of built-in magic. Each GPU has two or more hardware texture sampling units that typically work in parallel. The `u_unitCube` variable declares an array of identifiers used to select among the GPU's texture units. It's stored as a uniform variable so its value can be programmatically changed prior to each submission of vertex attributes to the GPU. Only one texture sampling unit is needed by this program, so `u_unitCube` is an array that stores only one identifier.

The skybox uses cube texture sampling as explained in the section, "Skybox." The more common 2D positional texture sampling approach identifies texture sampler units with the built-in `sampler2D` data type. In practice, both `samplerCube` and `sampler2D` are synonyms for `GLuint`. Both data types correspond to OpenGL ES resource identifiers.

The third and final kind of variable is declared using the `varying` keyword. Varying variables are optional additional outputs that vertex shaders send on to fragment shaders. Like `uniform` variables, `varying` variables have specified precisions. Fragment shaders can't access vertex attributes, so one common use for varying variables is to store attributes obtained by a vertex shader. Most GPUs store varying variables in scarce GPU registers. The `varying` qualifier can only be used with the data types `float`, `vec2`, `vec3`, `vec4`, `mat2`, `mat3`, `mat4`, or arrays of those types. The OpenGL ES 2.0 standard requires that GPUs support at least 32 `varying` variables of type `float`. A `vec2` `varying` counts as two `float`s. A `mat4` `varying` counts as 16 `float`s.

The vertex program in example OpenGLES_Ch8_2 passes texture coordinates to the fragment program using the `varying lowp vec3 v_texCoord[1]` array. The variable has `lowp` precision because texture coordinates for a skybox always fall within the `lowp` range of –1.0 to 1.0. A more general-purpose shader couldn't make that assumption and would require `highp` precision for texture coordinates. The array only contains one set of texture coordinates because only one texture is used in the example. A multi-texturing fragment shader might need more texture coordinates for each vertex.

All Shading Language shaders have a `main()` function that the GPU uses as the entry point to the shader. The `main()` function in this example's vertex shader is about as simple as can be.

Each untransformed vertex position attribute serves dual purpose as texture coordinates inside the skybox cube. That's just an implementation detail enabled by this example's specific "unit cube" vertex positions. Texture coordinates are usually stored as vertex attributes separate from position attributes.

```
void main()
{
   v_texCoord[0] = a_position;
   gl_Position = u_mvpMatrix * vec4(a_position, 1.0);
}
```

As required for all vertex shaders, the gl_Position built-in variable is set. The u_mvpMatrix uniform variable stores the combined model-view and projection matrices that define the point of view. Transforming the a_position attribute by the u_mvpMatrix produces the corresponding position in the pixel color render buffer coordinate system. The expression, vec4(a_position, 1.0), extends the three-coordinate position vector into a four-coordinate vector. Setting the fourth coordinate to 1.0 causes the subsequent transformation to include any translation encoded in u_mvpMatrix. If the fourth coordinate is set to 0.0, the position is rotated and scaled but not translated.

The Fragment Shader

One of the keys to understanding fragment shaders is the realization that fragments don't correspond one to one with positions output by vertex shaders. The rendering step that converts geometric shape data into colored pixels in the frame buffer is called *rasterizing*. To rasterize geometry, the GPU keeps track of which vertices define each point, line segment, or triangle to be rendered. It then executes the fragment shader to calculate the color of each fragment produced for each point, line segment, or triangle. Fragments are calculated for all the positions between vertices as well as the positions of the vertices themselves.

The GPU interpolates values for all the varying variables set by a vertex shader. For example, a vertex shader executes once for each of the two vertices that define a line segment, and each time the vertex shader runs, it stores a different pixel color render buffer position in gl_Position. The GPU must calculate fragment colors all along the line segment between the two vertex positions separately assigned to gl_Position. It does that using linear interpolation so that a position halfway between the two vertices is approximately equal to the average of each end vertex position, $\{(x0 * 0.5 + x1 * 0.5), (y0 * 0.5 + y1 * 0.5)\}$. A position three-fourths of the way between the first vertex than the second might be calculated as $\{(x0 * 0.25 + x1 * 0.75), (y0 * 0.25 + y1 * 0.75)\}$. In practice, the calculations aren't always quite that simple because foreshortening produced by perspective influences the interpolated positions of fragments between vertices.

The fragment shader executes once for every interpolated set of varying values. It's not just positions that are interpolated. Texture coordinates and colors are also interpolated. When calculating per-fragment lighting in a fragment program, even the normal vectors are interpolated between vertices.

The following code implements example OpenGLES_Ch8_2's fragment shader. Just like vertex shaders set the special built-in `gl_Position` variable, fragment shaders must set the built-in `gl_FragColor` variable to the final color calculated for each fragment. Within the following code, the assignment is shown in bold:

```
//
//   AGLKSkyboxShader.fsh
//
//

/////////////////////////////////////////////////////////////
// UNIFORMS
/////////////////////////////////////////////////////////////
uniform highp mat4      u_mvpMatrix;
uniform samplerCube     u_unitCube[1];


/////////////////////////////////////////////////////////////
// Varyings
/////////////////////////////////////////////////////////////
varying lowp vec3       v_texCoord[1];


void main()
{
   gl_FragColor = textureCube(u_unitCube[0], v_texCoord[0]);
}
```

The fragment shader is about as simple as possible. The final fragment color is calculated by calling the built-in `textureCube()` function specifying first the identifier for the texture sampling unit to use and then the texture coordinates for the fragment. Remember that the texture coordinates are actually values interpolated by the GPU.

There are many nuances, limitations, and quirks to writing OpenGL ES 2.0 Shading Language programs. The OpenGL ES 2.0 Shading Language forms a subset the OpenGL Shading Language used on the desktop so be wary of examples intended for desktop use. A handy quick reference card at http://www.khronos.org/opengles/sdk/docs/reference_cards/ OpenGL-ES-2_0-Reference-card.pdf helps to find the right built-in functions, types, precisions, and built-in variable names when you first get started.

Tying OpenGL ES 2.0 Shading Language Programs to Your Code

Apple supplies sample code including the following four methods reused by each of the custom Shading Language examples in this book:

```
- (BOOL)loadShaders;
- (BOOL)compileShader:(GLuint *)shader
    type:(GLenum)type
    file:(NSString *)file;
- (BOOL)linkProgram:(GLuint)prog;
- (BOOL)validateProgram:(GLuint)prog;
```

The methods simplify many of the process steps shown in Figure 8.3 for creating, compiling, linking, and verifying Shading Language programs.

Step 1: Create Shading Language program identifier

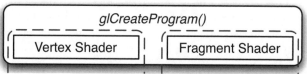

Step 2: Create separate vertex and fragment shaders; Provide the text of each shader; Compile each shader; Attach each shader to the program.

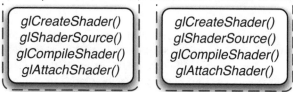

Step 3: Bind program vertex attribute locations to identifiers used with glEnableVertexAttribArray() and glVertexAttribPointer().

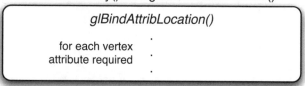

Step 4: Get the storage locations for each of the program's uniform variables.

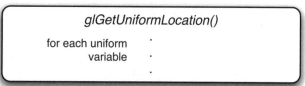

Step 5: Link and validate Shading Language program.

glLinkProgram()
glValidateProgram()

Step 6: Delete the shaders and Shading Language program.

glDeleteShader()
glDeleteProgram()

Figure 8.3   Steps for creating OpenGL ES 2.0 Shading Language programs.

A complete description of the steps for creating OpenGL EE 2.0 Shading Language Program objects falls outside the scope of this book. It's not as difficult as it might seem. With the aid of Apple's sample methods, it's as simple as including the following code in the −prepareToDraw method of custom classes such as AGLKSkyboxEffect, AGLKTextureTransformBaseEffect, or AGLKArmatureBaseEffect.

```
if(0 == program)
{
   [self loadShaders];
}
```

The −loadShaders method is identical in each of this book's examples except for the names of the files containing vertex and fragment shader source code and the specific attributes and uniforms used by the shaders. Examine the −loadShaders method in example OpenGLES_Ch8_2's AGLKSkyboxEffect class for a representative implementation.

Figure 8.4 lists the steps for using a custom Shading Language program after the program has been compiled, linked, and verified.

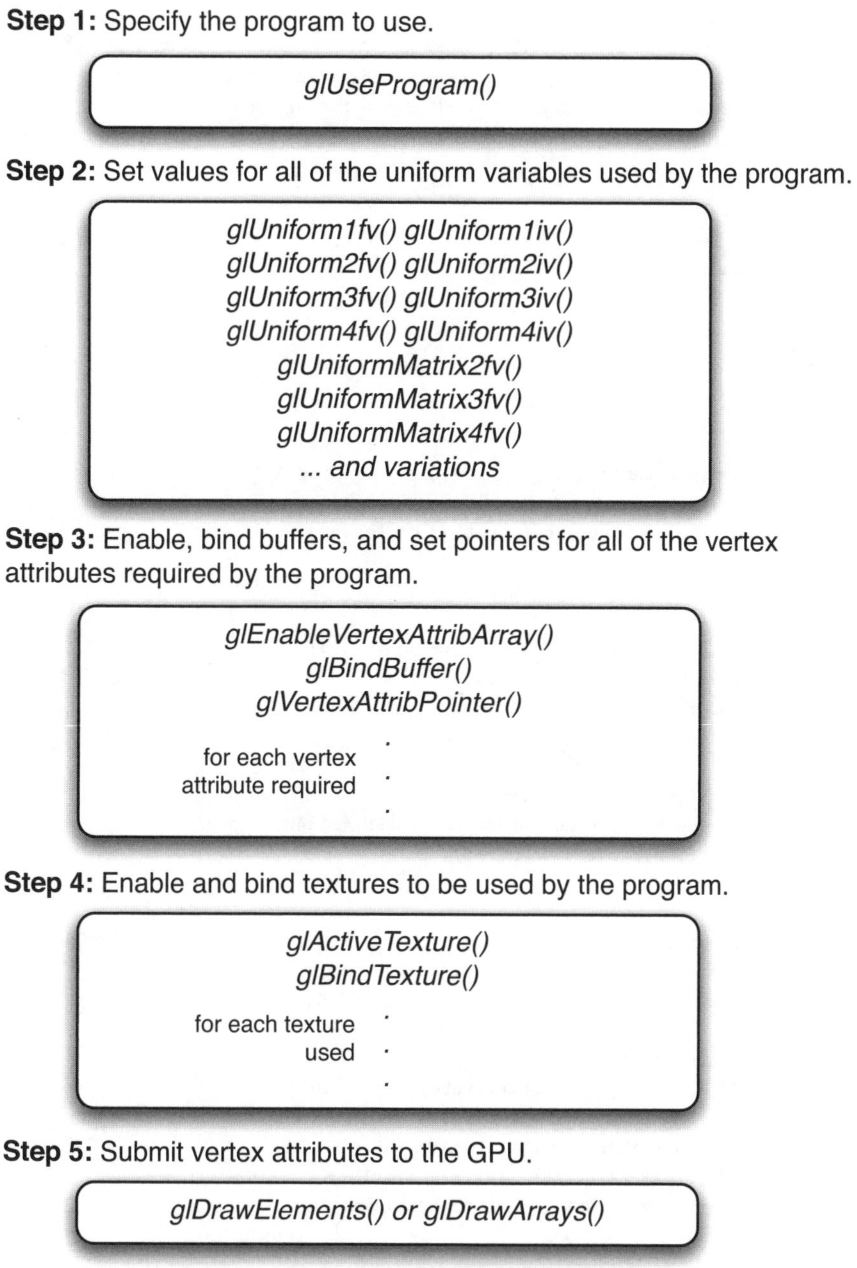

Step 1: Specify the program to use.

> *glUseProgram()*

Step 2: Set values for all of the uniform variables used by the program.

> *glUniform1fv() glUniform1iv()*
> *glUniform2fv() glUniform2iv()*
> *glUniform3fv() glUniform3iv()*
> *glUniform4fv() glUniform4iv()*
> *glUniformMatrix2fv()*
> *glUniformMatrix3fv()*
> *glUniformMatrix4fv()*
> *... and variations*

Step 3: Enable, bind buffers, and set pointers for all of the vertex attributes required by the program.

> *glEnableVertexAttribArray()*
> *glBindBuffer()*
> *glVertexAttribPointer()*
>
> for each vertex   ·
> attribute required   ·
>   ·

Step 4: Enable and bind textures to be used by the program.

> *glActiveTexture()*
> *glBindTexture()*
>
> for each texture   ·
>   used   ·
>   ·

Step 5: Submit vertex attributes to the GPU.

> *glDrawElements() or glDrawArrays()*

Figure 8.4   Steps for using a compiled OpenGL ES 2.0 Shading Language program.

The –prepareToDraw and –draw methods of AGLKSkyboxEffect, AGLKTextureTransformBaseEffect, and AGLKArmatureBaseEffect as well as GLKit's GLKBaseEffect, GLKSkyboxEffect, and GLKReflectionMapEffect combine to perform all the steps listed in Figure 8.4. The following code shows the complete implementations of –prepareToDraw and –draw in the simple AGLKSkyboxEffect class. Code in bold shows each of the steps:

```
- (void) prepareToDraw
{
   if(0 == program)
   {
      [self loadShaders];
   }

   if(0 != program)
   {
      glUseProgram(program);                          // Step 1

      // Translate skybox cube to specified center and scale to
      // specified size
      GLKMatrix4 skyboxModelView = GLKMatrix4Translate(
         self.transform.modelviewMatrix,
         self.center.x, self.center.y, self.center.z);
      skyboxModelView = GLKMatrix4Scale(
         skyboxModelView,
         self.xSize, self.ySize, self.zSize);

      // Pre-calculate the mvpMatrix
      GLKMatrix4 modelViewProjectionMatrix = GLKMatrix4Multiply(
         self.transform.projectionMatrix,
         skyboxModelView);

      // Standard matrices
      glUniformMatrix4fv(uniforms[AGLKMVPMatrix], 1, 0,
         modelViewProjectionMatrix.m);                // Step 2

      // One texture sampler
      glUniform1i(uniforms[AGLKSamplersCube], 0);// Step 2

      glEnableVertexAttribArray(GLKVertexAttribPosition);
      glBindBuffer(GL_ARRAY_BUFFER, vertexBufferID);
      glVertexAttribPointer(GLKVertexAttribPosition,
         3,
         GL_FLOAT,
         GL_FALSE,
         0,
         NULL);                                       // Step 3
```

```
    glBindBuffer(GL_ELEMENT_ARRAY_BUFFER, indexBufferID);

    // Bind the texture to be used
    if(self.textureCubeMap.enabled)
    {
       glBindTexture(GL_TEXTURE_CUBE_MAP,
          self.textureCubeMap.name);              // Step 4
    }
    else
    {
       glBindTexture(GL_TEXTURE_CUBE_MAP, 0);  // Step 4
    }
   }
}


- (void)draw
{
   glDrawElements(GL_TRIANGLE_STRIP,
      AGLKSkyboxNumVertexIndices,
      GL_UNSIGNED_BYTE,
      NULL);                                   // Step 5
}
```

Don't worry if this chapter's deep dive into the implementation of AGLKSkyboxEffect
overwhelms you. GLKit and classes such as GLKBaseEffect and GLKSkyboxEffect exist
so that you don't need to know the intricacies of OpenGL ES 2.0 Shading Language or all
the steps involved to use Shading Language programs. It's more important to absorb the
graphics concepts first and come back to implementation details later as needed. Custom
Shading Language programs correspond almost exactly to custom assembly language in other
programming contexts. Not everyone needs to resort to such low-level implementations, but
there's a degree of control only available at the lowest levels.

The next section includes a custom Shading Language program for managing another special
effect, particles. Look for similarities between the particles program and the AGLKSkyboxEffect
Shading Language program.

Particles

In computer graphics, *particle* typically refers to any colored or textured geometrical object
that can be defined by a single position in the 3D viewing volume. Applications often
render hundreds or thousands of particles at a time making efficient rendering paramount.
Applications rapidly reposition particles to create dramatic animation. Figure 8.5 shows one of
several particle effects demonstrated by example OpenGLES_Ch8_3. Play with the example to
get a sense of the impact animation provides.

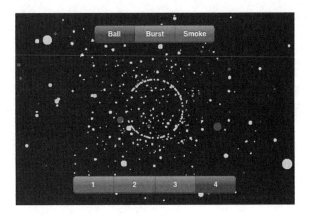

Figure 8.5   Screenshot of particles.

Particles can be implemented using points, lines, or triangles just like any other GPU-rendered graphics. A very computationally expensive way to implement particles uses geometric spheres composed of many triangles for every particle onscreen. Conceptually, spheres make ideal particles because they are positioned using a single point, the location of the sphere's center, and they have radial symmetry, which means they have the same shape from any point of view.

Fortunately, the illusion of spherical particles can be created using textured rectangles oriented parallel to the near and far planes of the viewing frustum. The viewing frustum defines the 3D volume visible each time the scene is rendered and is explained in the "Perspective and the Viewing Frustum" section of Chapter 5. Rectangles oriented parallel to the near and far planes are a type of billboard explained in the "Billboards" section. However, OpenGL ES includes a feature called *point sprites* that render even more efficiently than the two triangles needed to define a billboard rectangle.

OpenGL ES 2.0 renders point sprites any time you specify the GL_POINTS mode with glDrawArrays() or glDrawElements(). Point sprites produce a fragment for each pixel color render buffer position inside a square centered at the point sprite's location. The point sprite square has length and width equal to the current point sprite size in the pixel color render buffer coordinate system. Unfortunately, a custom Shading Language program is required to control the size of each point sprite.

Example OpenGLES_Ch8_3 creates the AGLKPointParticleEffect class to encapsulate the needed custom Shading Language program and provide other options to control particles. Each particle has an initial position, velocity, and size. A force vector specified per particle changes the particle's velocity over time. An overall simulated gravity affects every particle's velocity, too. Finally, each particle fades into complete transparency over time and has a life span after which the particle is no longer drawn.

The following code declares the interface for `AGLKPointParticleEffect`:

```
//
//  AGLKPointParticleEffect.h
//  OpenGLES_Ch8_3
//

#import <GLKit/GLKit.h>

////////////////////////////////////////////////////////////////
// Default gravity acceleration vector matches Earth's
// {0, (-9.80665 m/s/s), 0} assuming +Y up coordinate system
extern const GLKVector3 AGLKDefaultGravity;

@interface AGLKPointParticleEffect : NSObject  <GLKNamedEffect>

@property (nonatomic, assign) GLKVector3 gravity;
@property (nonatomic, assign) GLfloat elapsedSeconds;
@property (strong, nonatomic, readonly) GLKEffectPropertyTexture
   *texture2d0;
@property (strong, nonatomic, readonly) GLKEffectPropertyTransform
   *transform;

- (void)addParticleAtPosition:(GLKVector3)aPosition
   velocity:(GLKVector3)aVelocity
   force:(GLKVector3)aForce
   size:(float)aSize
   lifeSpanSeconds:(NSTimeInterval)aSpan
   fadeDurationSeconds:(NSTimeInterval)aDuration;

- (void)prepareToDraw;
- (void)draw;

@end
```

`AGLKPointParticleEffect` works like `GLKBaseEffect` and other effects presented so far. The `texture2d0` property defines the texture used for each particle. The `transform` property stores the point of view defined by `transform.projectionMatrix` and `transform. modelviewMatrix`. Two new properties, `gravity` and `elapsedSeconds`, control the physics simulation that governs particle motion. Gravity defaults to match Earth's gravity: –9.80665 meters per second per second (falling objects fall 9.8 meters per second faster every second). The `elapsedSeconds` property must be updated prior to preparing an `AGLKPointParticleEffect` instance for drawing. The calculations that determine each particle's current position depend on continuously increasing `elapsedSeconds`.

As with other effects, you must set properties, call –`prepareToDraw`, and then call –`draw`. The following code excerpt from `OpenGLES_Ch8_3ViewController`'s –`update` method updates the `elapsedSeconds` property right before the scene is redrawn:

```
- (void)update
{
   NSTimeInterval timeElapsed = self.timeSinceLastResume;

   self.particleEffect.elapsedSeconds = timeElapsed;
```

Then, `OpenGLES_Ch8_3ViewController`'s `–glkView:drawInRect:` method configures the particle effect's point of view to match the base effect and draws the particles.

```
// Draw particles
self.particleEffect.transform.projectionMatrix =
   self.baseEffect.transform.projectionMatrix;
self.particleEffect.transform.modelviewMatrix =
   self.baseEffect.transform.modelviewMatrix;
[self.particleEffect prepareToDraw];
[self.particleEffect draw];
```

Playing with the options provides the best way to get a feeling for the interactions of particle forces and velocities. `OpenGLES_Ch8_3ViewController` already implements four sample methods to explore a range of particle configuration options: `–spawnFireRing`, `–spawnPulse`, `–spawnSparkle`, and `–spawnBallCannon`. For example, `–spawnBallCannon` uses the following code to create particles that shoot up and into the scene with random velocities in the X axis direction. The particles fall with normal gravity once launched and fade out over the last half second of a 3.2 second life span.

```
// Turn on gravity
self.particleEffect.gravity = AGLKDefaultGravity;

float randomXVelocity = -0.5f + 1.0f *
   (float)random() / (float)RAND_MAX;

[self.particleEffect
   addParticleAtPosition:GLKVector3Make(0.0f, 0.0f, 0.9f)
   velocity:GLKVector3Make(randomXVelocity, 1.0f, -1.0f)
   force:GLKVector3Make(0.0f, 9.0f, 0.0f)
   size:4.0f
   lifeSpanSeconds:3.2f
   fadeDurationSeconds:0.5f];
```

Experiment adding your own particle dynamics by modifying the sample methods already implemented.

The Particle Shading Language Program

`AGLKPointParticleEffect` uses custom vertex and fragment shaders in part to show off the range of capabilities enabled by Shading Language programs. Physics calculations use the same Linear Algebra vector and matrix operations that underlay computer graphics. All particle physics simulation in example OpenGLES_Ch8_3 happens on the GPU.

> **Note**
>
> Beyond physics simulations, a trend called "general-purpose GPUs" exploits GPUs to execute algorithms for fields like audio processing, radar signal processing, protein molecule analysis, and other non-graphics applications. GPUs often perform linear algebra operations faster than general-purpose central processing units (CPUs).

`AGLKPointParticleEffect` defines the following somewhat unconventional attributes for each vertex:

```
////////////////////////////////////////////////////////////////
// Type used to define particle attributes
typedef struct
{
    GLKVector3 emissionPosition;
    GLKVector3 emissionVelocity;
    GLKVector3 emissionForce;
    GLKVector2 size;
    GLKVector2 emissionTimeAndLife;
}
AGLKParticleAttributes;
```

The vertex shader performs physics calculations using each of the per-vertex attributes and uniform values for gravity, elapsed seconds, a texture sampler identifier, and a combined model-view-projection matrix. Each particle's position is recalculated and stored in the built-in `gl_Position` variable by applying classic Newtonian physics equations based solely on initial position (which never changes after the particle is created), initial velocity, forces, and elapsed time. Each particle's size is stored in another built-in variable, `gl_PointSize`. The required assignments are shown in bold:

```
//
//   AGLKParticleShader.vsh
//
//


////////////////////////////////////////////////////////////////
// VERTEX ATTRIBUTES
////////////////////////////////////////////////////////////////
attribute vec3 a_emissionPosition;
attribute vec3 a_emissionVelocity;
attribute vec3 a_emissionForce;
attribute vec2 a_size;
attribute vec2 a_emissionAndDeathTimes;


////////////////////////////////////////////////////////////////
// UNIFORMS
////////////////////////////////////////////////////////////////
uniform highp mat4      u_mvpMatrix;
```

```
uniform sampler2D        u_samplers2D[1];
uniform highp vec3       u_gravity;
uniform highp float      u_elapsedSeconds;

///////////////////////////////////////////////////////////////
// Varyings
///////////////////////////////////////////////////////////////
varying lowp float       v_particleOpacity;


void main()
{
    highp float elapsedTime = u_elapsedSeconds -
        a_emissionAndDeathTimes.x;

    // Mass is assumed to be 1.0, so acceleration = force (a = f/m)
    // v = v0 + at : v is current velocity; v0 is initial velocity;
    //               a is acceleration; t is elapsed time
    highp vec3 velocity = a_emissionVelocity +
        ((a_emissionForce + u_gravity) * elapsedTime);

    // s = s0 + 0.5 * (v0 + v) * t : s is current position;
    //                               s0 is initial position;
    //                               v0 is initial velocity;
    //                               v is current velocity;
    //                               t is elapsed time
    highp vec3 untransformedPosition = a_emissionPosition +
        0.5 * (a_emissionVelocity + velocity) * elapsedTime;

    gl_Position = u_mvpMatrix * vec4(untransformedPosition, 1.0);
    gl_PointSize = a_size.x / gl_Position.w;

    // if emission life > elapsed time then non-zero with maximum
    // opacity of 1.0; otherwise 0.0. Fades over a_size.y seconds
    v_particleOpacity = max(0.0, min(1.0,
        (a_emissionAndDeathTimes.y - u_elapsedSeconds) /
        max(a_size.y, 0.00001)));
}
```

The per-vertex point size is divided by the w component of the particle's position in pixel color render buffer coordinates. The w component roughly corresponds to the distance of the particle from the near plane of the frustum. Dividing by w simulates perspective-based shrinking as particles recede into the distance.

The vertex shader also calculates the translucency of each particle and passes that value to the fragment shader in the `v_particleOpacity` varying variable. As a result, there isn't much work left to be done in the fragment shader.

```
//
//  AGLKParticleShader.fsh
//
//


/////////////////////////////////////////////////////////////
// UNIFORMS
/////////////////////////////////////////////////////////////
uniform highp mat4      u_mvpMatrix;
uniform sampler2D       u_samplers2D[1];
uniform highp vec3      u_gravity;
uniform highp float     u_elapsedSeconds;


/////////////////////////////////////////////////////////////
// Varyings
/////////////////////////////////////////////////////////////
varying lowp float      v_particleOpacity;


void main()
{
   lowp vec4 textureColor = texture2D(u_samplers2D[0],
      gl_PointCoord);
   textureColor.a = textureColor.a * v_particleOpacity;

   gl_FragColor = textureColor;
}
```

The fragment color is obtained from the built-in `texture2D()` function using the sampler specified by the `u_samplers2D` uniform variable and texture coordinates provided by another bit of built-in Shading Language magic. The built-in read-only `gl_PointCoord` variable is a two-component vector with components in the range 0.0 to 1.0 corresponding to the current fragment's {`s`, `t`} texture position within the point sprite being rendered.

The alpha value of `textureColor` used to determine `gl_FragColor` is multiplied by `v_particleOpacity` to implement particle translucency.

Limitations of AGLKPointParticleEffect

All particles drawn with an instance of `AGLKPointParticleEffect` have the same texture. To render scenes containing particles with different textures, multiple instances of `AGLKPointParticleEffect` must be used.

A significant downside manifests when calculating particle positions on the GPU. You might notice some visual artifacts such as dark outlines on some particles when you play with example OpenGLES_Ch8_3. The artifacts result from the order in which particles are rendered. Each particle is blended with the pre-existing contents of the pixel color render buffer. The first particle rendered is blended with the background color, but subsequent particles blend with the background color and previously rendered particles. The only way to avoid artifacts is to sort the particles based on their distance from the near frustum plane and render them in order from far to near.

There is no way to sort the order of vertices within an OpenGL ES 2.0 Shading Language program. Vertices are always processed in the order they're submitted to the GPU. The `AGLKPointParticleEffect` class could be reimplemented to calculate particle positions on the CPU, sort the particles from back to front, and resubmit correctly ordered current particle positions to the GPU, but that's left as an exercise for the reader. The billboards in the next section are sorted back to front and can provide inspiration for modifying `AGLKPointParticleEffect`. Particles can even be implemented using billboards instead of point sprites, but point sprites provide better performance. Example OpenGLES_Ch12_1 in Chapter 12, "Putting It All Together," demonstrates a billboard-based implementation of particles.

Billboards

Billboards are textured rectangles that always face the viewer. There are two common variations: The first, cylindrical billboards, are oriented to face the viewer but remain aligned with the "up" vector. The other, spherical billboards, are always oriented parallel to the frustum's near plane just like point sprites. Figure 8.6 shows trees rendered using cylindrical billboards.

Figure 8.6   Cylindrical billboard trees.

Figure 8.6 provides the illusion of highly detailed trees except in the lower-right corner where the tree is revealed to be paper thin. The cylindrical billboards in Figure 8.6 become unconvincing when the point of view looks along the "up" vector to the billboard.

Figure 8.7 shows spherical billboards. Many of the billboards present convincing illusions, but trees in the foreground appear to be lying on the ground instead of standing above the ground. The trunks of the trees in the center of Figure 8.7 disappear entirely. When the billboards are aligned with the near viewing plane, the trunks of some of the trees end up rendered behind the ground.

Figure 8.7   Spherical billboard trees.

Example OpenGLES_Ch8_4 animates the point of view to demonstrate the billboard effect by flying around and over trees. Toggle the "Render Spherical" user interface switch to compare spherical versus cylindrical billboards from varying points of view. Neither implementation of billboards works in every situation.

Several attributes of billboards make them much less efficient than point sprites. Each billboard requires a minimum of four vertices, and every time the point of view changes, the positions of those vertices must be recalculated and re-sent to the GPU. Fortunately, calculating billboard vertex positions is not too difficult or computationally expensive.

Figure 8.8 illustrates the relationship between the look-at vector and the up vector when defining a point of view. The same information enables calculation of vertex positions needed to orient a billboard toward the viewer. Recall from Chapter 4, "Shedding Some Light," that the cross product of two vectors defines a third vector perpendicular to the first two. The cross product of the up vector and the look-at vector is called the "Left Vector" in Figure 8.8. It might look to you like the left vector in Figure 8.8 points to the right, but from the point of view of an eye looking along the look-at vector, it's on the left. Imagine the viewer looking out of the sheet of paper.

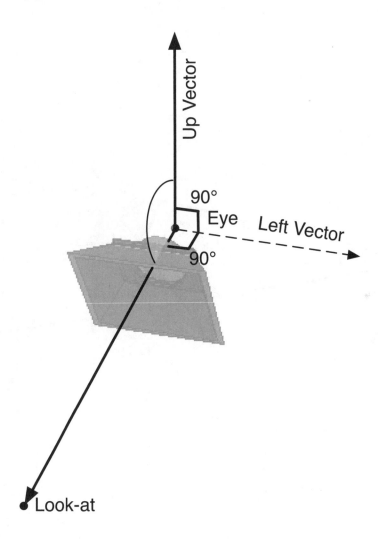

Figure 8.8   Calculating left vector from point of view.

The left vector defines a horizontal direction parallel to the view frustum's near and far planes. However, the angle between the up vector and the look-at vector is not necessarily 90 degrees and doesn't define the vertical direction of the near and far planes. Figure 8.9 shows the complete view frustum. The "Frustum Up Vector" is the cross product of the look-at vector and the left vector.

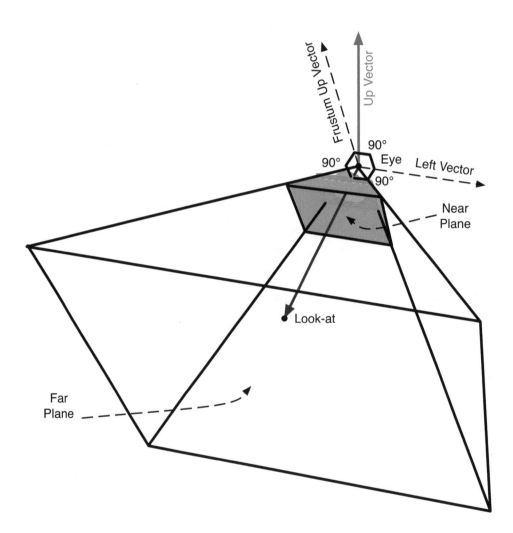

Figure 8.9   Calculating the frustum up vector.

Given a position, a size, and the left vector, we can calculate vertex positions for cylindrical billboards. Figure 8.10 illustrates the geometry for a cylindrical billboard with its origin in the center bottom and helps to visualize equations for calculating vertices defining a billboard's corners.

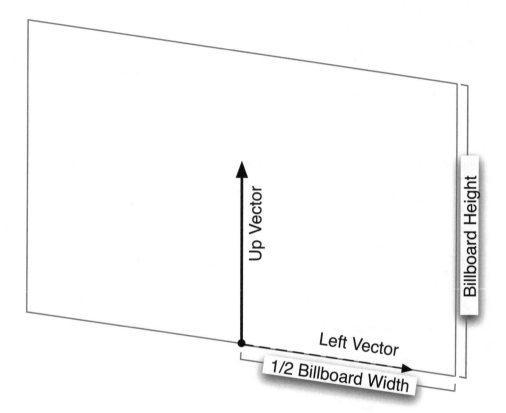

Figure 8.10   Cylindrical billboard with its origin in the center bottom.

The normalized left vector is the cross product of the normalized up vector and the normalized look-at vector.

```
GLKVector3 leftVector = GLKVector3CrossProduct(
   GLKVector3Normalize(upVector),
   GLKVector3Normalize(lookAtVector));
```

The left vector is normalized, meaning that it has length 1.0. Multiply the left vector by half the width of the billboard to produce a new vector with the desired length and the same direction as the left vector. The bottom-left vertex position is found by adding the new vector to the billboard's center bottom:

```
GLKVector3 leftBottomPosition =
   GLKVector3Add(GLKVector3MultiplyScalar(
   leftVector, billboard.size.x * 0.5f),
   billboard.position);
```

The bottom-right vertex position is the same distance in the opposite direction.

```
GLKVector3 rightBottomPosition =
   GLKVector3Add(GLKVector3MultiplyScalar(
   leftVector, billboard.size.x * -0.5f),
   billboard.position);
```

The top vertex positions are billboard height distance from the bottom positions in the direction of the up vector.

```
GLKVector3 leftTopPosition =
   GLKVector3Add(leftBottomPosition,
      GLKVector3MultiplyScalar(
         upVector, billboard.size.y));
GLKVector3 rightTopPosition =
   GLKVector3Add(rightBottomPosition,
      GLKVector3MultiplyScalar(
         upVector, billboard.size.y));
```

Use the frustum up vector instead of the up vector to calculate spherical billboard vertices as illustrated in Figure 8.11. Example OpenGLES_Ch8_4 calculates the frustum up vector and temporarily reassign the up vector as follows to keep all the other equations for finding vertex positions the same:

```
if(self.shouldRenderSpherical)
{  // Recalculate up vector
   upVector = GLKVector3CrossProduct(
      normalizedLookAtVector,
      leftVector);
}
```

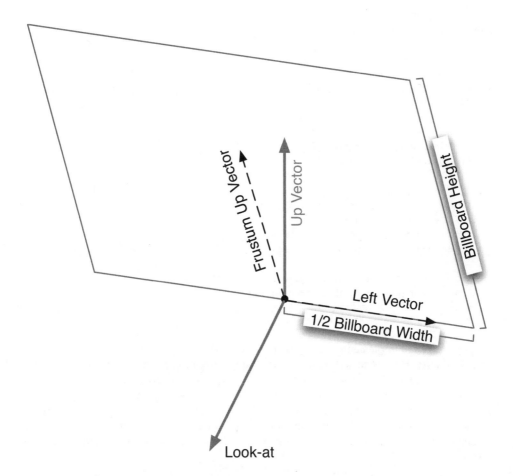

Figure 8.11   Spherical billboard with its origin in the center bottom.

Example OpenGLES_Ch8_4 includes a simple UtilityBillboard class to store the position, size, and texture coordinates for each billboard.

```
//
//  UtilityBillboard.h
//
//

#import <GLKit/GLKit.h>


@interface UtilityBillboard : NSObject
```

```
@property (assign, nonatomic, readonly)
   GLKVector3 position;
@property (assign, nonatomic, readonly)
   GLKVector2 minTextureCoords;
@property (assign, nonatomic, readonly)
   GLKVector2 maxTextureCoords;
@property (assign, nonatomic, readonly)
   GLKVector2 size;
@property (assign, nonatomic, readonly)
   GLfloat signedDistanceInLookDirection;


- (id)initWithPosition:(GLKVector3)aPosition
   size:(GLKVector2)aSize
   minTextureCoords:(GLKVector2)minCoords
   maxTextureCoords:(GLKVector2)maxCoords;


- (void)updateWithEyePosition:(GLKVector3)eyePosition
   lookDirection:(GLKVector3)lookDirection;

@end
```

UtilityBillboard implements the -updateWithEyePosition:lookDirection:
method to calculate the signed distance of the billboard from the eye position using
GLKVector3DotProduct(). The signed distances are used for comparison to sort the billboards
from far to near. The signed distance is negative when the billboard is behind the viewer. That
convenient fact enables a simple optimization: Given an array of billboards sorted by distance,
the first time a billboard with negative distance is encountered, it's safe to just stop drawing
more billboards. None of the rest in the array will be visible anyway because they're behind the
viewer.

```
/////////////////////////////////////////////////////////////////////
// Calculate the current distance of the receiver from
// eyePosition to enable sorting for render order.
- (void)updateWithEyePosition:(GLKVector3)eyePosition
   lookDirection:(GLKVector3)lookDirection;
{
   const GLKVector3 vectorFromEye = GLKVector3Subtract(
      eyePosition, position_);
   signedDistanceInLookDirection_ =
      GLKVector3DotProduct(vectorFromEye, lookDirection);
}
```

A UtilityBillboardManager class keeps track of billboards and renders them in much the
same way the UtilityModelManager class from Chapter 7 keeps track and renders models.
Add billboards to be managed by calling -addBillboard:. Call UtilityBillboardManager's
-updateWithEyePosition:lookDirection: right before drawing billboards.

UtilityBillboardManager updates all the managed billboards and sorts the billboards
from far to near. UtilityBillboardManager's —drawWithEyePosition:lookDirection:
upVector: method recalculates the vertices of each triangle in each billboard using either
cylindrical or spherical math depending on the value of UtilityBillboardManager's
shouldRenderSpherical property and then draws all visible billboards using
glDrawArrays( ).

```
//
//   UtilityBillboardManager.h
//
//

#import <GLKit/GLKit.h>

@class UtilityBillboard;


@interface UtilityBillboardManager : NSObject

@property (strong, nonatomic, readonly)
   NSArray *sortedBillboards;
@property (assign, nonatomic, readwrite)
   BOOL shouldRenderSpherical;

- (void)updateWithEyePosition:(GLKVector3)eyePosition
   lookDirection:(GLKVector3)lookDirection;

- (void)addBillboard:(UtilityBillboard *)aBillboard;

- (void)addBillboardAtPosition:(GLKVector3)aPosition
    size:(GLKVector2)aSize
    minTextureCoords:(GLKVector2)minCoords
    maxTextureCoords:(GLKVector2)maxCoords;


@end

@interface UtilityBillboardManager (viewAdditions)

- (void)drawWithEyePosition:(GLKVector3)eyePosition
    lookDirection:(GLKVector3)lookDirection
    upVector:(GLKVector3)upVector;

@end
```

Sorting leverages built-in Cocoa Touch capabilities. The NSArray class provides the needed
-sortedArrayUsingFunction:context: method. UtilityBillboard provides a function

named `UtilityCompareBillboardDistance()` suitable for use with
`-sortedArrayUsingFunction:context:`.

```
/////////////////////////////////////////////////////////////////
//
- (void)updateWithEyePosition:(GLKVector3)eyePosition
   lookDirection:(GLKVector3)lookDirection;
{
   // Make sure lookDirection is a unit vector
   lookDirection = GLKVector3Normalize(lookDirection);

   for(UtilityBillboard *currentBillboard in
      self.sortedBillboards)
   {
      [currentBillboard updateWithEyePosition:eyePosition
         lookDirection:lookDirection];
   }

   // Sort from furthest to nearest and billboards behind the
   // viewer ordered after all others.
   [self.mutableSortedBillboards
      sortUsingFunction:UtilityCompareBillboardDistance
      context:NULL];
}
```

Explore the implementation of `UtilityBillboardManager` in `UtilityBillboardManager.m`. It's not very long and reuses many of the techniques for storing and managing vertex attributes that have been used previously in classes such as `UtilityMesh`. Billboards are one of the most common ways to organize geometry after meshes and models. However, billboards consume a lot of the precious memory bandwidth between the CPU and GPU because of constant updates to vertex positions. Point sprites were created and implemented in GPU hardware specifically to reduce the need for billboards.

Summary

Special effects add visual complexity to scenes while minimally increasing the GPUs processing load. Each special effect has limitations. Skyboxes must be positioned so the point of view does not distort the texture so much that the illusion is spoiled. Particles implemented as point sprites are efficient, but the GPU has no way to sort the particles from distant to near, and without sorting, translucent particles are sometimes rendered incorrectly. Billboards add detail to scenes, but like skyboxes, the illusion cannot be maintained in all cases. Constraining the point of view is necessary to avoid revealing that the billboards have no depth.

Performance is critical for embedded graphics applications, and special effects often provide impressive results with good performance. The next chapter explores optimization techniques that enhance performance when special effects are not enough.

9

Optimization

This chapter identifies optimization strategies to improve OpenGL ES 2.0 rendering performance for iOS devices. The first technique described in the section, "Render as Little as Possible," typically provides the largest benefit. Each subsequent technique provides diminishing returns but might still make the difference between "too slow" and "fast enough" in some cases.

For embedded devices, optimization includes dimensions beyond just the speed of rendering. For example, users might prefer a 30Hz update rate that preserves battery life over a 60Hz rate that makes the device guzzle from the battery. Consider a reasonable balance for each application. Above all, don't render anything unless it benefits the user. There's no benefit to re-rendering an unchanged scene. There's also no benefit to rendering frames faster than 60Hz on iOS devices because users will never see the extra updates.

Before optimizing, consider whether optimization is needed at all. Many reasons exist to avoid optimizing:

- Optimizing an application often introduces new bugs.

- Optimizing an application's code usually makes that code harder to read and maintain.

- A lot of time can be spent optimizing code for little gain in performance.

Even when clear opportunities exist to optimize software, wise programmers remain cautious. As Donald Knuth, the "father" of analysis of algorithms, wrote in 1974,

> We should forget about small efficiencies, say about 97% of the time: premature optimization is the root of all evil. Yet we should not pass up our opportunities in that critical 3%. A good programmer will not be lulled into complacency by such reasoning, he will be wise to look carefully at the critical code; but only after that code has been identified.

With Knuth's advice in mind, the performance-critical 3% of code might be within the OpenGL ES libraries, drivers, or other places outside your control. Many applications are naturally constrained by input/output (I/O) speeds or other factors not improved by changes to source code. Similarly, changes to code execution speed might have no benefit for applications limited by the graphics processing unit (GPU). When the bottleneck isn't in your code, the best approach is to avoid the bottlenecks: Reduce I/O, render fewer geometric objects, and access less memory.

Render as Little as Possible

GPUs accomplish amazing amounts of number crunching within the 33 milliseconds available to render at a 30Hz update rate. Nevertheless, a GPU can only render so many points, lines, and triangles within the allotted time. No amount of optimization achieves the desired update rate when the sheer number of geometric primitives exceeds the GPU's capacity. This section explains a technique called *culling* to minimize the number of geometric primitives submitted to the GPU without diminishing output quality.

Culling encompasses a variety of techniques to avoid processing geometric objects that don't contribute fragments to the color render buffer. Culling often dramatically reduces GPU workload. If you don't implement any other optimizations, implement this one.

OpenGL ES includes some built-in culling capabilities. For example, Chapter 7, "Loading and Using Models," took advantage of "back face culling." Every triangle has a front side and a back side defined by the order OpenGL ES receives the triangle's vertices. Back face culling instructs OpenGL ES to discard triangles facing away from the viewer. It's an almost-free optimization in applications that model solid objects because users normally never see triangles that face away.

One of the most effective optimizations avoids rendering objects outside the current viewing frustum. Scenes usually contain geometric objects the user doesn't see at any given moment. Only objects currently within the viewing frustum produce fragments in the frame buffer's pixel color render buffer. Chapter 2, "Making the Hardware Work for You," introduced render buffers. Chapter 5, "Changing Your Point of View," and Chapter 8, "Special Effects," explain the viewing frustum.

Frustum-Based Culling

Example OpenGLES_Ch8_4 in the preceding chapter applies a simple form of frustum-based culling: A simple distance calculation determines whether a point, the location of a billboard, is in front or behind the viewer. The example avoids rendering geometry for billboards positioned behind the viewer. The approach applies to more geometric objects than just billboards. Assuming a viewpoint positioned in the center of a complex scene, half of the geometric objects are likely to be behind the viewpoint and therefore outside the viewing frustum. The computationally simple distance calculation potentially culls half the scene's geometry from rendering.

Slightly more complex calculations enable even more culling. Figure 9.1 illustrates objects positioned relative to a viewing frustum. An object may be completely within the frustum, partly within the frustum, or completely outside the frustum. The code needed to identify objects completely outside the frustum almost always executes more quickly than code to submit the object's geometry to the GPU and avoids wasted processing for objects with no chance to affect the appearance of the rendered scene.

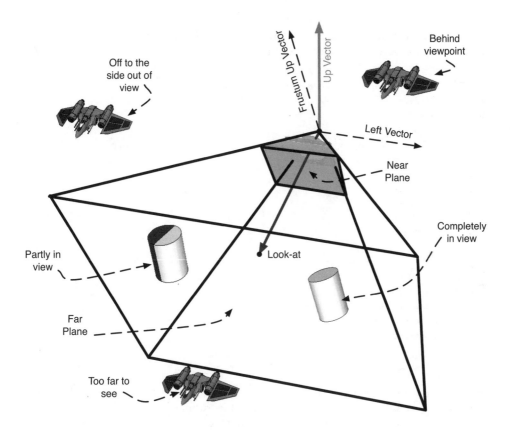

Figure 9.1   Objects in and out of frustum.

In Figure 9.1, the spaceships are positioned completely outside the viewing frustum. One is too far to be seen, another is behind the viewpoint, and a third is off to the side out of view. In contrast, each of the cylinders falls completely or partially within the frustum.

Example OpenGLES_Ch9_1 contains 81 complex spaceship models scattered throughout a scene and applies frustum culling to dramatically reduce the amount of geometry processed by the GPU. A user interface switch in the example turns culling off and on to show the impact. On a first generation iPad with culling enabled, the scene updates at about 30 frames per second. Without culling, updates drop to about 7 frames per second or less. Culling is effective in the example because only five or six spaceships are in view at any one time. Culling reduces the number of models processed by the GPU each frame from 81 to 5 or 6.

The bold elements of the following AGLKFrustum data type define a frustum as illustrated in Figure 9.2. The other elements derive from the frustum definition and help determination whether geometric objects intersect the frustum.

```
///////////////////////////////////////////////////////////////
// This data type is used to store the parameters that define a
// viewing frustum
typedef struct
{   // Frustum definition
    GLKVector3 eyePosition;
    GLKVector3 xNormalVector;
    GLKVector3 yNormalVector;
    GLKVector3 zNormalVector;
    GLfloat aspectRatio;
    GLfloat nearDistance;
    GLfloat farDistance;

    // Derived frustum properties
    GLfloat nearWidth;
    GLfloat nearHeight;
    GLfloat tangentOfHalfFieldOfView;
    GLfloat sphereFactorX;
    GLfloat sphereFactorY;
}
AGLKFrustum;
```

Three normal vectors, two distances, an aspect ratio, and a field of view collectively define a frustum, as shown in Figure 9.2. Not coincidentally, the frustum data structure stores the same information encoded in projection and modelview matrices. The frustum data structure is just an alternative representation convenient for testing whether or not geometry intersects the frustum. Equivalent projection and modelview matrices can be extracted from an initialized frustum.

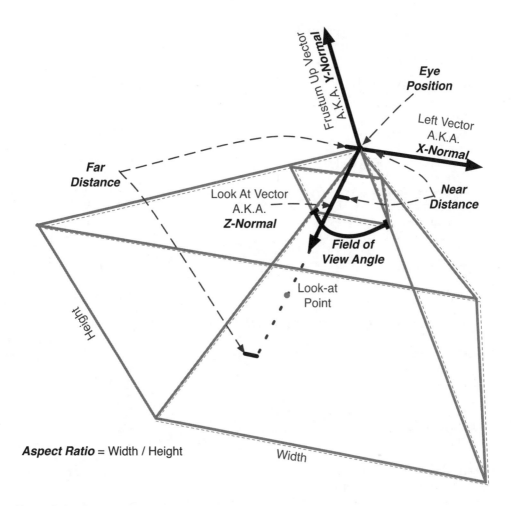

Figure 9.2   The geometry definition of a frustum.

The following AGLKFrustumMakeFrustumWithParameters(GLfloat fieldOfViewRad, GLfloat aspectRatio, GLfloat nearDistance, GLfloat farDistance) function accepts the same arguments as GLKMatrix4MakePerspective() and returns an initialized AGLKFrustum data structure. The related GLKMatrix4 AGLKFrustumMakePerspective(const UtilityFrustum *frustumPtr) function extracts a projection matrix from a frustum. The returned matrix is identical to the one returned from a call to GLKMatrix4MakePerspective() with the same parameters used to initialize the frustum.

```
AGLKFrustum AGLKFrustumMakeFrustumWithParameters
(
    GLfloat fieldOfViewRad,
    GLfloat aspectRatio,
    GLfloat nearDistance,
    GLfloat farDistance)
{
    AGLKFrustum frustum;

    AGLKFrustumSetPerspective(
        &frustum,
        fieldOfViewRad,
        aspectRatio,
        nearDistance,
        farDistance);

    return frustum;
}


/////////////////////////////////////////////////////////////////
//
extern void AGLKFrustumSetPerspective
(
    AGLKFrustum *frustumPtr,
    GLfloat fieldOfViewRad,
    GLfloat aspectRatio,
    GLfloat nearDistance,
    GLfloat farDistance)
{
    NSCAssert(NULL != frustumPtr,
        @"Invalid frustumPtr parameter");
    NSCAssert(0.0f < fieldOfViewRad && M_PI > fieldOfViewRad,
        @"Invalid fieldOfViewRad");
    NSCAssert(0.0f < aspectRatio, @"Invalid aspectRatio");
    NSCAssert(0.0f < nearDistance, @"Invalid nearDistance");
    NSCAssert(nearDistance < farDistance, @"Invalid farDistance");

    const GLfloat halfFieldOfViewRad = 0.5f * fieldOfViewRad;

    // store the information
    frustumPtr->aspectRatio = aspectRatio;
    frustumPtr->nearDistance = nearDistance;
    frustumPtr->farDistance = farDistance;
```

```
// compute width and height of the near section
frustumPtr->tangentOfHalfFieldOfView =
    tanf(halfFieldOfViewRad);
frustumPtr->nearHeight = nearDistance *
    frustumPtr->tangentOfHalfFieldOfView;
frustumPtr->nearWidth = frustumPtr->nearHeight * aspectRatio;

// Calculate sphere factors (used when testing sphere
// intersection with frustum)
frustumPtr->sphereFactorY =
    1.0f/cosf(frustumPtr->tangentOfHalfFieldOfView);
const GLfloat angleX =
    atanf(frustumPtr->tangentOfHalfFieldOfView * aspectRatio);
frustumPtr->sphereFactorX = 1.0f/cosf(angleX);

}
```

In addition to storing perspective information, a viewing frustum stores values defining a point of view for rendering a scene. The following AGLKFrustumSetPositionAndDirection (AGLKFrustum *frustumPtr, GLKVector3 eyePosition, GLKVector3 lookAtPosition, GLKVector3 upVector) function updates a frustum's point of view based on similar parameters to GLKMatrix4MakeLookAt(). A modelview matrix corresponding to the frustum's point of view can be obtained with the related GLKMatrix4 AGLKFrustumMakeModelview(const AGLKFrustum *frustumPtr) function that returns the same modelview matrix that GLKMatrix4MakeLookAt() calculates when called with the parameters used to set the frustum's position and direction.

```
void AGLKFrustumSetPositionAndDirection
(
    AGLKFrustum *frustumPtr,
    GLKVector3 eyePosition,
    GLKVector3 lookAtPosition,
    GLKVector3 upVector)
{
    NSCAssert(NULL != frustumPtr,
        @"Invalid frustumPtr parameter");

    frustumPtr->eyePosition = eyePosition;

    // compute the Z normal of the frustum. The Z normal points in
    // the direction from eye position to look at position
    const GLKVector3 lookAtVector =
        GLKVector3Subtract(eyePosition, lookAtPosition);
    NSCAssert(0.0f < AGLKVector3LengthSquared(lookAtVector),
            @"Invalid eyeLookPosition parameter");
        frustumPtr->zNormalVector = GLKVector3Normalize(lookAtVector);
```

```
// The frustum's X normal is the cross product of the
// normalized "up" vector and the frustum's Z normal
frustumPtr->xNormalVector = GLKVector3CrossProduct(
   GLKVector3Normalize(upVector),
   frustumPtr->zNormalVector);

// The frustum's Y normal is the cross product of the
// frustum's Z normal and the frustum's X normal.
frustumPtr->yNormalVector = GLKVector3CrossProduct(
   frustumPtr->zNormalVector,
   frustumPtr->xNormalVector);
}
```

To test whether a point falls within a frustum, the first step is to calculate a vector from the eye position to the point being tested and then extract the frustum axis–aligned components of that vector. Recall the "The Geometry of a 3D Scene" section of Chapter 1, "Using Modern Mobile Graphics Hardware": Every 3D vector can be expressed as three separate axis-aligned component vectors added together. Figure 9.3 shows component vectors aligned with each frustum axis. The sum of the component vectors equals the vector from the eye position to the point being tested.

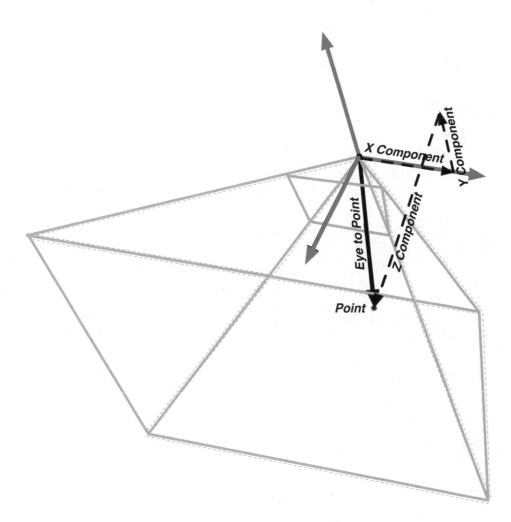

Figure 9.3   Frustum axis–aligned components of a vector from eye to point.

The lengths of the component vectors are computed using the dot product of the "eye to point" vector with each of the frustum's normalized axis vectors. The first and fastest test determines whether the point is beyond the frustum's far plane or behind the frustum's near plane. If the first test fails, there's no need to do any more work. The following excerpt from example OpenGLES_Ch9_1's `AGLKFrustumComparePoint(const AGLKFrustum` `*frustumPtr, GLKVector3 point)` function calculates the vector-from-eye position to the point being tested. It then extracts the frustum Z axis–aligned component of that vector. If the Z axis component is greater than the far distance or less than the near distance, the point is outside the frustum.

```
// compute vector from camera position to point
const GLKVector3 eyeToPoint = GLKVector3Subtract(
   frustumPtr->eyePosition, point);

// compute and test Z coordinate within frustum
const GLfloat pointZComponent = GLKVector3DotProduct(
   eyeToPoint, frustumPtr->zNormalVector);

if(pointZComponent > frustumPtr->farDistance ||
   pointZComponent < frustumPtr->nearDistance)
{  // The point is not within frustum
      result = AGLKFrustumOut;
}
```

Next, the eye-to-point vector's Y component must be shorter than the height of the frustum at the point being tested's Z position. That height, shown in Figure 9.4, is calculated by multiplying the tangent of half the field of view angle by the point being tested's Z position.

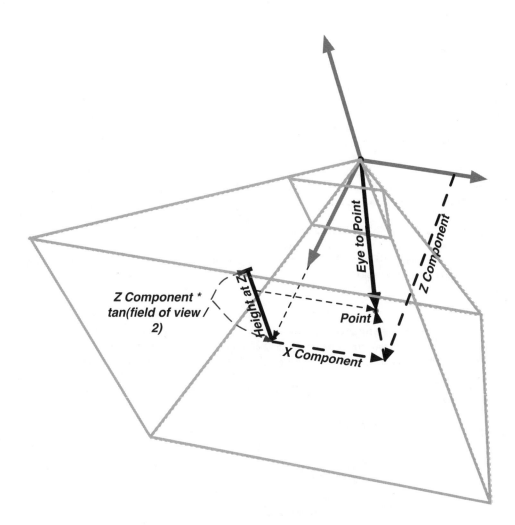

Figure 9.4   Frustum height at Z position.

Finally, the eye-to-point vector's X component must be shorter than the width of the frustum at the point being tested's Z position. The width of the frustum equals the height times the aspect ratio. The following code excerpt tests whether the X and Y components are within the frustum:

```
// compute and test Y coordinate within frustum
const GLfloat pointYComponent =
   GLKVector3DotProduct(eyeToPoint,
      frustumPtr->yNormalVector);
const GLfloat frustumHeightAtZ = pointZComponent *
   frustumPtr->tangentOfHalfFieldOfView;
```

```
if(pointYComponent > frustumHeightAtZ ||
   pointYComponent < -frustumHeightAtZ)
{  // The point is not within frustum
   result = AGLKFrustumOut;
}
else
{  // compute and test the X coordinate within frustum
   const GLfloat pointXComponent =
      GLKVector3DotProduct(eyeToPoint,
         frustumPtr->xNormalVector);
   const GLfloat frustumWidthAtZ = frustumHeightAtZ *
      frustumPtr->aspectRatio;

   if(pointXComponent > frustumWidthAtZ ||
      pointXComponent < -frustumWidthAtZ)
   {  // The point is not within frustum
      result = AGLKFrustumOut;
   }
}
```

Testing whether a sphere intersects the viewing frustum is a bit more complicated. Checking whether the distance from the sphere's center to a point within the frustum is less than the sphere's radius is almost sufficient. Unfortunately, that test misses a special case illustrated in Figure 9.5.

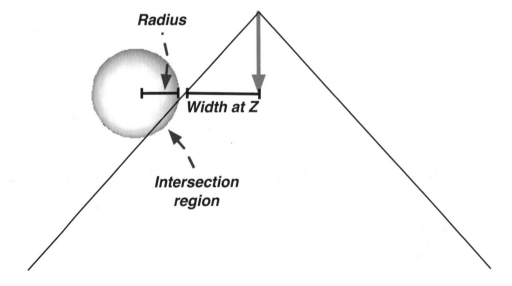

Figure 9.5   A special case for testing sphere intersection with a frustum.

Example OpenGLES_Ch9_1's AGLKFrustum data type includes elements named sphereFactorX and sphereFactorY specifically to handle the special case with spheres. The factors have values slightly greater than 1.0 and are multiplied with a sphere's radius when testing for intersection with the frustum. Figure 9.6 illustrates the geometric relationship of a sphere factor to a radius.

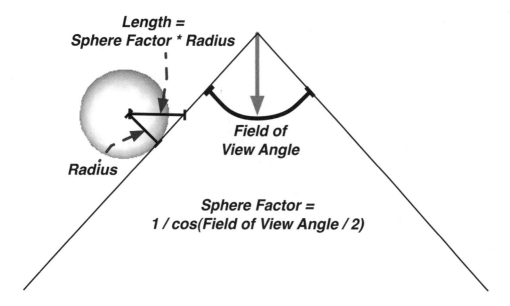

Figure 9.6   The geometric relationship between sphere factors and radius.

Sphere factors are calculated as follows based on the frustum's field of view:

```
// Calculate sphere factors (used when testing sphere
// intersection with frustum)
frustumPtr->sphereFactorY =
   1.0f/cosf(frustumPtr->tangentOfHalfFieldOfView);
const GLfloat angleX =
   atanf(frustumPtr->tangentOfHalfFieldOfView * aspectRatio);
frustumPtr->sphereFactorX = 1.0f/cosf(angleX);
```

All the geometric relationships are in place to efficiently test whether a sphere intersects with a viewing frustum. Examine example OpenGLES_Ch9_1's implementation of the AGLKFrustumCompareSphere(const AGLKFrustum *frustumPtr, GLKVector3 center, float radius) function to see the practical application. To determine whether a model intersects the frustum, testing whether a sphere enclosing the model intersects the frustum is sufficient. The example's —drawModels method attempts to draw 81 models scattered around the scene using code similar to examples from Chapters 7 and 8. A quick test, shown in bold in the following code, culls models that aren't visible in the frame being rendered:

```
/////////////////////////////////////////////////////////////
// Draw models positioned throughout the scene
- (void)drawModels
{
   const float modelRadius = 7.33f; // Used to cull models

   self.baseEffect.texture2d0.name =
      self.modelManager.textureInfo.name;
   self.baseEffect.texture2d0.target =
      self.modelManager.textureInfo.target;

   [self.modelManager prepareToDraw];

   // Draw an arbitrary large number of models
   for(NSInteger i = -4; i < 5; i++)
   {
      for(NSInteger j = -4; j < 5; j++)
      {
         const GLKVector3 modelPosition = {
            -100.0f + 150.0f * i,
            0.0f,
            -100.0f + 150.0f * j
         };

         if(!self.shouldCull ||
            AGLKFrustumOut != AGLKFrustumCompareSphere(
               &frustum_, modelPosition, modelRadius))
         {
            // Save the current matrix
            GLKMatrix4 savedMatrix =
               self.baseEffect.transform.modelviewMatrix;

            // Translate to the model position
            self.baseEffect.transform.modelviewMatrix =
               GLKMatrix4Translate(savedMatrix,
                  modelPosition.x,
                  modelPosition.y,
                  modelPosition.z);
            [self.baseEffect prepareToDraw];

            // Draw the model
            [self.model draw];

            // Restore the saved matrix
            self.baseEffect.transform.modelviewMatrix =
               savedMatrix;
         }
}
```

```
      }
   }
}
```

To keep example OpenGLES_Ch9_1 simple, it tests every model for frustum intersection every time the scene is rendered. Many of the tests can be avoided by storing model positions within a data structure called a scene graph.

Scene Graph–Assisted Culling

A *scene graph* is a hierarchical organization of geometric objects using a tree data structure. There's one root element in the tree. The root element is the "parent" that conceptually contains all the other elements in the data structure. Each "child" of the root element may also be a "parent" containing other elements. The *view hierarchy* within Cocoa Touch applications implements a scene graph for 2D UIView instances, as shown in Apple's documentation at http://developer.apple.com/library/ios/documentation/General/Conceptual/Devpedia-CocoaApp/View%20Hierarchy.html. The same concept applies to hierarchies of 3D objects. Because "parent" elements spatially contain all of their children, testing the parent for intersection with the frustum is sufficient. If the parent is outside, then by definition all of its children are also outside, and no need exists to individually test children.

Wikipedia contains a thorough explanation of scene graphs at http://en.wikipedia.org/wiki/Scene_graph. High-performance graphics applications often use a related data structure called an *octree*: http://en.wikipedia.org/wiki/Octree. None of the examples in this book contain enough objects to benefit from a full octree-based scene graph. However, example OpenGLES_Ch10_1 in Chapter 10, "Terrain and Picking," uses a simple form of spatial optimization for culling when drawing a simulated *terrain* composed of hills and valleys. The terrain itself is a large mesh like the meshes in Chapter 6, "Animation."

Example OpenGLES_Ch10_1's terrain mesh contains more vertices than a single call to glDrawElements() can access. Therefore, the terrain mesh is separated into "tiles" that each reference a subset of the vertices. Tiles are small enough to be drawn via glDrawElements() and collectively compose a simple scene graph. Models and other geometric objects are positioned as "children" within tiles. If a tile doesn't intersect the frustum, then none of the objects positioned within the tile are visible either.

Simplify

If you can't avoid drawing something, keep the drawing simple. Use special effects such as billboards to reduce the complexity of geometric objects passed to the GPU. Reduce the number of vertices in meshes. Use the smallest textures that preserve render quality and consider using compressed textures as described in the "Texture Compression" section of Chapter 3, "Textures." Use multi-texturing as explained in Chapter 3 to avoid multi-pass rendering. If possible, avoid multi-texturing, too. Use baked-in lighting as described in Chapter 4, "Shedding Some Light," to offload light calculations from the GPU. Lighting requires some of the most computationally expensive operations performed by GPUs. Example OpenGLES_Ch10_1 in the next chapter uses pre-computed lighting for terrain meshes to reduce the burden on the GPU.

Culling and simplifying almost always provide the best return on your time spent optimizing. No amount of improved efficiency when rendering objects will save as much time as simply rendering fewer objects. No amount of optimization to lighting effects will save as much time as not computing lighting at all.

Don't Guess: Profile

As a general rule, 80% of a program's execution time is spent on 20% of the code. In the rare case that an application spends the same amount of time in every block of code, the task of optimizing is gigantic. In such cases, every block must be optimized to get noticeable improvements. Fortunately for most applications, after the significant 20% of the code has been identified, focused optimization of only that code provides maximum benefit for minimum effort. Even optimizing 20% of the code might be too aggressive. Knuth recommends focus on the most performance critical 3%. The key is finding the critical code.

Apple's Xcode Integrated Development Environment (IDE) includes some tools to identify performance bottlenecks. Performance might be limited by the central processing unit (CPU) or the GPU or synchronization events forcing one processor to wait for the other. However, before you apply industrial-strength analysis tools, there's a quick and simple approach to narrow the search for performance problems: Comment out all the application's drawing code and measure the resulting "update rate." The contents of the screen won't actually change because nothing is drawn, but if the application doesn't even call the commented drawing code at the desired rate, no amount of optimization to drawing will solve the problem. In that case, the performance bottleneck isn't in the drawing code.

When OpenGL ES rendering does constrain application performance, apply Apple's OpenGL ES Performance Detective tool to identify any GPU bottlenecks. In many cases, it can direct you to the application code, if any, that limits OpenGL ES performance. It even generates performance improvement recommendations.

OpenGL ES Performance Detective

OpenGL ES Performance Detective runs on your development Mac. To use it, make sure the application to analyze is installed on an iOS device connected to the computer. Start OpenGL ES Performance Detective using the Xcode, Open Developer Tool, OpenGL ES Performance Detective menu item. OpenGL ES Performance Detective presents a dialog enabling you to choose which connected device and which application to analyze. After the iOS application starts running, interact with your iOS application until it's in the state you want to test, and then click OpenGL ES Performance Detective's Collect Evidence button. OpenGL ES Performance Detective generates a report.

For example, with frustum culling enabled in example OpenGLES_Ch9_1, OpenGL ES Performance Detective generates the following report:

Summary
The frame rate of your app is not limited by the graphics pipeline.

Your performance is not limited by the OpenGL ES commands issued by
your app. Use the Instruments tool to investigate where your
application is bottlenecked.

Example OpenGLES_Ch9_1 reliably generates 30 frames per second, the default value of `GLKViewController`'s `preferredFramesPerSecond` property. The GPU finishes rendering each frame before it's time to start rendering the next frame. What OpenGL ES Performance Detective doesn't report is how much time remains after rendering each frame. An attempt to render faster by setting the view controller's `preferredFramesPerSecond` property to 60 might reveal new bottlenecks depending on the speed of your iOS device's GPU.

With frustum-based culling turned off, OpenGL ES Performance Detective immediately detects a problem and recommends solutions:

Summary
The frame rate of your app is limited by the graphics pipeline.
Your performance is limited by the OpenGL ES commands issued by your app.

Top Suspect
GPU Vertex Processing

Reduce the number of vertices sent to OpenGL ES by simplifying your geometry. For
example:

1. Employ a polygon reduction algorithm.
2. Do not send unused vertex attributes. For example, do not send a normal when
lighting is disabled.
3. Use a Level of Detail (LOD) algorithm to avoid processing 1000's of triangles for
an object 10's of pixels on the screen.
4. Submit sorted indexed triangles. Sort both the index list and triangle list in
strip order.
5. Perform coarse object culling on the CPU.

OpenGL ES Performance Detective's numbered recommendations aren't listed in the order they should be applied. For example OpenGLES_Ch9_1, turning frustum-based culling back on in compliance with recommendation number 5 makes all the difference.

Instruments

Apple's Instruments application runs on Mac OS X and enables detailed analysis of almost every aspect of iOS application execution. The Instruments application itself loads separate tools called "instruments" to collect information. You pick and choose loadable instruments to refine analysis. For example, the Time Profiler instrument efficiently collects statistics about application code execution and helps identify code consuming the most runtime. If the Time Profiler instrument indicates excessive time spent in system calls, the System Trace instrument is available to record all system calls made by the application. If the Time Profiler instrument indicates excessive time spent in memory allocation, the Allocations instrument locates the sources of memory allocations. OpenGL ES Analyzer and OpenGL ES Driver instruments measure OpenGL ES activity. Use instruments on a case-by-case basis to drill down until the exact bottlenecks are found.

Xcode 4's Product, Profile menu starts the Instruments application. From there, the best approach is to experiment with the available instruments and get a feel for the information they provide. Creating custom loadable instruments is possible as well. Apple provides the Instruments User Guide at http://developer.apple.com/library/ios/DOCUMENTATION/ DeveloperTools/Conceptual/InstrumentsUserGuide/AboutTracing/AboutTracing.html. Apple frequently updates, improves, and extends Instruments, making online documentation the best place to turn for up-to-date guidance.

Minimize Buffer Copying

The GPU needs to access vertex attribute buffers, texture buffers, and render buffers millions of times per second. As a general rule, the GPU cannot access a buffer at the same time the CPU accesses the same buffer. Attempts by the CPU to read or write buffer contents likely force the CPU or the GPU (in some cases both) to stop and wait. The wait is called a *stall*. To mitigate the danger of stalls, OpenGL ES contexts and in some cases the low-level OpenGL ES hardware device driver create private copies of buffers. Copying buffers consumes memory and processor time, but OpenGL ES usually performs the copying at the least disruptive times to avoid stalls.

The best way to minimize buffer copying is to initialize buffers, hand them to OpenGL ES using the GL_STATIC_DRAW hint to the glBufferData() function, and then never modify or read the buffer from programs executing on the CPU. OpenGL ES copies the buffer initialized by glBufferData() into GPU-controlled memory and then accesses the buffer with optimal efficiency. Similarly, the GPU writes data into render buffers in GPU-controlled memory. Attempts by the CPU to read the contents of render buffers via the glReadPixels() function might cause stalls and usually force OpenGL ES to create time- and memory-consuming copies of the render buffer contents.

Of course, sometimes dynamically updating buffers or reading the contents of render buffers is necessary. There might be no other way to accomplish the application's goals or alternatives have even worse performance. In those cases, the recommended approach uses double buffers. For example: provide one vertex attribute buffer to the GPU and start modifying another via the CPU. After all OpenGL ES rendering commands that depend on the buffer used in the GPU have been sent, swap the buffers by calling glBindBuffer() so the one just updated by the CPU is used for subsequent rendering, making the buffer previously used by the GPU available for update by the CPU. Ensure that the GPU and CPU don't work in the same buffer at the same time.

Apple describes double buffering techniques in more detail at https://developer.apple. com/library/ios/documentation/3DDrawing/Conceptual/OpenGLES_ProgrammingGuide/ OpenGLESApplicationDesign/OpenGLESApplicationDesign.html.

Minimize State Changes

OpenGL ES contexts store a large amount of information to control rendering operations. Some of the information is cached in CPU controlled memory and other information is stored within registers in the GPU. Changes to the context's state always require some CPU overhead and might slow the GPU's as register values change. In particular, avoid unnecessary calls to `glBindBuffer()` and `glVertexAttribPointer()` as well as `glEnable()` and `glDisable()` in all their variants such as `glEnableVertexAttribArray()`. After a mode is enabled, it doesn't need to be reenabled. Calling `glEnable()` more than once for the same mode provides no benefit and wastes CPU time. For example, calling `glEnable(GL_DEPTH_TEST)` more than once wastes time updating the context's state even if the value is identical to the current value.

OpenGL ES implementations for iOS 4.0 and later include a recent non-standard extension to OpenGL ES to help consolidate context state changes. Many applications call `glBindBuffer()`, `glEnableVertexAttribArray()`, and `glVertexAttribPointer()` multiple times per rendered frame. For example, applications may render multiple meshes with different vertex attributes. The new vertex array objects (VAOs) extension records the current context state related to vertex attribute and stores that information in a small buffer. The entire state can then be restored with a single call to `glBindVertexArrayOES()` instead of separate calls to `glBindBuffer()`, `glEnableVertexAttribArray()`, and `glVertexAttribPointer()`. The "OES" extension denotes non-standard extensions proposed by Khronos Group, Inc., the maintainers of the OpenGL ES standard.

Following the pattern used for other types of buffers, vertex array objects are generated, bound, and initialized in multiple steps:

```
glGenVertexArraysOES(1,                    // STEP 1
    &vertexArrayObjectID);


glBindVertexArrayOES(vertexArrayObjectID); // STEP 2

// STEP 3: initialize the bound VAO by calling
// glBindBuffer(), glEnableVertexAttribArray(), and
// glVertexAttribPointer()to configure needed vertex
// attributes
```

To restore the entire vertex array attribute state represented by a vertex array object, it's only necessary to bind the VAO again. OpenGL ES functions use the restored state just as if the individual explicit calls to `glBindBuffer()`, `glEnableVertexAttribArray()`, and `glVertexAttribPointer()` had been made.

```
glBindVertexArrayOES(vertexArrayObjectID);


glDrawElements(...
```

Because vertex array objects are non-standard, avoid them unless profiling indicates that context state changes involving vertex array attribute buffers represent a significant bottleneck.

VAO will likely become an official part of the OpenGL ES standard in future versions, but there are no guarantees, and the application programming interface (API) to use VAO might change slightly as part of the standardization process. If the eventual standard differs from the non-standard implementation in any way, iOS applications using nonstandard VAO extensions might require changes to work with the new standard.

Summary

The GPUs in iOS devices render complex scenes at reasonable frame rates, but they have limits. The most effective optimization you can make is to simply draw less. Use frustum-based culling to avoid wasting processor cycles on geometry the user can't see. Profile application performance to find bottlenecks and concentrate optimization on the bottlenecks. Don't bother to make a block of code execute ten times faster if that block rarely executes. Users will never notice the speed-up. Remember that iOS devices have relatively small screens. Small textures and simple geometry often provide adequate visual quality. Don't make geometric models so complex that triangles end up smaller than a single pixel onscreen. Users will never see the detail.

Chapter 10 introduces more 3D graphics tricks of the trade, including techniques to enable user interaction with rendered objects. Touch input becomes compelling when users feel like they are reaching in and interacting with objects they see.

Terrain and Picking

This chapter presents a method for drawing expansive outdoor scenes with rolling terrain by reusing many of the 3D graphics concepts and sample classes introduced in prior chapters. Approaches for 3D terrain rendering apply to any application for visualizing large data sets, including medical imaging and molecular modeling. Large data sets require special handling within 3D applications. Partitioning data into subsets suitable for access by the graphics processing unit (GPU) is necessary.

This chapter also introduces a technique called *picking* to detect user interaction with 3D geometry. When a user touches the screen, what 3D objects are under the user's finger? What terrain location is touched?

Terrain Implementation

Chapter 6, "Animation," introduces meshes as efficient representations of complex geometry. Meshes store collections of triangles sharing vertices or sides. In addition to representing models such as the bumper cars in Chapter 6, meshes can define rolling hills and valleys providing the illusion of terrain spanning kilometers. Example OpenGLES_Ch10_1 demonstrates the loading and display of terrain meshes. Figure 10.1 shows a simplified terrain mesh.

Figure 10.1   Sample terrain mesh.

Height Map

Terrain meshes form a rectangular a grid in the coordinate system's X, Z plane. The Y position of each vertex in the grid corresponds to an altitude (also known as "elevation" or height). Figure 10.2 reveals the mesh grid for the same terrain shown in Figure 10.1.

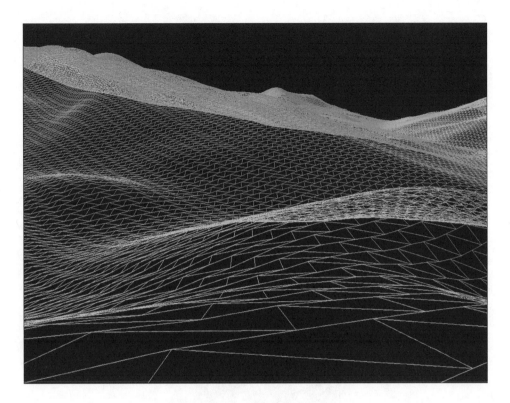

Figure 10.2   Sample terrain mesh grid.

Hard coding the positions of every vertex in a complex mesh is impractical. The easiest way to obtain height values is to load them at runtime from files. Many 3D modeling tools include features to generate terrain elevation data. Sites such as the U.S. Geological Survey at http://earthexplorer.usgs.gov provide free files containing Digital Elevation Model (DEM) data for real places. DEM data exists in many formats. The current standard is Multi-resolution Terrain Elevation Data 2010 (GMTED2010) that can be converted to ordinary image files via the USGS web-based GMTED_viewer.

Example OpenGLES_Ch10_1 loads heights from a compact binary file representation generated by a Mac OS X TerrainEditor application available as source code at http://opengles.cosmicthump.com/learning-opengl-es-sample-code/. `TerrainEditor.app` reads ordinary image files and interprets the brightness of each pixel in the image as normalized values from `0.0` (black) to `1.0` (white). Example OpenGLES_Ch10_1 loads and scales normalized height values to produce desired terrain. As an implementation detail, both `TerrainEditor.app` and example OpenGLES_Ch10_1 use Apple's Core Data framework to provide the compact binary representation.

> **Note**
>
> Core Data adapts database concepts to simplify storage, retrieval, and processing of model data for Mac OS X and iOS applications. Core Data automates common tasks for managing interrelated objects including change validation and built-in undo/redo support. Mixing Core Data with GLKit and OpenGL ES provides the same advantages available for less graphical applications. Reference: http://developer.apple.com/technologies/ios/data-management.html.

Figure 10.3 shows the image used to supply height values for example OpenGLES_Ch10_1. The image is 300 pixels high and 300 pixels wide representing a square with 3-kilometer sides. Each of the 90,000 pixels (300 times 300) in the image corresponds to an X, Z position in the rectangular mesh, and each pixel's brightness value provides a Y position. Two triangles compose each rectangle in the mesh. Therefore, 180,000 triangles must be rendered to draw the whole terrain.

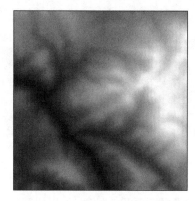

Figure 10.3   The source of height values in example OpenGLES_Ch10_1.

Terrain Tiles

In prior examples, entire meshes were drawn with a single call to glDrawElements(). A mesh containing 90,000 vertices and 180,000 triangles far exceeds the limits of the OpenGL ES glDrawElements() implementation. Therefore, example OpenGLES_Ch10_1 submits mesh data to glDrawElements() in multiple smaller batches called *tiles*. The complete terrain mesh is stored by a class named TETerrain that Core Data automatically generates from a model created graphically in Xcode and shown in Figure 10.4.

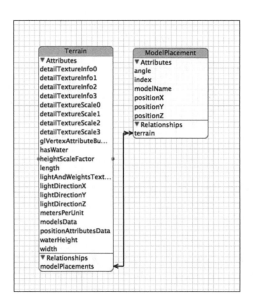

Figure 10.4   Core Data model for a terrain.

Having Xcode generate Objective-C classes corresponding to a Core Data model is not always necessary. However, generating Objective-C classes for use in example OpenGLES_Ch10_1 and adding methods unrelated to data storage is convenient. There is a trick: Don't modify the generated files, because you might want to regenerate them sometime if you change the data model. Regenerating clobbers any edits you made to the previously generated files. Instead, add methods to the generated classes using Objective-C categories implemented in separate files from the generated ones.

> ### Note
>
> Objective-C categories add methods to existing classes even when the source code for the existing classes is not available, or as in this case, it's desirable to avoid editing the existing/ generated classes. Categories make it possible for the implementation of a class to span multiple files. Methods added via a category are indistinguishable at runtime from methods defined in the main class implementation. More information is available at http://developer.apple.com/ library/ios/documentation/General/Conceptual/DevPedia-CocoaCore/Category.html.

The following code defines categories of the TETerrain class. Categories are often named based on the name of the class being extended. This example includes categories named TETerrain+viewAdditions and TETerrain+modelAdditions. The categories add methods to obtain information about the terrain, subdivide the entire terrain into tiles, and draw the tiles.

```
//
//   TETerrain+viewAdditions.h
//
//

#import "TETerrain+modelAdditions.h"
#import <GLKit/GLKit.h>

@class GLKTextureInfo;
@class UtilityCamera;
@class UtilityTerrainEffect;
@class UtilityPickTerrainEffect;
@class UtilityModelEffect;
@class UtilityModelManager;


/////////////////////////////////////////////////////////////////
// The only vertex attribute needed for terrain rendering is
// "position".
typedef enum
{
   TETerrainPositionAttrib,
   TETerrainNumberOfAttributes
} TETerrainAttribute;


@interface TETerrain (viewAdditions)

- (NSArray *)tiles;

- (void)prepareTerrainAttributes;

- (void)drawTerrainWithinTiles:(NSArray *)tiles
   withCamera:(UtilityCamera *)aCamera
   terrainEffect:(UtilityTerrainEffect *)aTerrainEffect;

- (void)drawModelsWithinTiles:(NSArray *)tiles
   withCamera:(UtilityCamera *)aCamera
   modelEffect:(UtilityModelEffect *)aModelEffect
   modelManager:(UtilityModelManager *)modelManager;

- (void)prepareToPickTerrain:(NSArray *)tiles
   withCamera:(UtilityCamera *)aCamera
   pickEffect:(UtilityPickTerrainEffect *)aPickEffect;

@end
```

```
//
//   TETerrain+modelAdditions.h
//
//

#import "TETerrain.h"
#import <GLKit/GLKit.h>


@interface TETerrain (modelAdditions)

- (GLfloat)calculatedHeightAtXPosMeters:(GLfloat)x
    zPosMeters:(GLfloat)z
    surfaceNormal:(GLKVector3 *)aNormal;
- (GLfloat)calculatedHeightAtXPos:(GLfloat)x
    zPos:(GLfloat)z
    surfaceNormal:(GLKVector3 *)aNormal;
- (GLfloat)heightAtXPos:(NSInteger)x zPos:(NSInteger)z;
- (GLfloat)heightAtXPosMeters:(GLfloat)x zPosMeters:(GLfloat)z;
- (GLfloat)maxHeightNearXPosMeters:(NSInteger)x
    zPosMeters:(NSInteger)z;
- (GLfloat)regionalHeightAtXPosMeters:(NSInteger)x
    zPosMeters:(NSInteger)z;
- (BOOL)isHeightValidAtXPos:(NSInteger)x zPos:(NSInteger)z;
- (BOOL)isHeightValidAtXPosMeters:(NSInteger)x
    zPosMeters:(NSInteger)z;

- (GLfloat)widthMeters;
- (GLfloat)heightMeters;
- (GLfloat)lengthMeters;

@end
```

The `TETerrainAttribute` type defines OpenGL ES vertex attributes used to render the terrain mesh. The –tiles method returns an array of tiles that each references a subset of the total terrain. The tiles are created as needed the first time the –tiles method is invoked. The – prepareTerrainAttributes method configures the OpenGL ES state needed to render terrain including creation of vertex attribute buffers. After calling – prepareTerrainAttributes, call -drawTiles:(NSArray *)tiles to render the portions of the overall terrain mesh referenced by the tiles in the specified `tiles` array. The remaining methods in the categories enable queries to obtain the dimensions of the terrain and heights at positions within the terrain.

Example OpenGLES_Ch10_1 encapsulates tiles via the `TETerrainTile` class. Each instance of `TETerrainTile` manages an OpenGL ES element array buffer containing indices for a subset of vertices in the overall terrain. Element array buffers are explained in the "Using Indexed Vertices" section of Chapter 6. The interesting work is performed in `TETerrainTile`'s –draw method, which binds an element array buffer and calls `glDrawElements()` to submit vertices for processing.

```
//
//  TETerrainTile.h
//
//

#import <Foundation/Foundation.h>

@class TETerrain;


@interface TETerrainTile : NSObject

@property (assign, nonatomic, readonly) NSInteger originX;
@property (assign, nonatomic, readonly) NSInteger originY;
@property (strong, nonatomic, readonly) NSSet *
   containedModelPlacements;

- (id)initWithTerrain:(TETerrain *)aTerrain
   tileOriginX:(NSInteger)x
   tileOriginY:(NSInteger)y
   tileWidth:(NSInteger)aWidth
   tileLength:(NSInteger)aLength;

- (void)draw;

- (void)manageContainedModelPlacements:(NSSet *)somePlacements;
- (NSSet *)containedModelPlacements;

@end

static const NSInteger TETerrainTileDefaultWidth = 32;
static const NSInteger TETerrainTileDefaultLength = 32;
```

Explore the implementations of the `TETerrain+viewAdditions` category and the `TETerrainTile` class in example OpenGLES_Ch10_1. The implementations of each method are straightforward and short. Most of the code is similar or identical to code introduced in preceding chapters for managing and rendering meshes.

Terrain Effect

A custom OpenGL ES Shading Language program renders terrain by combining four "detail" textures mixed according to blending weights stored in a fifth texture called `lightAndWeightsTextureInfo`. The textures combine to provide the illusion of details such as bumps, ripples, leaves, dirt, or sand when the mesh is rendered. The lightAndWeightsTextureInfo texture also includes pre-calculated baked-in lighting for a fixed light direction. Chapter 4, "Shedding Some Light," briefly describes lighting baked into a texture. The following UtilityTerrainEffect class manages the OpenGL ES Shading Language program for terrain rendering:

```
//
//  UtilityTerrainEffect.h
//
//

#import "UtilityEffect.h"
#import <GLKit/GLKit.h>

@class TETerrain;
@class UtilityTextureInfo;


@interface UtilityTerrainEffect : UtilityEffect

@property (assign, nonatomic, readwrite)
   GLKVector4 globalAmbientLightColor;
@property (assign, nonatomic, readwrite)
   GLKMatrix4 projectionMatrix;
@property (assign, nonatomic, readwrite)
   GLKMatrix4 modelviewMatrix;
@property (assign, nonatomic, readwrite)
   GLKMatrix3 textureMatrix0;
@property (assign, nonatomic, readwrite)
   GLKMatrix3 textureMatrix1;
@property (assign, nonatomic, readwrite)
   GLKMatrix3 textureMatrix2;
@property (assign, nonatomic, readwrite)
   GLKMatrix3 textureMatrix3;
@property (strong, nonatomic, readwrite)
   UtilityTextureInfo *lightAndWeightsTextureInfo;
@property (strong, nonatomic, readwrite)
   UtilityTextureInfo *detailTextureInfo0;
@property (strong, nonatomic, readwrite)
   UtilityTextureInfo *detailTextureInfo1;
@property (strong, nonatomic, readwrite)
   UtilityTextureInfo *detailTextureInfo2;
@property (strong, nonatomic, readwrite)
   UtilityTextureInfo *detailTextureInfo3;

// Designated initializer
- (id)initWithTerrain:(TETerrain *)aTerrain;
```

```
- (void)prepareToDraw;

@end
```

The Shading Language program individually transforms each texture using supplied texture matrices called `textureMatrix0`, `textureMatrix1`, `textureMatrix2`, and `textureMatrix3` affecting `detailTextureInfo0` through `detailTextureInfo3`, respectively, within the `UtilityTerrainEffect` class. Call `UtilityTerrainEffect`'s `−prepareToDraw` method right before submitting terrain vertex attributes via `TETerrain`'s `−drawTiles:` method.

> ### Note
>
> Example OpenGLES_Ch10_1 implements several "Effect" classes that encapsulate separate Shading Language programs for terrain rendering, model rendering, and picking. To avoid unnecessary code duplication, example OpenGLES_Ch10_1 introduces the `UtilityEffect` abstract base class to load, compile, link, and validate Shading Language programs. `UtilityEffect` conforms to GLKit's `GLKNamedEffect` protocol. In the context of the Objective-C language, `UtilityEffect` is "abstract" because `UtilityEffect` implements two methods, `−bindAttribLocations` and `−configureUniformLocations`, to generate exceptions if they are ever invoked directly. Subclasses of `UtilityEffect` must override the two methods.

The following Shading Language program for terrain rendering transforms vertex position attributes using a combined Model View Projection matrix like previous vertex shader examples. In this case, vertex position attributes serve double duty as texture coordinates so that detail textures automatically cover the entire terrain mesh. However, the shader transforms texture coordinates for each of the detail textures using separate matrices. Each texture may have separate translation, rotation, and scale applied. Scaling a detail texture controls how many times the texture repeats over the entire mesh. For example, textures may be scaled to repeat hundreds of times across the terrain or to exactly fit the terrain without repeating. Chapter 3, "Textures," explains texture transformation and repeating. Reviewing examples in Chapter 3 helps to visualize the more complex transformations used in this example.

```
//
//   UtilityTerrainShader.vsh
//
//


/////////////////////////////////////////////////////////////
// VERTEX ATTRIBUTES
/////////////////////////////////////////////////////////////
attribute vec3 a_position;


/////////////////////////////////////////////////////////////
// TEXTURE
/////////////////////////////////////////////////////////////
#define MAX_TEXTURES    5
```

```
#define MAX_TEX_COORDS  5

///////////////////////////////////////////////////////////////
// UNIFORMS
///////////////////////////////////////////////////////////////
uniform highp mat4      u_mvpMatrix;
uniform highp mat3      u_texMatrices[MAX_TEXTURES];
uniform sampler2D       u_units[MAX_TEXTURES];
uniform lowp vec4       u_globalAmbientColor;


///////////////////////////////////////////////////////////////
// Varyings
///////////////////////////////////////////////////////////////
varying highp vec2      v_texCoords[MAX_TEX_COORDS];


void main()
{
   vec3 coords = u_texMatrices[0] * a_position;
   v_texCoords[0] = vec2(coords.x, coords.z);
   coords = u_texMatrices[1] * a_position;
   v_texCoords[1] = vec2(coords.x, coords.z);
   coords = u_texMatrices[2] * a_position;
   v_texCoords[2] = vec2(coords.x, coords.z);
   coords = u_texMatrices[3] * a_position;
   v_texCoords[3] = vec2(coords.x, coords.z);
   coords = u_texMatrices[4] * a_position;
   v_texCoords[4] = vec2(coords.x, coords.z);

   gl_Position = u_mvpMatrix * vec4(a_position, 1.0);
}
```

Mixing texture colors with weight factors works much the same way vertex positions
are influenced by weights, as described in Chapter 7, "Loading and Using Models."
UtilityTerrainEffect and UtilityTerrainShader use detailTextureInfo3 to provide
the default terrain fragment color. In other words, if all the texture mixing weights are zero,
100% of each terrain fragment color comes from texels within detailTextureInfo3. Blending
based on weight works just like the GL_ONE_MINUS_SRC_ALPHA blending function explained in
Chapter 3. OpenGL ES Shading Language even provides a built-in function called mix(
first_color, second_color, weight) that returns ((1.0 - weight) * first_color)
+ (weight * second_color). In the following fragment shader, the default textureColor
provided by detailTextureInfo3 is mixed with textureColor0 based on weights.x,
which corresponds to lightAndWeightsTextureInfo's texel red component. Then
textureColor1 is mixed in using weights.y obtained from lightAndWeightsTextureInfo's
texel green component. Finally, textureColor2 is mixed in using weights.z obtained from
lightAndWeightsTextureInfo's texel blue component.

The last texel color component in `lightAndWeightsTextureInfo` would ordinarily be interpreted as Alpha or W in an (X, Y, Z, W) coordinate system, but in this case, the last component defines the light intensity for each rendered fragment. The light intensities are pre-calculated in the Mac OS X TerrainEditor application and saved in the `lightAndWeightsTextureInfo` loaded by example OpenGLES_Ch10_1.

```
//
//  UtilityTerrainShader.fsh
//
//


/////////////////////////////////////////////////////////////////
// TEXTURE
/////////////////////////////////////////////////////////////////
#define MAX_TEXTURES    5
#define MAX_TEX_COORDS  5


/////////////////////////////////////////////////////////////////
// UNIFORMS
/////////////////////////////////////////////////////////////////
uniform highp mat4      u_mvpMatrix;
uniform highp mat3      u_texMatrices[MAX_TEXTURES];
uniform sampler2D       u_units[MAX_TEXTURES];
uniform lowp vec4       u_globalAmbientColor;


/////////////////////////////////////////////////////////////////
// Varyings
/////////////////////////////////////////////////////////////////
varying highp vec2      v_texCoords[MAX_TEX_COORDS];


void main()
{
   // Extract light color from w component of light and weight
   // texture
   lowp vec4 lightAndWeights =
      texture2D(u_units[0], v_texCoords[0]);
   lowp vec4 lightColor = u_globalAmbientColor + lowp vec4(
      lightAndWeights.w,
      lightAndWeights.w,
      lightAndWeights.w,
      1.0);

   // Extract texture mixing weights from light and weight
   // texture
```

```
lowp vec3 weights = lowp vec3(
   lightAndWeights.x,
   lightAndWeights.y,
   lightAndWeights.z);

// Blend the terrain textures using weights
lowp vec4 textureColor0 = texture2D(u_units[1], v_texCoords[1]);
lowp vec4 textureColor1 = texture2D(u_units[2], v_texCoords[2]);
lowp vec4 textureColor2 = texture2D(u_units[3], v_texCoords[3]);
lowp vec4 textureColor3 = texture2D(u_units[4], v_texCoords[4]);
lowp vec4 textureColor = textureColor3;
textureColor = mix(textureColor, textureColor0, weights.x);
textureColor = mix(textureColor, textureColor1, weights.y);
textureColor = mix(textureColor, textureColor2, weights.z);

// Scale by light color
lowp vec4 color = lightColor * textureColor;

// Final terrain color is always opaque
color.a = 1.0;

gl_FragColor = color;
}
```

The example's `TETerrain`, `TETerrainTile`, and `UtilityTerrainEffect` classes presented so far work together to efficiently render complex terrain meshes. The "Optimization" section of this chapter describes opportunities to improve terrain rendering performance using culling and scene graph techniques introduced in Chapter 9, "Optimization."

Adding Models

Figure 10.5 is a screenshot of models rendered in a scene along with terrain. Example OpenGLES_Ch10_1 uses `UtilityMesh` and `UtilityModel` classes similar to the ones in previous examples. OpenGLES_Ch10_1 adds a –prepareToPick method to `UtilityMesh`. The new method works like the existing –prepareToDraw method but doesn't enable vertex attributes such as normal vectors and texture coordinates because those attributes aren't needed for picking.

A doesRequireLighting property has been added to the `UtilityModel` class. Some models, including the trees, have lighting baked into their textures. The doesRequireLighting property differentiates between models to be rendered using the OpenGL lighting model and models rendered with baked-in lighting.

Figure 10.5   Models rendered with terrain.

Model Placement

The TEModelPlacement class is generated by Xcode from the data definition shown in Figure 10.4 and stores properties for model name, position, and angle of rotation about the Y axis. A collection of TEModelPlacement instances stored along with the terrain specify the locations of trees, stones, and buildings. For example, the same palm tree model is rendered multiple times in Figure 10.5 because multiple instances of TEModelPlacement at different locations within the terrain reference the palm tree model's name.

Model Effect

Example OpenGLES_Ch10_1's terrain always has baked-in lighting and multiple textures. In contrast, models use a single texture and may have baked-in lighting or not on a case-by-case basis. The UtilityModelEffect class manages OpenGL ES Shading Language programs optimized for rendering models with or without baked-in lighting.

```
//
//   UtilityModelEffect.h
//
//

#import "UtilityEffect.h"
#import <GLKit/GLKit.h>


@interface UtilityModelEffect : UtilityEffect

@property (assign, nonatomic, readwrite) GLKMatrix4
    projectionMatrix;
@property (assign, nonatomic, readwrite) GLKMatrix4
    modelviewMatrix;
@property (assign, nonatomic, readwrite) GLKVector4
    globalAmbientLightColor;
@property (assign, nonatomic, readwrite) GLKVector3
    diffuseLightDirection;
@property (assign, nonatomic, readwrite) GLKVector4
    diffuseLightColor;
@property (strong, nonatomic, readwrite) GLKTextureInfo *
    texture2D;

- (void)prepareLightColors;
- (void)prepareModelview;
- (void)prepareModelviewWithoutNormal;

@end
```

When rendering models with lighting, the `UtilityModelEffect`'s `diffuseLightColor` and `globalAmbientLightColor` properties are set to match the `TETerrainEffect`'s values. The `UtilityModelEffect`'s `diffuseLightDirection` property is set to match the light direction used to bake lighting into the terrain's `lightAndWeightsTextureInfo`. The light direction is stored by the `TETerrain` object. When rendering models without lighting, the `diffuseLightColor` is set to black and the `globalAmbientLightColor` is set to full white, which prevents the OpenGL ES lighting equation from modifying the texture colors of the model.

The custom Shading Languages programs, `UtilityModelShader.vsh` and `UtilityModelShader.fsh`, for rendering models remain simple. The relevant portion of `UtilityModelShader.vsh` provides the fragment program with texture coordinates and transformed position coordinates along with calculated lighting for a single directional light.

```
void main()
{
    // Texture coords
```

```
    v_texCoords[0] = a_texCoords0;

    // Lighting
    lowp vec3 normal = normalize(u_normalMatrix * a_normal);
    lowp float nDotL = max(
        dot(normal, normalize(u_diffuseLightDirection)), 0.0);
    v_lightColor = (nDotL * u_diffuseLightColor) +
        u_globalAmbient;

    gl_Position = u_mvpMatrix * vec4(a_position, 1.0);
}
```

The following `UtilityModelShader.fsh` program uses a trick to enable correct rendering of models that have translucent textures. Chapter 8, "Special Effects," explained that rendering translucent textures produces unsightly visual artifacts unless the textured objects are rendered in sorted order–based distance from the near frustum plane. However, when textures contain only fully opaque and fully transparent texels (none are partially opaque), the need to sort can be avoided.

```
void main()
{
    lowp vec4 color = texture2D(u_units[0], v_texCoords[0]);
    if (color.a < 0.2)
    {   // discard nearly transparent fragments
        discard;
    }

    gl_FragColor = color * v_lightColor;
}
```

The bold code in `UtilityModelShader.fsh` tests whether the current fragment color is nearly transparent and if so discards the fragment. A discarded fragment has no effect on either the pixel color render buffer or the depth render buffer. That's exactly the desired result when rendering models such as the trees shown in Figure 10.5. Discarded transparent fragments don't obscure fragments produced for other 3D objects. The trick doesn't work with partially transparent texels because the final pixel color in the pixel color render buffer then depends on the blending of fragments generated from multiple 3D objects. The order in which the fragments are generated then becomes critical, and sorting is required.

Note

Conditional execution with "if" statements and the use of the `discard` command are among the most computationally intense and therefore slow operations performed by graphics processing units (GPUs). The implementation of example OpenGLES_Ch10_1 is a tradeoff between the time and complexity needed to sort models based on distance from the observer and the computational intensity of the Shading Language programs. Different applications might require a different tradeoff based on benchmarking.

OpenGL ES Camera

The viewing frustum defines a "point of view" as explained in the "Perspective and the Viewing Frustum" section of Chapter 5, "Changing Your Point of View," and elaborated in Chapter 9, "Optimization." Many 3D applications apply the metaphor of a "camera" through which scenes are viewed. Rather than working directly with a frustum data structure, a virtual camera is moved through the virtual world. When needed, the frustum corresponding to the camera's position, orientation, and field of view can be calculated.

Cameras make such a useful metaphor for defining the point of view that it's often convenient to create a class such as the following `UtilityCamera` class in OpenGLES_Ch10_1. The `UtilityCamera` class has methods such as `-(void)setPosition:(GLKVector3)aPosition lookAtPosition:(GLKVector3)lookAtPosition` and `-(void)moveBy:(GLKVector3)aVector`. Moving the camera through the virtual world animates the point of view using motions and terminology more familiar and intuitive than direct manipulation of the frustum data structure.

```
//
//  UtilityCamera.h
//
//


#include <GLKit/GLKit.h>
#import "AGLKFrustum.h"


@class UtilityCamera;


@protocol UtilityOpenGLCameraDelegate <NSObject>


/////////////////////////////////////////////////////////////
// Returning NO prevents changes.
@optional
- (BOOL)camera:(UtilityCamera *)aCamera
   willChangeEyePosition:(GLKVector3 *)eyePositionPtr
   lookAtPosition:(GLKVector3 *)lookAtPositionPtr;


@end



@interface UtilityCamera : NSObject

@property (nonatomic, assign, readwrite)
   __unsafe_unretained IBOutlet id delegate;
@property(assign, nonatomic, readonly)
   GLKMatrix4 projectionMatrix;
@property(assign, nonatomic, readonly)
   GLKMatrix4 modelviewMatrix;
```

```
@property(assign, nonatomic, readonly)
   GLKVector3 position;
@property(assign, nonatomic, readonly)
   GLKVector3 lookAtPosition;
@property(assign, nonatomic, readonly)
   GLKVector3 upUnitVector;
@property(nonatomic, readonly)
   const AGLKFrustum *frustumForCulling;

- (void)configurePerspectiveFieldOfViewRad:(GLfloat)angle
   aspectRatio:(GLfloat)anAspectRatio
   near:(GLfloat)nearLimit
   far:(GLfloat)farLimit;

- (void)rotateAngleRadiansAboutY:(GLfloat)anAngleRadians;
- (void)rotateAngleRadiansAboutX:(GLfloat)anAngleRadians;

- (void)moveBy:(GLKVector3)aVector;

- (void)setPosition:(GLKVector3)aPosition
   lookAtPosition:(GLKVector3)lookAtPosition;
- (void)setOrientation:(GLKMatrix4)aMatrix;

@end
```

The UtilityCamera class reuses and encapsulates the AGLKFrustum data structure introduced in Chapter 9. UtilityCamera's projectionMatrix and modelviewMatrix properties are directly calculated from the frustum corresponding to the camera's position, orientation, and field of view.

All UtilityCamera methods that change the frustum position or orientation call UtilityCamera's -setPosition:lookAtPosition: method, which in turn sends the - (BOOL)camera:(UtilityCamera *)aCamera willChangeEyePosition:(GLKVecto r3 *)eyePositionPtr lookAtPosition:(GLKVector3 *)lookAtPositionPtr message to the camera's delegate. The delegate performs extra processing to control what happens. The delegate can return NO to prevent the change to the camera's position.

> **Note**
>
> Delegation is a common pattern within Cocoa Touch. A delegate is an object given an opportunity to influence the behavior of another object. The basic idea is that two objects coordinate to solve a problem. One object suchas UtilityCamera is very general and intended for reuse in a wide variety of situations. It stores a reference to another object, its delegate, and sends messages to the delegate at critical times. The messages give the delegate an opportunity to perform extra processing or control what happens. Implement application-specific rules and logic in the delegate instead of modifying or subclassing the more general object.

Example OpenGLES_Ch10_1 uses the application's `OpenGLES_Ch10_1ViewController` instance as the camera's delegate. `OpenGLES_Ch10_1ViewController` implements `-camera:willChangeEyePosition:lookAtPosition:` to keep the camera from being positioned below the height of the terrain at the camera's position. A more sophisticated implementation of the delegate could prevent the camera from colliding with models or implement virtual gravity so the camera slides down hills within the terrain.

The following partial implementation of `UtilityCamera` reveals how the class manages the viewing frustum and communicates with a delegate object. The full implementation is available at http://opengles.cosmicthump.com/learning-opengl-es-sample-code/.

```
//
//  UtilityCamera.m
//
//

#import "UtilityCamera.h"
#import "AGLKFrustum.h"


@interface UtilityCamera ()
{
   AGLKFrustum frustum;
}

@property(assign, nonatomic, readwrite)
   BOOL isInCallback;

@end


/////////////////////////////////////////////////////////////////
// Instances of this class encapsulate a viewing frustum and
// enable point-of-view animation using the metaphor of a
// camera.
@implementation UtilityCamera

@synthesize delegate = delegate_;
@synthesize isInCallback = isInCallback_;


/////////////////////////////////////////////////////////////////
// Initialize the receiver with a default frustum
- (id)init
{
   self = [super init];
   if(nil != self)
```

```
{
    // Default 45 deg. field of view, square aspect ratio,
    // near distance of 0.5, and far distance of 5000
    frustum = AGLKFrustumMakeFrustumWithParameters(
        GLKMathDegreesToRadians(45.0f),
        1.0f,
        0.5f,
        5000.0f);
    // Default eye at origin, look down neg. Z axis,
    // Y axis is "up"
    AGLKFrustumSetPositionAndDirection(
        &frustum,
        GLKVector3Make(0.0f, 0.0f, 0.0f),
        GLKVector3Make(0.0f, 0.0f, -1.0f),
        GLKVector3Make(0.0f, 1.0f, 0.0f));
    }

    return self;
}


/////////////////////////////////////////////////////////////////
// Set the receiver's frustum shape
- (void)configurePerspectiveFieldOfViewRad:(GLfloat)angle
   aspectRatio:(GLfloat)anAspectRatio
   near:(GLfloat)nearLimit
   far:(GLfloat)farLimit;
{
    AGLKFrustumSetPerspective(
        &frustum,
        angle,
        anAspectRatio,
        nearLimit,
        farLimit);
}


/////////////////////////////////////////////////////////////////
// Set the receiver's eye and look-at positions and give optional
// delegate object opportunity to revise or constrain the
// specified positions.
- (void)setPosition:(GLKVector3)aPosition
   lookAtPosition:(GLKVector3)lookAtPosition;
{
    if(!self.isInCallback)
    { // Prevent recursive call to -setPosition:lookAtPosition:
        self.isInCallback = YES;
```

```
      BOOL shouldMakeChange = YES;

      if([self.delegate respondsToSelector:
         @selector(camera:willChangeEyePosition:lookAtPosition:)])
      {
         shouldMakeChange =
            [self.delegate camera:self
               willChangeEyePosition:&aPosition
               lookAtPosition:&lookAtPosition];
      }

      if(shouldMakeChange)
      {
         const GLKVector3 upUnitVector =
            GLKVector3Make(0.0f, 1.0f, 0.0f); // Assume Y up

         AGLKFrustumSetPositionAndDirection(
            &frustum,
            aPosition,
            lookAtPosition,
            upUnitVector);
      }

      self.isInCallback = NO;
   }
}


/////////////////////////////////////////////////////////////////
// Return's the receiver's look-at position
- (GLKVector3)lookAtPosition
{
   const GLKVector3 eyePosition = frustum.eyePosition;
   const GLKVector3 lookAtPosition = GLKVector3Add(
      eyePosition, frustum.zNormalVector);

   return lookAtPosition;
}


/////////////////////////////////////////////////////////////////
// Move the receiver's eye position and look-at position by the
// direction and distance of aVector. This method calls
// -setPosition:lookAtPosition: giving the receiver's optional
// delegate an opportunity to revise or constrain the resulting
// frustum positions.
- (void)moveBy:(GLKVector3)aVector;
```

```
{
   const GLKVector3 currentEyePosition = [self position];
   const GLKVector3 currentLookAtPosition = [self lookAtPosition];

   [self setPosition:GLKVector3Add(currentEyePosition, aVector)
      lookAtPosition:GLKVector3Add(currentLookAtPosition, aVector)];
}

@end
```

Picking

Example OpenGLES_Ch10_1 applies specialized rendering with false color to enable picking. When a user touch is recognized, the scene is rendered into a pixel color render buffer with `UtilityPickTerrainEffect`. Terrain X and Z position coordinates are encoded in the red and green color components of fragments. For example, fragments generated from the terrain mesh at position {150, 45, 78} have the floating-point RGB color {150.0 / `terrainWidth`, 78.0 / `terrainLength`, 0.0}. The pixel color under the touch position is then read from the pixel color render buffer. Examining the red and green components of the pixel color identifies the terrain position that was touched.

Users don't see false color rendering because the pixel color render buffer used for picking is never presented onscreen. The approach works regardless of the position and orientation of the camera. Terrain rendered in the foreground automatically occludes terrain in the background, so the terrain position closest to the viewpoint under the touch is always returned. Figure 10.6 helps to visualize the false color scene.

Figure 10.6   Rendering with fragment colors encoding position data.

`UtilityPickTerrainEffect` renders into an OpenGL ES *frame buffer object* (FBO). Frame buffers are introduced in Chapter 1, "Using Modern Mobile Graphics Hardware." Frame buffers receive the results of rendering. Examples up to now exclusively used frame buffers intended for presentation onscreen. Cocoa Touch's `GLKView` class creates a default frame buffer and an attached pixel color render buffer shared with a Cocoa Touch `CALayer` for the view. The `UtilityPickTerrainEffect` class creates an additional frame buffer represented by FBOs instead of `CALayers`.

The following `UtilityPickTerrainInfo` data type and the `UtilityPickTerrainEffect` class interface show how straightforward picking can be. After an instance of `UtilityPickTerrainEffect` has been initialized with terrain via `-initWithTerrain:`, calling that instance's `-terrainInfoForProjectionPosition:` method specifying the location of a touch event returns a `UtilityPickTerrainInfo` structure containing the X and Z coordinates of the terrain at the location.

```
//
//  UtilityPickTerrainEffect.h
//
//
```

```
#import "UtilityEffect.h"
#import <GLKit/GLKit.h>

@class TETerrain;
@class TEModelManager;


typedef struct
{
   GLKVector2 position;
   unsigned char modelIndex;
}
UtilityPickTerrainInfo;


@interface UtilityPickTerrainEffect : UtilityEffect

@property(assign, nonatomic, readwrite)
   GLKMatrix4 projectionMatrix;
@property(assign, nonatomic, readwrite)
   GLKMatrix4 modelviewMatrix;
@property(assign, nonatomic, readwrite)
   unsigned char modelIndex;

// Designated initializer
- (id)initWithTerrain:(TETerrain *)aTerrain;

- (UtilityPickTerrainInfo)terrainInfoForProjectionPosition:
   (GLKVector2)aPosition;

@end
```

The position passed to -terrainInfoForProjectionPosition: is in Cocoa Touch
coordinates relative to the position and size of the GLKView that was touched. The returned
UtilityPickTerrainInfo provides the corresponding terrain coordinates in the 3D virtual
world.

UtilityPickTerrainEffect's FBO doesn't need to match the size of the frame buffer
intended for presentation onscreen. In fact, the best size for an FBO uses power of 2
dimensions. UtilityPickTerrainEffect's FBO is 512 by 512 no matter what size is used
for the frame buffer presented onscreen. Power of 2 dimensions are explained in Chapter 3,
"Textures," and they are important because each FBO typically shares pixel color render buffer
storage with an OpenGL ES texture buffer. Rendering into an FBO is often called "render to
texture" and the resulting texture can be used for subsequent rendering. Example
OpenGLES_Ch10_1 doesn't reuse the texture buffer associated with the FBO, but Apple
provides a sample application, GLEssentials, that uses an FBO to render the reflection of a scene
within the scene itself. The sample is at http://developer.apple.com/library/ios/samplecode/
GLEssentials/Introduction/Intro.html.

UtilityPickTerrainEffect creates and configures its FBO for picking using the following method. The code is similar to the GLEssentials sample and code in example OpenGLES_Ch2_2 that shows how GLKView can be reimplemented. Code to create the texture used as the FBO's pixel color render buffer matches the code in example OpenGLES_Ch3_2 that shows how GLKTextureLoader works.

```objc
////////////////////////////////////////////////////////////
// Build a Frame Buffer Object with attached Pixel Color Render
// Buffer and Depth Buffer to receive the results of rendering
// in false color for picking.
-(GLuint)buildFBOWithWidth:(GLuint)fboWidth
                    height:(GLuint)fboHeight
{
   GLuint fboName;
   GLuint colorTexture;

   // Create a texture object to apply to model
   glGenTextures(1, &colorTexture);
   glBindTexture(GL_TEXTURE_2D, colorTexture);

   // Set up filter and wrap modes for this texture object
   glTexParameteri(GL_TEXTURE_2D, GL_TEXTURE_WRAP_S,
                GL_CLAMP_TO_EDGE);
   glTexParameteri(GL_TEXTURE_2D, GL_TEXTURE_WRAP_T,
                GL_CLAMP_TO_EDGE);
   glTexParameteri(GL_TEXTURE_2D, GL_TEXTURE_MAG_FILTER,
                GL_LINEAR);
   glTexParameteri(GL_TEXTURE_2D, GL_TEXTURE_MIN_FILTER,
                GL_LINEAR_MIPMAP_LINEAR);

   // Allocate a texture image we can render into
   // Pass NULL for the data parameter since we don't need to
   // load image data. We will be generating the image by
   // rendering to this texture.
   glTexImage2D(GL_TEXTURE_2D,
             0,
             GL_RGBA,
             fboWidth,
             fboHeight,
             0,
             GL_RGBA,
             GL_UNSIGNED_BYTE,
             NULL);

   GLuint depthRenderbuffer;
   glGenRenderbuffers(1, &depthRenderbuffer);
   glBindRenderbuffer(GL_RENDERBUFFER, depthRenderbuffer);
```

```
      glRenderbufferStorage(GL_RENDERBUFFER, GL_DEPTH_COMPONENT16,
                            fboWidth, fboHeight);

      glGenFramebuffers(1, &fboName);
      glBindFramebuffer(GL_FRAMEBUFFER, fboName);
      glFramebufferTexture2D(GL_FRAMEBUFFER,
                             GL_COLOR_ATTACHMENT0,
                             GL_TEXTURE_2D, colorTexture, 0);
      glFramebufferRenderbuffer(GL_FRAMEBUFFER,
         GL_DEPTH_ATTACHMENT, GL_RENDERBUFFER, depthRenderbuffer);

      if(glCheckFramebufferStatus(GL_FRAMEBUFFER) !=
         GL_FRAMEBUFFER_COMPLETE)
      {
         NSLog(@"failed to make complete framebuffer object %x",
            glCheckFramebufferStatus(GL_FRAMEBUFFER));

         UtilityPickTerrainEffectDestroyFBO(fboName);

         fboName = 0;
      }

      return fboName;
}
```

`UtilityPickTerrainEffect` destroys its FBO and returns resources to OpenGL ES via the following two functions that are also similar to Apple's GLEssentials sample:

```
/////////////////////////////////////////////////////////////////
// This function deletes the specified FBO including all of its
// attachments and returns resources to OpenGL
static void UtilityPickTerrainEffectDestroyFBO(GLuint fboName)
{
   if(0 == fboName)
   {
      return;
   }

   glBindFramebuffer(GL_FRAMEBUFFER, fboName);

   // Delete the attachment
   UtilityPickTerrainEffectDeleteFBOAttachment(
      GL_COLOR_ATTACHMENT0);

   // Delete any depth or stencil buffer attached
   UtilityPickTerrainEffectDeleteFBOAttachment(
      GL_DEPTH_ATTACHMENT);
```

```
    glDeleteFramebuffers(1, &fboName);
}


/////////////////////////////////////////////////////////////
// This function deletes the specified attachment and returns
// resources to OpenGL
static void UtilityPickTerrainEffectDeleteFBOAttachment(
    GLenum attachment)
{
    GLint param;
    GLuint objName;

    glGetFramebufferAttachmentParameteriv(
        GL_FRAMEBUFFER,
        attachment,
        GL_FRAMEBUFFER_ATTACHMENT_OBJECT_TYPE,
        &param);

    if(GL_RENDERBUFFER == param)
    {
        glGetFramebufferAttachmentParameteriv(
            GL_FRAMEBUFFER,
            attachment,
            GL_FRAMEBUFFER_ATTACHMENT_OBJECT_NAME,
            &param);

        objName = ((GLuint*)(&param))[0];
        glDeleteRenderbuffers(1, &objName);
    }
    else if(GL_TEXTURE == param)
    {
        glGetFramebufferAttachmentParameteriv(
            GL_FRAMEBUFFER,
            attachment,
            GL_FRAMEBUFFER_ATTACHMENT_OBJECT_NAME,
            &param);

        objName = ((GLuint*)(&param))[0];
        glDeleteTextures(1, &objName);
    }
}
```

UtilityPickTerrainEffect's —prepareToDraw configures OpenGL ES to render into the FBO as follows:

```
//////////////////////////////////////////////////////////////////
// Prepare OpenGL state for rendering into the FBO
- (void)prepareToDraw;
{
   [super prepareToDraw];
   glBindFramebuffer(GL_FRAMEBUFFER, pickFBO);
   glViewport(0, 0, UtilityPickTerrainFBOWidth,
      UtilityPickTerrainFBOHeight);
}
```

After the scene has been rendered with UtilityPickTerrainEffect,
-terrainInfoForProjectionPosition: reads the pixel color at the specified location in the
range the range 0.0 to 1.0 back into 3D X and Z coordinates:

```
//////////////////////////////////////////////////////////////////
// This method returns the 3D X,Z coordinates of any terrain
// at aPosition. The aPosition coordinates must be in the range
// 0.0 to 1.0 corresponding to the relative location of aPosition
// within a Cocoa Touch view a.k.a. "projection" coordinates.
- (UtilityPickTerrainInfo)terrainInfoForProjectionPosition:
   (GLKVector2)aPosition
{
   GLubyte pixelColor[4];  // Red, Green, Blue, Alpha color
   GLint readLocationX = MIN((UtilityPickTerrainFBOWidth - 1),
      (UtilityPickTerrainFBOWidth - 1) * aPosition.x);
   GLint readLocationY = MIN((UtilityPickTerrainFBOHeight - 1),
      (UtilityPickTerrainFBOHeight - 1) * aPosition.y);
   glReadPixels(readLocationX,
      readLocationY,
      1,
      1,
      GL_RGBA,
      GL_UNSIGNED_BYTE,
      pixelColor);

   UtilityPickTerrainInfo result;
   GLKVector2 position = {
      self.width * (GLfloat)pixelColor[0] /  // red component
         UtilityPickTerrainMaxIndex,
      self.length * (GLfloat)pixelColor[1] / // green component
         UtilityPickTerrainMaxIndex
   };
   result.position = position;
   result.modelIndex = pixelColor[2]; // blue component

   return result;
}
```

> **Note**
>
> Reading rendered values from an FBO back into central processing unit (CPU)–controlled memory can require time-consuming synchronization. The CPU must wait to read until the GPU has finished rendering the scene, and then the graphics processing unit (GPU) must wait until the CPU has finished reading before the GPU can proceed rendering anything else into the FBO. OpenGL ES automatically manages all necessary synchronization but can't always avoid synchronization delays. Picking occurs at most a few times per second compared to normal rendering, which ideally occurs 30 or 60 times per second. Example OpenGLES_Ch10_1 accepts the performance tradeoff that color-based picking entails, but other applications might need to make different tradeoffs.

As one last nuance, just like `UtilityPickTerrainEffect` encodes terrain vertex coordinates in the red and green components of each rendered pixel, an optional `modelIndex` is encoded in the blue component. If the blue color component of the pixel read from the FBO is not zero, the blue color is scaled into the range 1 to 255 and corresponds to the index of a model at the picked location. Due to the encoding scheme, at most 255 models can be available for picking at any one time in any one scene, but that enables more than enough pickable models for example OpenGLES_Ch10_1.

The following OpenGL ES 2.0 Shading language programs are used with `UtilityPickTerrainEffect` to render terrain and models with false color for picking:

```
//
//   UtilityPickTerrainShader.vsh
//
//


/////////////////////////////////////////////////////////////
// VERTEX ATTRIBUTES
/////////////////////////////////////////////////////////////
attribute vec3 a_position;


/////////////////////////////////////////////////////////////
// TEXTURE
/////////////////////////////////////////////////////////////


/////////////////////////////////////////////////////////////
// UNIFORMS
/////////////////////////////////////////////////////////////
uniform highp mat4      u_mvpMatrix;
uniform highp vec2      u_dimensionFactors;
uniform lowp float      u_modelIndex;


/////////////////////////////////////////////////////////////
// Varyings
/////////////////////////////////////////////////////////////
```

```
varying lowp vec4       v_color;


void main()
{
    float r = a_position.x * u_dimensionFactors.x;
    float g = a_position.z * u_dimensionFactors.y;

    v_color = vec4(r, g, u_modelIndex, 1.0);

    gl_Position = u_mvpMatrix * vec4(a_position, 1.0);
}

//
//  UtilityPickTerrainShader.fsh
//
//


/////////////////////////////////////////////////////////////////
// UNIFORMS
/////////////////////////////////////////////////////////////////
uniform highp mat4      u_mvpMatrix;
uniform highp vec2      u_dimensionFactors;
uniform lowp float      u_modelIndex;


/////////////////////////////////////////////////////////////////
// Varyings
/////////////////////////////////////////////////////////////////
varying lowp vec4       v_color;


void main()
{
    gl_FragColor = v_color;
}
```

Alternative Picking Approaches

Historically, the desktop version of OpenGL supported picking via a specialized rendering mode enabled with the function, `glRenderMode(GL_SELECT)`. The GL_SELECT picking mode is now discouraged even in desktop applications because few GPUs support the feature in hardware. Using the GL_SELECT rendering mode often forces OpenGL to fall back to software-based rendering that runs on the CPU instead of the GPU, which sits idle in the meantime.

Purely geometric approaches to picking avoid any extra rendering at all. The most common geometric approach is called ray casting. Imagine a ray cast from the location of the touch on the frustum's near plane to the spot on the frustum's far plane corresponding to the touch. The object intersected by that ray closest to the point of view is the object picked.

Unfortunately, purely geometric approaches such as ray casting often introduce a lot of software complexity and might require computationally expensive searches for intersected objects. Unless the calculation to detect intersection executes very quickly and there are relatively few objects to test for intersection, geometric approaches might introduce more delay than the color picking approach.

The physics simulation provided by the Bullet 3D Game Multiphysics Library provides state-of-the-art collision detection between rays and 3D objects. If you already use Bullet 3D to implement physics such as acceleration from gravity and object collision detection within your application, ray casting–based picking comes almost for free. The Bullet Collision Detection library can be used by itself without requiring the full suite of Bullet 3D libraries. Many iOS applications use Bullet 3D, and it's free for commercial use under the terms of the open source ZLib License: http://code.google.com/p/bullet/.

Optimizing

The following code in OpenGLES_Ch10_1ViewController's -drawTerrainAndModels method naively draws every terrain tile and every model each time the method is called:

```
- (void)drawTerrainAndModels
{
   TETerrain *terrain = [[self dataSource] terrain];

   if(nil == self.tiles)
   {  // Cache tiles
      self.tiles = terrain.tiles;
   }

   // The terrain is opaque, so there is no need to blend.
   glDisable(GL_BLEND);

   [terrain drawTerrainWithinTiles:self.tiles
      withCamera:self.camera
      terrainEffect:self.terrainEffect];

   // Assume subsequent rendering involves translucent objects.
   glEnable(GL_BLEND);

   // Configure modelEffect for texture and diffuse lighting
   self.modelEffect.texture2D =
      [self.dataSource.modelManager textureInfo];
   self.modelEffect.projectionMatrix =
      self.camera.projectionMatrix;
```

```
   self.modelEffect.modelviewMatrix =
      self.camera.modelviewMatrix;

   [self.modelEffect prepareToDraw];
   [self.dataSource.modelManager prepareToDraw];

   [terrain drawModelsWithinTiles:self.tiles
      withCamera:self.camera
      modelEffect:self.modelEffect
      modelManager:self.dataSource.modelManager];
}
```

Example OpenGLES_Ch10_2 demonstrates some modest and straightforward changes to OpenGLES_Ch10_1 that nevertheless approximately double the number of frames produced per second. Example OpenGLES_Ch10_2 follows the advice in Chapter 9, "Optimization," to render as little as possible. Frustum-based culling avoids rendering tiles that can't be seen. The following –drawTerrainAndModels implementation in OpenGLES_Ch10_2ViewController provides a more optimal result using code shown in bold:

```
- (void)drawTerrainAndModels
{
   TETerrain *terrain = [[self dataSource] terrain];

   if(nil == self.tiles)
   {  // Cache tiles
      self.tiles = terrain.tiles;
   }

   NSMutableArray *fullDetailTiles = [NSMutableArray array];
   NSMutableArray *simplifiedTiles = [NSMutableArray array];

   [terrain identifyTilesToDraw:self.tiles
      withCamera:self.camera
      fullDetail:fullDetailTiles
      simplified:simplifiedTiles
      simplificationDistanceTiles:
         OpenGLES_Ch10_2DefaultSimplifaicationDistanceInTiles];

   // The terrain is opaque, so there is no need to blend.
   glDisable(GL_BLEND);

   [terrain drawTerrainWithinFullDetailTiles:fullDetailTiles
      simplifiedTiles:simplifiedTiles
      withCamera:self.camera
      terrainEffect:self.terrainEffect];

   // Assume subsequent rendering involves translucent objects.
   glEnable(GL_BLEND);
```

```
    // Configure modelEffect for texture and diffuse lighting
    self.modelEffect.texture2D =
        [self.dataSource.modelManager textureInfo];
    self.modelEffect.projectionMatrix =
        self.camera.projectionMatrix;
    self.modelEffect.modelviewMatrix =
        self.camera.modelviewMatrix;

    [self.modelEffect prepareToDraw];
    [self.dataSource.modelManager prepareToDraw];

    [terrain drawModelsWithinTiles:fullDetailTiles
        withCamera:self.camera
        modelEffect:self.modelEffect
        modelManager:self.dataSource.modelManager];
}
```

Example OpenGLES_Ch10_2 adds the–identifyTilesToDraw:withCamera:fullDetail:
simplified:simplificationDistanceTiles: method to TETerrain+viewAdditions.m.
The method iterates through all terrain tiles and culls tiles that aren't visible because they don't
intersect the viewing frustum for the current camera position and orientation. The method
places visible tiles in one of two arrays. Tiles close to the camera's position are put in an array
of tiles to be rendered with full detail. Tiles far away are put in an array of tiles to be rendered
in a simplified form.

```
/////////////////////////////////////////////////////////////////
// This method adds visible tiles from someTiles to either
// fullDetailTiles or simplifiedTiles. Tiles that are not visible
// by aCamera are not added to fullDetailTiles or simplifiedTiles.
//
// Visible tiles are added to simplifiedTiles if and only if
// the tile is greater than aNumberOfTiles from
// aCamera's position. Otherwise, visible tiles are added to
// fullDetailTiles.
- (void)identifyTilesToDraw:(NSArray *)someTiles
  withCamera:(UtilityCamera *)aCamera
  fullDetail:(NSMutableArray *)fullDetailTiles
  simplified:(NSMutableArray *)simplifiedTiles
  simplificationDistanceTiles:(GLfloat)aNumberOfTiles;
{
    const AGLKFrustum *frustumForCulling =
        [aCamera frustumForCulling];
    const GLfloat tileMetersPerUnit =
        self.metersPerUnit;
    const GLfloat tileWidthMeters = TETerrainTileDefaultWidth *
        tileMetersPerUnit;
    const GLfloat tileLengthMeters = TETerrainTileDefaultLength *
```

```
      tileMetersPerUnit;
   const GLfloat tileRadiusMeters = hypotf(tileWidthMeters,
      tileLengthMeters);
   const GLKVector3 cameraPositionMeters = aCamera.position;
   const GLfloat simplificationDistance =
      aNumberOfTiles * MAX(tileWidthMeters, tileLengthMeters);
   const GLfloat simplificationDistanceSquared =
      simplificationDistance * simplificationDistance;

   NSAssert(NULL != frustumForCulling, @"No valid frustum");

   for(TETerrainTile *tile in someTiles)
   {
      GLfloat originXMeters = tile.originX * tileMetersPerUnit;
      GLfloat originYMeters = tile.originY * tileMetersPerUnit;
      GLKVector3 centerMeters = GLKVector3Make(
         originXMeters + tileWidthMeters/2,
         0,
         originYMeters + tileLengthMeters/2);

      if(AGLKFrustumOut != AGLKFrustumCompareSphere(
         frustumForCulling, centerMeters, tileRadiusMeters))
      { // Some part of the tile is visible
         if(simplificationDistanceSquared > distanceSquared(
            cameraPositionMeters, centerMeters))
         { // Remember to draw the tile with full detail
            [fullDetailTiles addObject:tile];
         }
         else
         { // Remember to draw the tile simplified
            [simplifiedTiles addObject:tile];
         }
      }
   }
}
```

Culling whole tiles improves rendering speed dramatically because large portions of the terrain can be skipped, and the models contained within the culled tiles are skipped as well. Even when tiles can't be skipped entirely, they can often be rendered with simplified geometry. Users generally don't detect any reduction of visual detail in distant tiles.

Example OpenGLES_Ch10_2 draws simplified tiles as triangle fans instead of triangle strips. Triangle fans are one of three OpenGL ES triangulation modes supported by glDrawArrays() and glDrawElements(). The GL_TRIANGLES mode directs OpenGL ES to form triangles out of each group of three consecutive vertices provided. The GL_TRIANGLE_STRIP mode is introduced in Chapter 6 as an optimal way to render meshes by composing triangles that each share two vertices with preceding triangle. The GL_TRIANGLE_FAN mode composes triangles that all share one "center" vertex and an edge vertex with the preceding triangle.

Figure 10.7 illustrates a triangle fan with geometry similar to terrain tiles but only eight vertices per side. The arrows in Figure 10.7 indicate the sequence in which OpenGL ES processes the vertices. The first vertex is the "center" vertex, but it doesn't have to be in the center of the shape. All the triangles in the fan share the "center" vertex. The fan in Figure 10.7 contains 28 triangles because 29 vertices are in the shape, but the first vertex is shared among all the triangles.

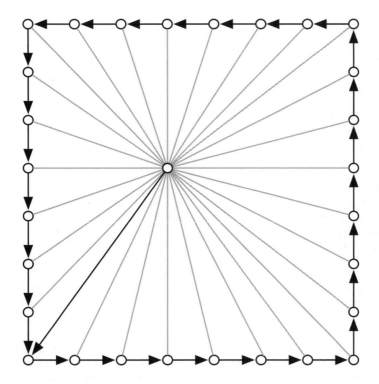

Figure 10.7   Triangle fans are one of the OpenGL ES built-in triangulation modes.

Using GL_TRIANGLE_FAN mode to render simplified terrain reduces the number of triangles rendered. For comparison, the mesh for a 32 by 32 vertex terrain tile has 31 rows and 31 columns. When rendered as a GL_TRIANGLE_STRIP, each terrain tile contains (31 * 31 * 2) + 31 = 1953 triangles because each rectangle in each row and column is composed of two triangles, and each row contains a "degenerate" triangle that has no area but preserves needed order for vertex processing. In contrast, a triangle fan formed by the center vertex of a terrain tile and including all the edge vertices contains only (4 * 31) = 124 triangles. There are four sides to the tile, and each side has either 31 rows or 31 columns, and every triangle shares the center vertex.

The following implementation of –drawSimplifiedTiles: in TETerrain+viewAdditions.m works just like the implementation of –drawTiles: except for the one line of code shown in bold:

```
////////////////////////////////////////////////////////////////////
// This method submits vertex data to OpenGL for each tile in
// tiles. The pointer to the start of vertex data for each tile
// is set prior to rendering so that the vertex data for each
// tile is within accessible range of a single glDrawElements()
// call per tile. Tiles are drawn via TETerrainTile's
// -drawSimplified method.
- (void)drawSimplifiedTiles:(NSArray *)tiles;
{
   for(TETerrainTile *tile in tiles)
   {
      // Set the pointer to the first vertex position in the
      // tile
      glVertexAttribPointer(
         TETerrainPositionAttrib,
         3,
         GL_FLOAT,
         GL_FALSE,
         sizeof(GLKVector3),
         ((GLKVector3 *)NULL) +
            (tile.originY * self.width) +
            tile.originX);

      [tile drawSimplified];
   }
}
```

The implementation of –drawSimplified in the TETerrainTile class creates an element array buffer containing vertex indices for the center vertex and all edge vertices in the tile. The glDrawElements() function is then called with GL_TRIANGLE_FAN mode to render the tile.

```
////////////////////////////////////////////////////////////////////
// This method configures OpenGL ES state by binding element
// array buffers, and if necessary by passing element index data
// to the GPU. Then the vertices corresponding to the receiver
// are passed to the GPU via a call to glDrawElements(). The
// receiver's center and perimeter vertices are drawn as a
// triangle fan.
- (void)drawSimplified;
{
   if(0 == simplifiedIndexBufferID_ &&
```

```
        0 < [self.simplifiedIndexData length])
    {   // Indices haven't been sent to GPU yet
        // Create an element array buffer for mesh indices
        glGenBuffers(1, &simplifiedIndexBufferID_);
        NSAssert(0 != self.simplifiedIndexBufferID,
            @"Failed to generate element array buffer");

        glBindBuffer(GL_ELEMENT_ARRAY_BUFFER,
            self.simplifiedIndexBufferID);
        glBufferData(GL_ELEMENT_ARRAY_BUFFER,
            [self.simplifiedIndexData length],
            [self.simplifiedIndexData bytes],
            GL_STATIC_DRAW);

        // No longer need local index storage
        self.simplifiedIndexData = nil;
    }
    else
    {
        glBindBuffer(GL_ELEMENT_ARRAY_BUFFER,
            self.simplifiedIndexBufferID);
    }

    glDrawElements(GL_TRIANGLE_FAN,
        self.numberOfSimplifiedIndices,
        GL_UNSIGNED_SHORT,
        ((GLushort *)NULL));
}
```

Examine the –generateIndicesForTileOriginX:tileOriginY:tileWidth:tileLength:
and –generateSimplifiedIndicesForTileOriginX:tileOriginY:tileWidth:
tileLength: methods in TETerrainTile.m to see how the methods identify detailed and
simplified vertex indices for each terrain tile. The two methods are relatively simple and follow
the examples set in the "Using Indexed Vertices" section of Chapter 6.

The optimizations provided by example OpenGLES_Ch10_2 impacts only two classes,
TETerrainTile and TETerrain, and doubles the display update rate. On an original iPad,
example OpenGLES_Ch10_1 achieves approximately 14 frames per second (FPS) rendering
the included sample terrain. Example OpenGLES_Ch10_2 consistently produces around 30
FPS rendering the same terrain. The iPad 2 produces approximately 24 FPS unoptimized and
consistently more than 50 FPS after optimizing.

Other Potential Optimizations

Numerous academic papers explore optimizations for real-time terrain rendering. The game-
focused website, Gamasutra.com, provides an explanation and sample code for one of the most

famous algorithms, Real-time Optimally Adapting Mesh (ROAM), by Mark Duchaineau et al. (http://www.gamasutra.com/view/feature/3188/realtime_dynamic_level_of_detail_.php).

ROAM dynamically adapts the level of detail within terrain meshes to provide high visual quality with a near minimal number of triangles. However, rendering a small number of unneeded triangles is usually more effective than burdening the CPU with complex calculations needed to achieve a true minimum number. Most implementations of ROAM also require frequent updates to vertex data stored in GPU-controlled memory. The balance between CPU, GPU, and memory copies must always be considered when optimizing. Example OpenGLES_Ch10_2 provides reasonable quality with very little CPU impact and no dynamic vertex data updates.

A handful of papers and samples at http://vterrain.org/LOD/Papers/ describe approaches "beyond" ROAM. Current research explores opportunities to dynamically control the level of detail in terrain using OpenGL ES Shading Language programs running on the GPU. The techniques store height values encoded within textures and leverage the built-in GPU texture sampling logic with MIP maps to select vertex heights and even interpolate between vertices to provide more detail than the exists within the texture. MIP maps and texture interpolation are explained in Chapter 3. Unfortunately, the Shading Language approaches rely on the ability to sample textures from within vertex programs. All OpenGL ES–compatible GPUs enable texture sampling within fragment programs, but few enable sampling from vertex programs even though the OpenGL ES 2.0 standard includes the capability as an option. The `UtilityTerrainEffect` class in both example OpenGLES_Ch10_1 and example OpenGLES_Ch10_2 uses the following statement to determine how many texture sampling units are available in vertex programs:

```
glGetIntegerv(GL_MAX_VERTEX_TEXTURE_IMAGE_UNITS,
    &maxVertexTextureImageUnits);
```

Unfortunately, none of the shipping iOS devices at the time of this writing make any texture sampling units available to vertex programs. Some of the GPUs used in iOS devices might be able to support texture sampling within vertex programs in the future if Apple supplies improved OpenGL ES drivers.

Summary

Terrain rendering adapts mesh rendering techniques for large vertex data sets. A collection of tiles organizes terrain vertex data into chunks small enough for access by calls to `glDrawElements()`. The tiles also constitute a simple scene graph to enable operations including the frustum-based culling introduced in Chapter 9.

Picking based on color information encoded in a frame buffer provides fast and simple determination of the terrain coordinates under the user's touch. The same approach works in the Mac OS X TerrainEditor application for selecting models placed within the terrain. Color-based picking provides the advantages of being relatively simple to implement and relatively fast; it takes approximately the same amount of time to render in false color for picking and it does to render normally. Almost all the computation for color-based picking runs on the GPU as opposed to the CPU. Nevertheless, other picking approaches such as ray casting that rely more heavily on the CPU might work better in some applications. For example, if the application already uses a physics simulation, ray based–picking might be available at no extra performance cost.

The TerrainEditor application loads terrain height values encoded as pixel brightness within an image file. The common theme of using color vectors (RGB) interchangeably with position vectors (XYZ) recurs with color-based picking in examples OpenGLES_Ch10_1 and OpenGLES_Ch10_2. The X and Z coordinates of terrain are encoded in the R and G components of a pixel color render buffer attached to an FBO.

Chapter 11, "Math Cheat Sheet," revisits the common math operations needed for 3D rendering. Geometry expressed as vectors might seem counterintuitive at first, but vector operations almost exclusively consist of addition and multiplication that GPUs can perform very rapidly and in parallel. Chapter 11 provides a concise reference and explanations for the common vector operations introduced in preceding chapters.

Math Cheat Sheet

Math forms the basis of computer science in general and computer graphics in particular. The term *linear algebra* encompasses the majority of mathematic operations used in modern computer graphics. Other common terms for the same operations include vector algebra and matrix math. Study of vectors and vector transformations began in the 1600s and matured into its current form in the 1790s. Charles Babbage designed his mechanical general-purpose computer called the "Analytical Engine" in 1837. With the Analytical Engine in mind, Augusta Ada King, Countess of Lovelace, wrote the first computer program in 1842. As a result, when transistors were invented in 1948 to replace mechanical switches and vacuum tubes, mathematicians already knew what to do with them, and the software industry was born.

Computer graphics algorithms are closely related to digital signal processing algorithms used for radars, cell phones, video encoding, and music synthesis. For example, radars analyze reflected radio waves to find the position of an object in three-dimensional (3D) space using the same math used to find the correct positions in a pixel color render buffer for fragments representing an object in a 3D scene. The operations described in this chapter apply across fields of study such as economics, natural sciences, and social sciences. Wrapping your mind around abstract math can be difficult. Fortunately, only a few key concepts are needed for most programs. This chapter reviews linear algebra concepts introduced gradually by preceding chapters and explains the key concepts, important formulas, and when to use them.

Note

As another common application of linear algebra, consider economics: Many problems in economics require a method of solving a large number of interrelated equations. The variables in the equations can be economic indicators or money supply or changes in productivity. With linear algebra, a matrix represents transformations from one set of values to another, and an economy can be modeled as a succession of those transformations. Linear algebra supplies tools to manage the huge number of factors involved and reduce the complexity of problems.

Overview

Linear algebra includes the study of vectors, coordinate systems (also known as vector spaces), and functions that transform vectors according to rules specified as systems of linear equations and matrices. Almost all aspects of computer graphics are implemented using linear algebra even when alternative approaches such as trigonometry apply. Linear algebra exploits simple operations such as addition, subtraction, and multiplication that computers perform very quickly.

Terms such as *point*, *vector*, and *axis* are introduced in Chapter 1, "Using Modern Mobile Graphics Hardware." Familiarity with the terms is necessary to follow the explanations in this chapter. Also recall from Chapter 1 that vectors can be added to form new vectors. Every 3D vector can be represented as the sum of three axis-aligned vectors. The locations of 3D points are stored using three coordinate values, {x, y, z}. A point's location is equally expressed as a vector from the coordinate system's origin to the point's location.

Coordinate systems are defined by matrices. Matrices enable efficient conversion of point locations from one coordinate system to another. Ultimately, the graphics processing unit (GPU) requires all point locations to be expressed in the OpenGL default coordinate system so the GPU knows where the point falls within a render buffer. The next section explains how matrices encode coordinate system definitions.

Decoding a Matrix

All possible 3D coordinate systems can be encoded using just 16 values. The values are organized in memory as an array of 16 consecutive floating-point values, shown in Figure 11.1. However, mathematic notation conventionally represents a 3D matrix as a 4 by 4 grid of values. Figure 11.1 shows the correlation between values in the values in memory and the mathematic notation.

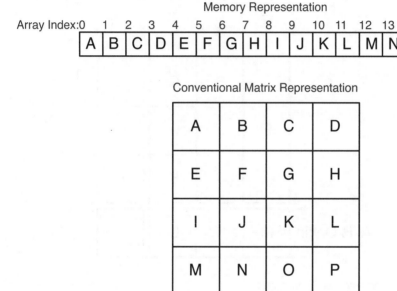

Figure 11.1   A 4 by 4 matrix defines a 3D coordinate system.

Each matrix encodes three unit vectors describing the directions of a coordinate system's positive X, Y, and Z axes. A fourth vector identifies the location of the axis origin. Figure 11.2 calls out individual vectors. The combination of axis directions and the origin effectively defines a coordinate system.

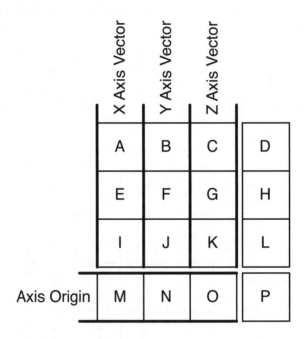

Figure 11.2   Vectors encoded within a matrix.

Figure 11.3 shows an "identity" matrix. When an identity matrix is concatenated (multiplied) with any other matrix, the result is identical to the other matrix. A unit vector, {1.0, 0.0, 0.0}, defines the X axis encoded in the identity matrix. Unit vectors always have length equal to 1.0. A unit vector, {0.0, 1.0, 0.0}, defines the Y axis encoded in the identity matrix. A unit vector ,{0.0, 0.0, 1.0}, defines the Z axis encoded in the identity matrix. The identity matrix axis origin is at position {0.0, 0.0, 0.0}.

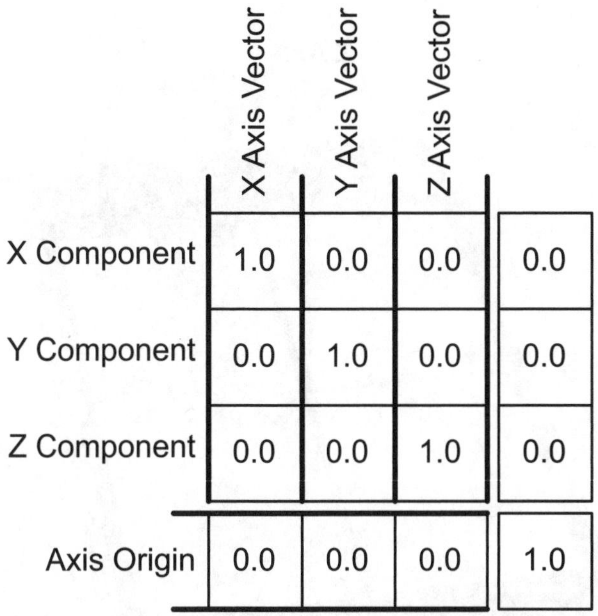

	X Axis Vector	Y Axis Vector	Z Axis Vector	
X Component	1.0	0.0	0.0	0.0
Y Component	0.0	1.0	0.0	0.0
Z Component	0.0	0.0	1.0	0.0
Axis Origin	0.0	0.0	0.0	1.0

Figure 11.3   The identity matrix.

Matrices define relative coordinate systems. You must answer the question, "relative to what," to interpret values encoded in a matrix. Figure 11.4 shows how OpenGL's default coordinate system aligns with a full screen Cocoa Touch UIView containing 3D content. The OpenGL origin is in the center of the view. The OpenGL X axis runs parallel to the top and bottom of the view with values of X increasing to the right. The OpenGL Y axis runs parallel to the left and right of the view with values of Y increasing up. The OpenGL Z axis has positive values increasing along a vector pointing out of the view toward the viewer.

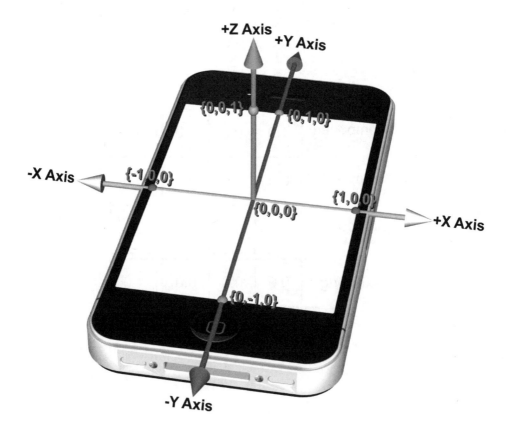

Figure 11.4   The OpenGL default coordinate system.

OpenGL applications define new coordinate systems relative to the default coordinate system. For an application to define a new 3D coordinate system with the origin in the bottom-left corner of the default coordinate system, the application creates a matrix like the one shown in Figure 11.5. The origin of the matrix in Figure 11.5 is at the position, {-1.0, -1.0, 0.0}, in the default coordinate system.

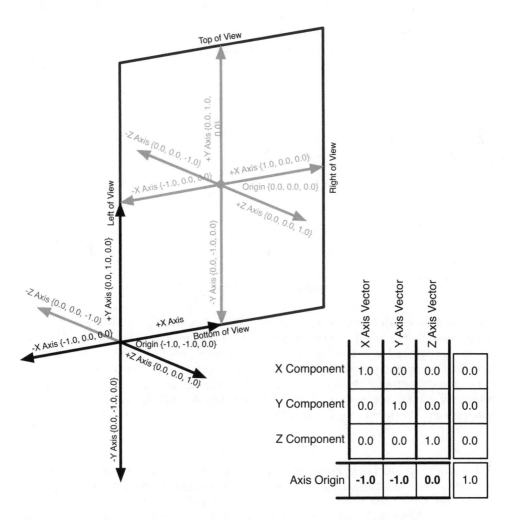

Figure 11.5   A translated coordinate system relative to the OpenGL default coordinate system.

Moving a coordinate system origin relative to another coordinate system is called "translation" and comprises one of the basic transformations introduced in Chapter 5, "Changing Your Point of View." Translation only affects the "axis origin" portion of a matrix. Two other basic transformations, rotation and scale, only affect the "axis vectors" encoded within a matrix. For example, rotation changes the direction that each axis vector points relative to another coordinate system. Scale changes the length of each "axis vector" relative to another coordinate system. Figure 11.6 illustrates changes to a coordinate system resulting from translation, rotation, and scale. Example OpenGLES_Ch5_4 provides a user interface to help you experiment and visualize the cumulative effects of coordinate system transformations.

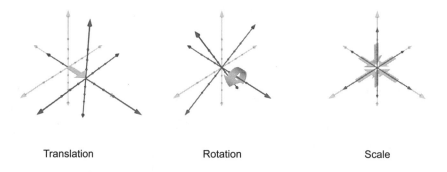

Translation   Rotation   Scale

Figure 11.6   Visualization of translation, rotation, and scale.

What about the fourth column in a matrix? None of the figures so far have used the fourth column for anything. It turns out that the fourth column is only used when a matrix includes perspective transformations. OpenGL historically maintains two separate matrices, the projectionMatrix and the modelviewMatrix, in part to keep the encoding of transformations simple. By convention, only the projectionMatrix contains perspective transformations. When the convention is followed, calculations involving the modelviewMatrix are free to ignore the fourth column.

Note

The modelviewMatrix and projectionMatrix are almost always concatenated together to create a single modelviewProjectionMatrix for use in OpenGL ES 2.0 Shading Language programs. Conventional distinctions between modelview transformations and projection transformations don't imply that there is any meaningful mathematic difference. The distinction has historically proven to be handy because some common operations use only one matrix or the other. For example, the transformation of normal vectors in lighting equations requires a specialized matrix derived from the modelviewMatrix.

Obtaining a Matrix from a Frustum

Given a point of view defined by a viewing frustum, the corresponding modelviewMatrix can be readily constructed. The viewing frustum is introduced in Chapter 8, "Special Effects," and further explained in Chapter 9, "Optimization." To see how matrices and frustums relate, consider how a frustum is represented.

Starting in Chapter 9, examples use an AGLKFrustum data structure and functions to manipulate the data structure. In particular, the AGLKFrustumSetPositionAndDirection() function specifies the position and orientation of a frustum.

```
void AGLKFrustumSetPositionAndDirection
(
 AGLKFrustum *frustumPtr,
 GLKVector3 eyePosition,
 GLKVector3 lookAtPosition,
 GLKVector3 upVector);
```

AGLKFrustumSetPositionAndDirection() calculates the look-at direction from the eyePosition and the lookAtPosition. The frustum's Z axis vector is a unit vector pointing in the look-at direction.

```
// Compute the Z axis of the frustum. The Z axis points in
// the direction from eye position to look at position
const GLKVector3 lookAtVector =
   GLKVector3Subtract(eyePosition, lookAtPosition);
   frustumPtr->zNormalVector = GLKVector3Normalize(lookAtVector);
```

The cross product of any two non-parallel unit vectors produces a third unit vector perpendicular to the first two. Cross products are introduced in Chapter 4, "Shedding Some Light," and described again in the "Vector Cross Product" section of this chapter.

Given an up direction and a look-at direction, the X axis vector of the frustum is the cross product of "up" and "look-at." Figure 11.7 shows the relationships between the up direction, the look-at direction, and the calculated frustum X axis vector.

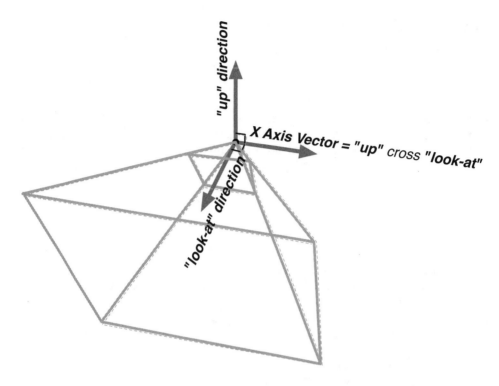

Figure 11.7   "Look-at" and "up" vectors define the orientation of a frustum.

The frustum's X axis is the normalized cross product of the look-at vector and the up vector. In the following code, the zNormalVector is the normalized look-at vector:

```
// The frustum's X normal is the cross product of the
// normalized "up" vector and the frustum's Z normal
frustumPtr->xNormalVector = GLKVector3CrossProduct(
   GLKVector3Normalize(upVector),
   frustumPtr->zNormalVector);
```

The upVector passed to AGLKFrustumSetPositionAndDirection() can't always be used unmodified as the frustum's Y axis because the upVector might not be a unit vector and might not be perpendicular to both the X axis and the Z axis. The frustum's true Y axis is calculated as the cross product of the Z axis and the X axis.

```
// The frustum's Y axis is the cross product of the
// frustum's Z normal and the frustum's X normal.
frustumPtr->yNormalVector = GLKVector3CrossProduct(
   frustumPtr->zNormalVector,
   frustumPtr->xNormalVector);
```

Figure 11.8 identifies the relationship between the frustum's axis vectors and the corresponding matrix. The frustum's axes provide the axis vectors in the "look-at" modelview matrix corresponding to the frustum. The axis origin in Figure 11.8 is derived from the frustum's `eyePosition`.

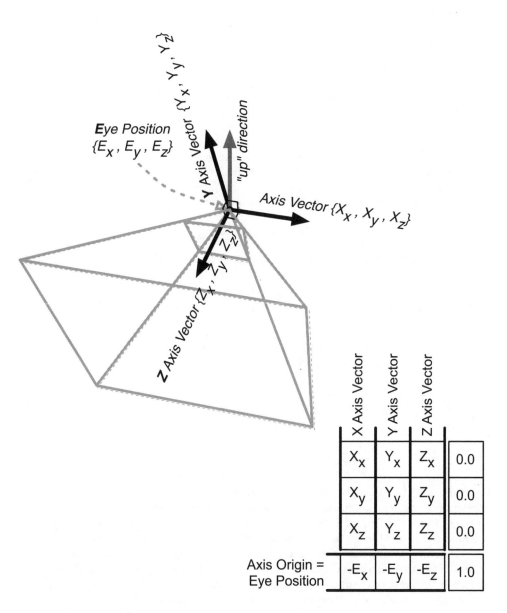

Figure 11.8   Axis vectors corresponding to a frustum.

The following `GLKMatrix4 AGLKFrustumMakeModelview(const AGLKFrustum *frustumPtr)` function returns a modelview matrix encoding the position and direction of the specified frustum:

```
//////////////////////////////////////////////////////////////////
// Returns a modelview matrix that encodes the point of view
// matching the specified frustum
GLKMatrix4 AGLKFrustumMakeModelview
(
 const AGLKFrustum *frustumPtr)
{
   NSCAssert(AGLKFrustumHasDimention(frustumPtr),
      @"Invalid frustumPtr parameter");

   const GLKVector3 eyePosition = frustumPtr->eyePosition;
   const GLKVector3 xNormal = frustumPtr->xNormalVector;
   const GLKVector3 yNormal = frustumPtr->yNormalVector;
   const GLKVector3 zNormal = frustumPtr->zNormalVector;
   const GLfloat xTranslation = GLKVector3DotProduct(
      xNormal, eyePosition);
   const GLfloat yTranslation = GLKVector3DotProduct(
      yNormal, eyePosition);
   const GLfloat zTranslation = GLKVector3DotProduct(
      zNormal, eyePosition);

   GLKMatrix4 m = {
      // X Axis      Y Axis      Z Axis
      xNormal.x, yNormal.x, zNormal.x,              0.0f,
      xNormal.y, yNormal.y, zNormal.y,              0.0f,
      xNormal.z, yNormal.z, zNormal.z,              0.0f,

      // Axis Origin
      -xTranslation, -yTranslation, -zTranslation, 1.0f
   };

   return m;
}
```

The translation components of the modelview matrix for a frustum are expressed as a displacement from the coordinate system in which the frustum is defined. The relationship is easiest to visualize in Figure 11.5. Stated in a different way, the origin of a coordinate system is defined as a position in another coordinate system, the one to which the new coordinate system is relative. Translation moves a coordinate system's origin. Translation amounts are negated in the `AGLKFrustumMakeModelview()` function because to convert from the eye position in the previous coordinate system to the origin, {0, 0, 0}, in a new coordinate system, subtracting each component of the eye position is necessary.

Perspective

Just like the `AGLKFrustumSetPositionAndDirection()` function sets the position and orientation of a frustum, the `AGLKFrustumSetPerspective(AGLKFrustum *frustumPtr, GLfloat fieldOfViewRad, GLfloat aspectRatio, GLfloat nearDistance, GLfloat farDistance)` function defines the shape of a frustum. Figure 11.9 shows the geometric relationships between the parameters to `AGLKFrustumSetPerspective()` and the resulting frustum.

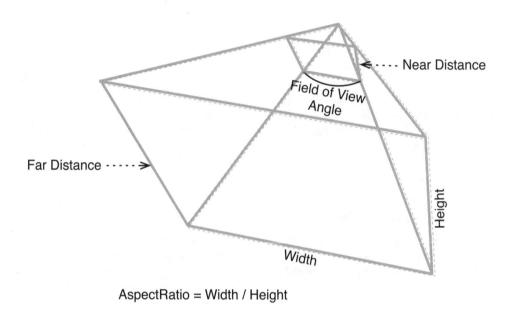

AspectRatio = Width / Height

Figure 11.9   Defining the shape of a frustum.

The frustum's shape determines the "perspective" projection matrix corresponding to the frustum. The following `GLKMatrix4 AGLKFrustumMakePerspective(const AGLKFrustum *frustumPtr)` function returns a projection matrix corresponding to the shape of the frustum.

```
////////////////////////////////////////////////////////////////
// Returns a projection matrix that encodes perspective
// matching the specified frustum
extern GLKMatrix4 AGLKFrustumMakePerspective
(
 const AGLKFrustum *frustumPtr)
{
   NSCAssert(AGLKFrustumHasDimention(frustumPtr),
      @"Invalid frustumPtr parameter");
```

```
const GLfloat cotan =
    1.0f / frustumPtr->tangentOfHalfFieldOfView;
const GLfloat nearZ = frustumPtr->nearDistance;
const GLfloat farZ = frustumPtr->farDistance;

GLKMatrix4 m = {
    cotan / frustumPtr->aspectRatio, 0.0f, 0.0f, 0.0f,
    0.0f, cotan, 0.0f, 0.0f,
    0.0f, 0.0f, (farZ + nearZ) / (nearZ - farZ), -1.0f,
    0.0f, 0.0f, (2.0f * farZ * nearZ) / (nearZ - farZ), 0.0f
};

return m;
}
```

The cotan value calculated from the tangent of half the field of view in AGLKFrustumMakePerspective() expresses the relationship between the width and height of an object and the distance of the object from the coordinate system origin. The cotan value controls how perspective makes objects in the distance appear smaller than close objects. Reducing the field of view has the visual effect of magnifying objects and thus making them appear closer as if they are being seen through a telescope.

Axis Components of Vectors

The dot product of two vectors extracts the component of each vector in the direction of the other. The dot product operation is introduced in Chapter 4. Imagine a triangle defined by two vectors, vector A and vector B, as depicted in Figure 11.10.

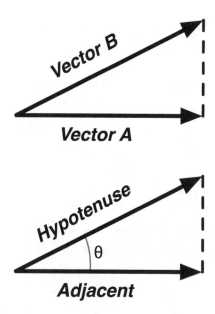

$$cos\ \theta = Length\ of\ Adjacent\ /\ Length\ of\ Hypotenuse$$

$$cos\ \theta = GLKVector3DotProduct(Adjacent,\ Hypotenuse)$$

Figure 11.10   Visualizing the dot product.

Following standard naming conventions for right triangles, vector A is the "adjacent" side of the triangle, and vector B is the hypotenuse of the triangle. The definition of the cosine function for an angle, θ, is the length of the adjacent side divided by the length of the hypotenuse for a right triangle with angle θ. Very conveniently, the dot product operation returns the same value, length of the adjacent side divided by the length of the hypotenuse, without requiring any trigonometry.

Figure 11.11 provides another way to visualize the dot product of two vectors. In Figure 11.11, the dot product of Unit Vector A with the X Axis Unit Vector provides the fraction of the length of Unit Vector A in the direction of the X Axis. The dot product of Unit Vector A with the Y Axis Unit Vector provides the fraction of the length of Unit Vector A in the direction of the Y Axis.

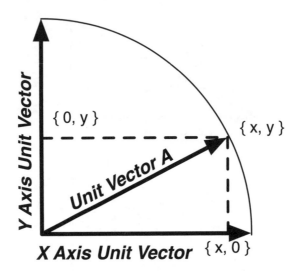

Figure 11.11   The length of a vector in the direction of another vector.

The ability to find the length of one vector in the direction of another has countless uses. Keep in mind that the dot product operation works with any pair of vectors. The operation doesn't need to include an axis-aligned vector. For example, Figure 11.12 uses a dashed line to help visualize the fraction of Unit Vector A in the direction of Unit Vector B. In other words, the intersection of the dashed line with Unit Vector B in Figure 11.12 shows the dot product of Unit Vector A and Unit Vector B.

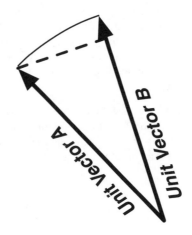

Figure 11.12   The dot product works with any pair of unit vectors.

Apple provides the C code to calculate the dot product of two 3D vectors in GLKVector3.h, which is part of GLKit. The code looks similar to the following. Only multiplication and addition, two of the fastest operations performed by GPUs, are used in the calculation of dot products:

```
float GLKVector3DotProduct(
    GLKVector3 vectorLeft,
    GLKVector3 vectorRight)
{
    return vectorLeft.x * vectorRight.x +
           vectorLeft.y * vectorRight.y +
           vectorLeft.z * vectorRight.z;
}
```

Transforming Points

After you have a matrix, what's it good for? Matrices are used to calculate the location of a point in one coordinate system that corresponds to the location of the same point in another coordinate system. Converting a point's location from one coordinate system to another is called "transforming" or sometimes "projecting." The two terms are interchangeable. In other words, the location of any one point can be defined in terms of different coordinate systems. The same point at position {55.5, 11.0, 100.2} in one coordinate system might be at position {10.0, -100.0, 20.0} in another coordinate system.

Recall that any point location can be interpreted as a vector from the coordinate system origin to the point. To transform a vector, multiply the vector with a matrix. The result is the same vector expressed in the coordinate system to which the matrix is relative. The iOS examples in this book almost never transform vectors in Objective-C or C code because the operation is best performed by the GPU. Instead of C code, many of the OpenGL ES 2.0 Shading Language examples in this book include a statement such as the following: gl_Position = u_mvpMatrix * vec4(a_position, 1.0); When a position is multiplied by the combined modelviewProjectionMatrix, mvpMatrix, the result is the same position expressed in the OpenGL default coordinate system.

If you need to transform a vector using C code, Apple's GLKit framework provides the GLKMatrix4MultiplyVector3(GLKMatrix4 matrixLeft, GLKVector3 vectorRight) and GLKMatrix4MultiplyVector3WithTranslation(GLKMatrix4 matrixLeft, GLKVector3 vectorRight) functions. GLKMatrix4MultiplyVector3() performs the transform, ignoring any translation encoded in the axis origin portion of the matrix. GLKMatrix4MultiplyVector3WithTranslation() includes translation in the transform. What is really happening is that there is no mathematically defined operation to multiply a three-component vector with a 4 by 4 matrix. Both GLKit functions extend the 3D vector to be a four-component vector. GLKMatrix4MultiplyVector3() extends the vector with zero to convert the 3D vector, {x, y, z}, into the 4D vector, {x, y, z, 0.0}. When the zero component is multiplied with the translation encoded in the axis origin portion of the matrix, the translation has no effect. GLKMatrix4MultiplyVector3WithTranslation() extends the

3D vector to create a 4D vector, {x, y, z, 1.0}. When the 4D vector is multiplied with the matrix, the encoded translation in the axis origin portion of the matrix is multiplied by 1.0 and therefore included in the transformation.

You can see the C code implementation of 4D vector transformation in Apple's `GLKMatrix4.h`, which is part of GLKit. The following function implementation shows the code formatted to emphasize operations used to compute each component of the transformed vector:

```
GLKMatrix4 GLKMatrix4MultiplyVector4(
    GLKMatrix4 matrix,
    GLKVector4 vector)
{
    GLKVector4 v = {
        matrix.m[0]  * vector.x +
        matrix.m[4]  * vector.y +
        matrix.m[8]  * vector.z +
        matrix.m[12] * vector.w,

        matrix.m[1]  * vector.x +
        matrix.m[5]  * vector.y +
        matrix.m[9]  * vector.z +
        matrix.m[13] * vector.w,

        matrix.m[2]  * vector.x +
        matrix.m[6]  * vector.y +
        matrix.m[10] * vector.z +
        matrix.m[14] * vector.w,

        matrix.m[3]  * vector.x +
        matrix.m[7]  * vector.y +
        matrix.m[11] * vector.z +
        matrix.m[15] * vector.w
    };

    return v;
}
```

It's no coincidence that the calculations in `GLKMatrix4MultiplyVector4()` look familiar. They are the dot product calculation performed in four dimensions. Transforming a point using a matrix extracts components of a vector from the coordinate system origin to the point. The components of interest are the components aligned with each of the axes encoded in the matrix. The transformed X coordinate is the portion of the vector in the direction of the matrix X axis. The transformed Y coordinate is the portion of the vector in the direction of the matrix Y axis. The transformed Z coordinate is the portion of the vector in the direction of the matrix Z axis. The bold code in the implementation of `GLKMatrix4MultiplyVector4()` highlights the interaction of the final component, w, of the four-component vector and the translation encoded within the matrix axis origin.

Transpose Matrix and Inverse Matrix

A matrix defines the relationship of one coordinate system to another. The relationship can be reversed. A matrix that maps coordinate system A to coordinate B can be transposed to map coordinate system B to coordinate system A. Transposing a matrix is accomplished by swapping the rows and columns within a matrix. Figure 11.13 depicts a matrix and the corresponding transpose matrix.

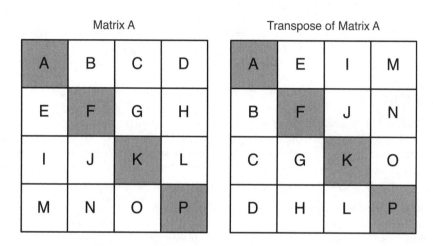

Figure 11.13   A matrix and the corresponding transpose matrix.

Notice that the shaded matrix elements along the diagonal of Matrix A in Figure 11.13 are the same in the Transpose of Matrix A. One way to think about the transpose operation is that the transpose matrix is a reflection of the original matrix with symmetry along the diagonal. Also notice that the transpose of a transpose matrix yields the original matrix again: The transpose of Transpose of Matrix A in Figure 11.13 reproduces Matrix A.

GLKit provides the `GLKMatrix4 GLKMatrix4Transpose(GLKMatrix4 matrix)` function that returns the transpose of `matrix`.

The inverse of a matrix is another matrix that when multiplied with the original matrix produces the identity matrix. Given Matrix A and its inverse, Matrix B, then multiplying Matrix A and Matrix B produces the identity matrix. Calculating the inverse of the matrix requires a lot of work for general matrices. However, when a matrix has uniform scale applied to all of its axes, the inverse of the matrix is equal to the transpose of the matrix. Not all matrices are invertible. For example, if a matrix contains a scale factor of zero, there is no inverse matrix.

GLKit provides the `GLKMatrix4 GLKMatrix4Invert(GLKMatrix4 matrix, bool *isInvertible)` function. The `isInvertible` parameter returns a Boolean value by reference telling you whether `matrix` was invertible or not.

GLKit also provides the `GLKMatrix4InvertAndTranspose(GLKMatrix4 matrix, bool *isInvertible)` that returns the transpose of the inverse of `matrix` if possible and tells you whether the matrix was invertible via the `isInvertible` parameter. The transposed inverse of the modelview matrix is needed to correctly calculate lighting based on normal vectors when using the standard OpenGL lighting equations. The `GLKBaseEffect` class calculates the transposed inverse of the modelview matrix as needed to return the value of the base effect's `normalMatrix` property. The `UtilityArmatureBaseEffect` class in example OpenGLES_Ch7_3 and the `UtilityModelEffect` class from examples in Chapter 10, "Terrain and Picking," both calculate a `normalMatrix` property using `GLKMatrix4InvertAndTranspose()`. The examples indirectly show how lighting equations use the `normalMatrix` within OpenGL ES Shading Language programs.

Quaternions

Quaternions were first described by Irish mathematician Sir William Rowan Hamilton. Hamilton's breakthrough came on Monday, October 16, 1843, in Dublin. While walking along the towpath of the Royal Canal with his wife, the idea of quaternions struck him. To preserve the idea for posterity, he carved the formula for quaternions into the stone of Brougham Bridge as he paused on it. The carving remains to this day as a historical landmark.

GLKit includes the `GLKQuaternion` data type and functions to manipulate quaternions. Each quaternion is composed of a vector, v, and a scalar value, s, that specifies an amount of rotation about v. 3D graphics applications apply quaternions because when using a quaternion, it's possible to compose any rotation about any combination of axes without ever suffering the dreaded "gimbal lock." For example, the math used by the implementation of `GLKMatrix4MakeLookAt()` cannot produce a useful point of view that looks directly along the "up" vector. The limitation exists because when looking directly "up" or "down," the math used by `GLKMatrix4MakeLookAt()` attempts to calculate the tangent of 90 degrees, which is mathematically undefined. This "undefined" phenomenon occurs in the real world when mechanical gimbals encounter "gimbal lock" and seize or produce wobbling unreliable behavior. Wikipedia provides an animation at http://en.wikipedia.org/wiki/Gimbal_lock to help visualize gimbal lock.

Conversions between quaternions and matrices work in both directions. The `GLKMatrix4 GLKMatrix4MakeWithQuaternion(GLKQuaternion quaternion)` function returns a matrix containing the same rotation as `quaternion`. `GLKQuaternion GLKQuaternionMakeWithMatrix4(GLKMatrix4 matrix)` returns a quaternion that encodes all rotation with `matrix`. The ability to convert back and forth provides flexibility. None of the examples in this book use quaternions, but converting the bumper cars examples, OpenGLES_Ch6_1 and OpenGLES_Ch7_1, to use quaternions makes an interesting advanced project when you've mastered the other concepts in this book. There are many cases where using quaternions can simplify your code. For example, quaternion-based camera classes are popular in several third-party 3D game frameworks.

A concise explanation of quaternions is available at http://www.cprogramming.com/tutorial/3d/quaternions.html. GLKit's `GLKQuaternion.h` file reveals Apple's implementation of quaternions in the form of inline C code. The math is straightforward but beyond the scope of this book. Quaternions take advantage of 4D space to represent 3D angles. As you can imagine, representing four dimensions on the pages of a book imposes quite a challenge. For that reason, online presentations and explanations of quaternions provide a better resource.

Surviving Graphics Math

This chapter contains a crash course in 3D graphics math. If it makes your head spin, don't worry too much. This section lists the most common 3D math operations that applications perform. Even without a deep understanding of the implementations, these recipes and techniques will solve most of the problems you might encounter.

Simple Vector Arithmetic

The following common operations are performed with vectors:

- **Reversing direction**—`GLKVector3 GLKVector3Negate(GLKVector3 vector)` returns a new vector with the same length as `vector` but opposite direction. See `GLKVector3Negate()` used by the `SceneCar` class in Chapter 6, "Animation."

- **Length scaling**—`GLKVector3 GLKVector3MultiplyScalar(GLKVector3 vector, float value)` scales the length of `vector` by `value` but does not change vector's direction unless `value` is negative. `GLKVector3MultiplyScalar(vector, -1.0)` returns the same vector as `GLKVector3Negate(vector)`. `GLKVector3MultiplyScalar()` is used in Chapter 4 to average surface normal vectors for smooth lighting simulation. The `SceneCar` sample class, the AGLKit sample classes, and the Utility sample classes also apply the function.

- **The vector between points**—`GLKVector3 GLKVector3Subtract(GLKVector3 position1, GLKVector3 position2)` returns the vector from `position2` to `position1`. Chapter 4 calculates the vectors between points as one of the steps to calculating surface normal vectors for lighting simulation. Multiple AGLKit and the Utility sample classes apply the function.

- **Vector addition**—`GLKVector3 GLKVector3Add(GLKVector3 vectorA, GLKVector3 vectorB)` returns a new vector equivalent to first traveling the length of `vectorA` in the direction of `vectorA` and then traveling the length of `vectorB` in the direction of `vectorB` as illustrated back in Chapter 1's Figure 1.11. Chapter 4 applies vector addition as one of the steps to average surface normal vectors for smooth lighting simulation.

- **Vector normalizing**—`GLKVector3 GLKVector3Normalize(GLKVector3 vector)` returns a new vector with the same direction as `vector` and a length of 1.0. Vectors with length 1.0 are called unit vectors. Chapter 4 explains normal vectors.

- **Distance between points**—`float GLKVector3Distance(GLKVector3 positionA, GLKVector3 positionB)` returns the distance between `positionA` and `positionB`. It is equivalent to `GLKVector3Length(GLKVector3Subtract(positionB, positionA))`. The `SceneCar` class in Chapter 6 calls `GLKVector3Distance()`.

Vector Dot Product

The "Axis Components of Vectors" section of this chapter shows the implementation of the dot product function, `float GLKVector3DotProduct(GLKVector3 vectorA, GLKVector3 vectorB)`. The dot product has the following common uses:

- **The angle between vectors**—The dot product is the cosine of the angle between two vectors. Therefore `acosf(GLKVector3DotProduct(vectorA, vectorB))` provides the angle between two vectors. The `SceneCar` class in Chapter 6 calls `GLKVector3DotProduct()` to determine the rotation angle needed to make a bumper car model face the direction it's moving.

- **Length squared calculation**—The dot product of a vector with itself equals the length squared of the vector. The length squared is useful in many cases because if `lengthA` squared is greater than `lengthB` squared, then `lengthA` is also greater than `lengthB`. It's often enough to know which length is greater without needing to know the precise value of the length. See the `UtilityVector3LengthSquared()` function implementation in the TerrainEditor example from Chapter 10.

- **Length calculation**—`sqrtf(GLKVector3DotProduct(vectorA, vectorA))` calculates the length of `vectorA` and is equivalent to `float GLKVector3Length(GLKVector3 vectorA)`. The `sqrtf()` function is one of the most computationally expensive functions in the standard C library. Avoid calling it whenever possible. In many cases, the length squared of a vector can be used instead of the actual length. The `SceneCar` class implementation in Chapter 6 calls `GLKVector3Length()` and examples in Chapter 10 use it to control camera motion.

- **Identifying points behind the point of view**—If `GLKVector3DotProduct(GLKVector3Subtract(position, eyePosition), lookAtVector)` is negative, then `position` is behind `eyePosition` and therefore cannot be seen. This technique is introduced in Chapter 8 to avoid drawing billboard special effects that can't be seen.

- **Diffuse light calculation**—The intensity of the diffuse light hitting a triangle is equal to `GLKVector3DotProduct(diffuseLightDirection, surfaceNormalvector)`. Chapter 4 explains application of the dot product for lighting simulation.

- **Separating vector components**—`GLKVector3DotProduct(vectorA, vectorB)` returns the fractional component of `vectorA` in the direction of `vectorB`. `GLKVector3DotProduct(vectorA, zAxisVector)` returns the component of `vectorA` that's aligned with the Z axis. `GLKVector3DotProduct(vectorA, yAxisVector)` returns the component of `vectorA` that's aligned with the Y axis. `GLKVector3DotProduct(vectorA, xAxisVector)` returns the component of `vectorA` that's aligned with the X axis. See the `AGLKFrustum` sample class introduced in Chapter 9 and the "Axis Components of Vectors" section of this chapter.

Vector Cross Product

The cross product of two non-parallel unit vectors is a third unit vector perpendicular to both of the non-parallel unit vectors, as shown in Figure 11.14.

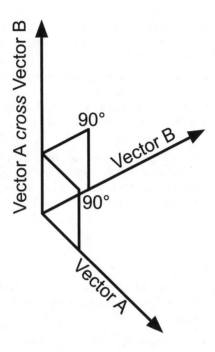

Figure 11.14   Visualization of the cross product.

Only multiplication and subtraction, two of the fastest operations performed by GPUs, are used in the calculation of cross products.

```
GLKVector3 GLKVector3CrossProduct(
   GLKVector3 vectorLeft,
   GLKVector3 vectorRight)
{
   GLKVector3 v = {
     vectorLeft.y * vectorRight.z - vectorLeft.z * vectorRight.y,
     vectorLeft.z * vectorRight.x - vectorLeft.x * vectorRight.z,
     vectorLeft.x * vectorRight.y - vectorLeft.y * vectorRight.x };

   return v;
}
```

The cross product is primarily used as follows:

- **Surface normal vector**—A surface normal vector is a unit vector perpendicular to the plane defined by two vectors. `GLKVector3CrossProduct(GLKVector3Normalize (vectorA), GLKVector3Normalize(vectorB))` returns the surface normal for the plane defined by `vectorA` and `vectorB`. Chapter 4 explains the calculation of surface normal vectors for lighting simulation. Chapter 12, "Putting It All Together," uses the same calculations to keep models of rocket-powered bumper cars parallel with the terrain as the cars race over hills and valleys.

- **Frustum geometry**—The cross product of a frustum's look-at direction vector and the up direction vector produces the frustum's X axis vector. Chapters 8 and 9 explain the geometric definition of the visible area in a 3D scene. The "Obtaining a Matrix from a Frustum" section of this chapter introduces the relationships between the geometric definition of a frustum and the corresponding matrix representation.

- **Billboard orientation**—Billboards are aligned parallel to the frustum's near plane. The cross product of a frustum's look-at direction vector and the up direction times the half the billboard's width identifies the location of the billboard's bottom-left corner. As described in Chapter 8, the remaining corners of the billboard are calculated relative to the bottom-left corner.

The Modelview Matrix

The modelview matrix defines the coordinate system used to describe the position and orientation of objects within a scene. The modelview matrix defines the position and orientation of the viewing frustum.

- **Initializing a modelview matrix**—The most common way to initialize a modelview matrix is to call `GLKMatrix4 GLKMatrix4MakeLookAt(float eyeX, float eyeY, float eyeZ, float centerX, float centerY, float centerZ, float upX, float upY, float upZ)`. The modelview matrix can also be calculated from a viewing frustum or from a quaternion.

- **Relationship to default coordinates**—The modelview matrix is used to transform points from the modelview coordinate system to the projection coordinate system. The concatenation of the modelview and projection matrices produces a single matrix for transforming points all the way from the modelview coordinate system to the OpenGL default coordinate system.

- **Concatenation**—Two matrices may be concatenated to create a third matrix that includes all the coordinate system transformations from both matrices. `GLKMatrix4 GLKMatrix4Multiply(GLKMatrix4 matrixA, GLKMatrix4 matrixB)` returns the concatenation of `matrixA` and `matrixB`.

- **Cumulative transformations**—The modelview matrix typically contains all coordinate system transformations that are unrelated to perspective. `GLKMatrix4 GLKMatrix4Scale(GLKMatrix4 matrix, float sx, float sy, float sz)` returns a new matrix produced by scaling the axes encoded in `matrix` by the specified factors.

GLKMatrix4 GLKMatrix4Translate(GLKMatrix4 matrix, float tx, float ty, float tz) returns a new matrix produced by translating the axis origin encoded in matrix by the specified axis-aligned distances. GLKMatrix4 GLKMatrix4RotateWithVector3(GLKMatrix4 matrix, float radians, GLKVector3 axisVector) returns a new matrix produced by rotating the axes encoded in matrix by the specified number of radians about axisVector.

The Projection Matrix

The projection matrix defines either an orthographic or a perspective projection. Orthographic projections do not alter the apparent size of objects based on their distance from the coordinate system origin. Perspective projections cause objects further away from the coordinate system origin to appear smaller. The projection matrix defines the shape of the viewing frustum and is most commonly initialized by calling GLKMatrix4 GLKMatrix4MakePerspective(float fovyRadians, float aspect, float nearZ, float farZ) or GLKMatrix4 GLKMatrix4MakeOrtho(float left, float right, float bottom, float top, float nearZ, float farZ). The projection matrix can also be calculated based on the shape of an existing frustum.

Summary

This chapter explores the math underlying 3D graphics. The chapter is hardly comprehensive. Several books thicker than this one are needed to cover the depth and breadth of linear algebra.

Matrices encode coordinate systems by storing unit vectors that define the directions of three axes and by storing the location of the coordinate system origin within a reference coordinate system. All coordinate systems are relative to some other coordinate system. The default OpenGL coordinate system provides a basis reference upon which other coordinate systems are defined.

Matrices also define the shape, position, and orientation of viewing frustums. Converting back and forth between matrices and a frustum data structure is possible. Quaternions encode rotation about any vector and are used to avoid undefined behavior in cases when rotating a matrix causes errors. Converting back and forth between matrices and quaternions is possible.

Chapter 12 describes an example combining techniques ranging from terrain rendering to skyboxes, particle systems, animation, changing points of view, lighting, models, and collision detection. Picturing when and why topics described in isolation by previous chapters should be used in an application can be difficult. Chapter 12 ties it all together.

Putting It All Together

This chapter describes the design and construction of a simple simulation, example OpenGLES_Ch12_1. The simulation incorporates terrain, special effects, models, animation, varying points of view, textures, lighting, and optimization. Pulling it all together produces a moderately complex application incorporating almost all the code introduced by preceding chapters.

For example OpenGLES_Ch12_1, you control one of three rocket-propelled hovering carts shown in Figure 12.1. You steer by tilting the iOS device and accelerate by pressing the Boost button. Carts collide with each other and can be knocked off course. The simulation includes gravity, air resistance, and some simplistic artificial intelligence (AI) to control the other two carts.

Figure 12.1   Screenshot of simulation.

Overview

Example OpenGLES_Ch12_1 expands upon examples from Chapter 10, "Terrain and Picking," by adding classes to the Model and View subsystems within the iOS standard *Model-View-Controller* application architecture. New TECart and TEParticleEmitter classes extend the Model subsystem to represent hovering carts and encapsulate 3D positions that emit particles. Within the View subsystem, OpenGLES_Ch12_1 adds a new UtilityBillboardParticleEffect class along with OpenGL ES 2.0 Shading Language programs to render particles composed of billboards. The billboard special effect renders textured geometric objects oriented to face the viewer as explained in Chapter 8, "Special Effects."

Model-View-Controller

The Model-View-Controller (MVC) application architecture is one of the oldest and most successfully reused software design patterns. It was first introduced with the Smalltalk programming language in the 1970s. MVC defines the overall organization of the Cocoa Touch frameworks. It's a high-level pattern for organizing large groups of cooperating objects into distinct subsystems: the Model, the View, and the Controller.

To understand the roles that subsystems play in the MVC pattern, analyzing the capabilities and behavior of common applications is useful. Most applications store information, retrieve information, present information to a user, and enable a user to edit or otherwise manipulate the information. In an object-oriented application, information isn't just bytes; objects encapsulate information along with methods for using the information. Each object within a complex application should fit into one of the following subsystems:

- **Model**—The Model subsystem contains the objects that provide the unique capabilities and information storage for an application. Don't confuse the 3D graphics concept of a model with the Model subsystem. The MVC Model subsystem contains all the rules for processing application data. It's critically important that the Model subsystem stands alone without dependencies on either the View or Controller subsystems. In example OpenGLES_Ch12_1, terrain elevation data resides within the Model subsystem. Elevation data and the operations performed with the data exist independent of the many potential ways to visualize the terrain ranging from flat topological maps to interactive textured 3D meshes.

- **View**—The View subsystem presents information gathered from the Model and provides a way for users to interact with information. A multitude of Views can exist to present the same Model. For example, there may be a 3D View, a 2D View, a View composed of tables, a printed report View, a command-line View, a Web-based View, and a scripting language View all interacting with the same Model. The COLLADAViewer and TerrainEditor applications introduced in Chapter 7, "Loading and Using Models," and Chapter 10 demonstrate multiple Views of data including 3D rendering and tabular presentation.

- **Controller**—The Controller subsystem decouples the Model from the Views. User interaction with a View results in requests made to the Controller subsystem, which in turn might change information in the Model. The Controller also handles data translation and formatting for presentation to a user. For example, a Model may store data in meters, but based on a user's preference, the Controller might convert the data to feet or pixels. A Model might store objects in unordered collections, but the Controller might sort the objects before providing them to a View for presentation to a user.

MVC ensures the ability to modify the implementation of the Model subsystem without impact to the Views and vice versa. In example OpenGLES_Ch12_1, a user presses the "Boost" button, which is part of the View subsystem. The button sends an Objective-C message, `-startBoosting:`, to an instance of `OpenGLES_Ch12_1ViewController`, which then sends a message to the player-controlled `TECart` instance within the Model subsystem. In response, the `TECart` instance recalculates acceleration vectors applied to the physics simulation to calculate a new velocity and position for the cart. The next time the View subsystem renders the scene, the player's cart occupies a new 3D position resulting from the acceleration.

In the MVC architecture, the cart computes acceleration, velocity, and position by applying its own physics rules irrespective of the reason acceleration started or the way the cart will be presented visually. Rendering the cart at a position within the 3D scene occurs irrespective of the calculations performed to determine the cart's position. Changes to the implementation of cart physics have no impact on the code to render carts, and changes to rendering have no impact on the implementation of cart physics. Figure 12.2 depicts the MVC relationships in example OpenGLES_Ch12_1. Arrows in the figure represent communication between subsystems.

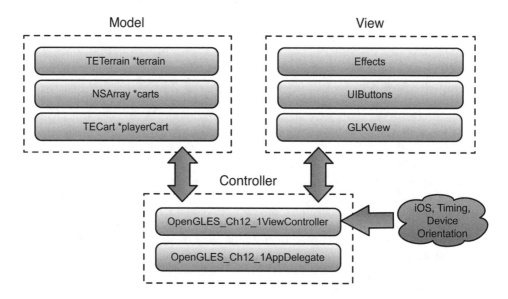

Figure 12.2   Communication between subsystems within example OpenGLES_Ch12_1.

Cocoa Touch refines the MVC architecture by introducing the concepts of Model-Controllers and View-Controllers. In example OpenGLES_Ch12_1, the OpenGLES_Ch12_1AppDelegate class fills the role of Model-Controller. It's part of the Controller subsystem with responsibility for loading and saving the Model subsystem objects such as terrain and carts. The OpenGLES_Ch12_1ViewController class fills the role of View-Controller by coordinating communication between the Model subsystem and the View subsystem. OpenGLES_Ch12_1ViewController manages timing, instructs Model objects to update internal state, and receives messages from a GLKView instance to coordinate rendering.

Everything All the Time

Early examples in this book demonstrate 3D concepts entirely within the View and Controller subsystems. Simple examples either lack a Model subsystem altogether or the Model is something trivial such as a single triangle or simple mesh encapsulated within a View-Controller. As application complexity increases, the motivation to segregate code into separate

MVC subsystems increases. Many decades of use prove the value of the MVC architecture for organizing complex applications. More importantly, effective use of Cocoa Touch requires adherence to MVC. The names of Cocoa Touch classes such as UIView, GLKView, UIViewController, and GLKViewController emphasize their roles. When pulling together all the components needed for a full-featured iOS application, the MVC architecture almost always provides the best available code organization.

The following subsections briefly document the classes comprising example OpenGLES_Ch12_1. The roles, relationships, and interactions described here clarify the ways each technique might apply in your own applications.

The Controller Subsystem

Only two classes compose example OpenGLES_Ch12_1's Controller subsystem, and each class approaches the maximum reasonable implementation size with approximately 1,200 lines of code split between them.

OpenGLES_Ch12_1AppDelegate

Like the examples from Chapter 10, example OpenGLES_Ch12_1 loads terrain data and 3D models using Apple's Core Data framework. Core Data exists to simplify storage of complex objects and relationships within a Model subsystem. The OpenGLES_Ch12_1AppDelegate class contains all the code needed to interact with Core Data.

OpenGLES_Ch12_1AppDelegate also loads the 3D model of a rocket-powered hover cart from a .modelplist file applying the approach introduced in Chapter 7, "Loading and Using Models," and continued through Chapter 9, "Optimization." Chapter 7 explains the compact binary .modelplist file format and its advantages. OpenGLES_Ch12_1AppDelegate insulates the rest of the application from details about storage of Model objects. A different implementation of OpenGLES_Ch12_1AppDelegate could load terrain and models using entirely different technology without any impact to the rest of example OpenGLES_Ch12_1.

OpenGLES_Ch12_1ViewController

The OpenGLES_Ch12_1ViewController class manages periodic update of Model and View subsystem objects. A skybox provides the expansive vista needed to complete the illusion of terrain. Particles add interactivity to the rendered scene and help convey the illusion that rocket-powered carts hover above the ground. Chapter 8 explains skybox and particle special effects.

OpenGLES_Ch12_1ViewController also keeps track of the display update rate and attempts to gracefully reduce graphical detail when the rate drops too low, as it might on the oldest iOS devices or in the iPad and iPhone simulators. Rendering complex terrain meshes and thousands of particles every frame can tax the graphics processing unit (GPU). OpenGLES_Ch12_1ViewController reduces the threshold distance for drawing simplified terrain meshes and discontinues particle rendering when update rates fall below 20Hz.

According to profiling and Apple's OpenGL ES Performance Detective application, example OpenGLES_Ch12_1 is not constrained by GPU performance when running on an iPad 2.

OpenGLES_Ch12_1ViewController organizes methods into groups: "Load time configuration," "Device orientation," "View lifecycle," "Accessors," "GLKViewDelegate updating," "GLKViewDelegate drawing," "Camera delegate," and "Responding to gestures and actions." The organization covers all the roles played by GLKViewController subclasses plus camera management. There's no particular reason all the method groups need to be in one class, but typical GLKit-based applications include all the method groups somewhere.

The Model Subsystem

The simulation of terrain, carts, and physics takes place in the model. A Core Data "Entity Relationship" document, OpenGLES_Ch12_1.xcdatamodeld, within the OpenGLES_Ch12_1 Xcode project catalogs information needed to represent terrain and model placements. Core Data provides storage for the terrain and model placements so the information can be readily loaded when example OpenGLES_Ch12_1 starts. The Xcode project also contains two classes, TETerrain and TEModelPlacement, generated by Xcode from the Core Data document. Generating classes to encapsulate Core Data "Entities" is usually unnecessary. It's done for example OpenGLES_Ch12_1 primarily to enable the creation of Objective-C categories adding methods to interact with terrain and models.

The generated TETerrain and TEModelPlacement classes form the core of the Model subsystem, but several other classes described in this section are needed. For example, the TECart class encapsulates information about the racing hover carts. TECart instances are created by OpenGLES_Ch12_1AppDelegate in the Controller subsystem as needed to fulfill the principal responsibility of a Model-Controller, loading or creating Model subsystem objects. The remaining Model subsystem classes are used by the implementations of TETerrain, TEModelPlacement, and TECart. For example, TETerrain stores terrain texture data using instances of UtilityTextureInfo and 3D models using instances UtilityMesh and UtilityModel. TECart calls functions declared in AGLKCollision and AGLKFilters to implement the physics.

AGLKCollision

The AGLKCollision.h and AGLKCollision.m files contain functions useful for collision detection between 3D objects. In particular, the following AGLKRayDoesIntersectTriangle() function calculates the point of intersection between a ray and a triangle. Recall that the terrain mesh is composed of thousands of triangles. Given a ray cast directly down from an object's X and Z position above the terrain, the intersectionPoint returned by reference from AGLKRayDoesIntersectTriangle() provides the point along the ray where the ray touches the surface of a terrain triangle. AGLKRayDoesIntersectTriangle() is used to make carts seem to hover above the terrain surface.

```
extern BOOL AGLKRayDoesIntersectTriangle(
    GLKVector3 rayDirection,
    GLKVector3 pointOnRay,
```

```
GLKVector3 trianglePointA,
GLKVector3 trianglePointB,
GLKVector3 trianglePointC,
GLKVector3 *intersectionPoint)
```

AGLKRayDoesIntersectTriangle() returns YES if an intersection was found and NO if there is no intersection between the ray and the triangle. A result of NO indicates an object is no longer above the terrain; the object has fallen off the edge.

Rays are defined by any point, pointOnRay, along the ray and a vector, rayDirection, providing the direction of the ray. To cast a ray down from a cart, the position of the cart provides a convenient point and the direction is simply a vector pointing straight down the Y axis, {0.0, -1.0, 0.0}. Any three points, trianglePointA, trianglePointB, and trianglePointC, define a triangle. The three corners composing a terrain mesh triangle are used when calculating an intersection with terrain.

AGLKFilters

The AGLKFilters.h and AGLKFilters.m files contain functions for low pass filtering as described in Chapter 6, "Animation." Low pass filter functions are used in many places throughout example OpenGLES_Ch12_1 to apply incremental changes needed for smooth animation. For example, when a hover cart turns, it turns gradually rather than just snapping to a new direction. The gradual turn is implemented using the AGLKVector3LowPassFilter() filter function to incrementally update the vector identifying the cart's current forward direction until the vector equals a new target direction.

```
extern GLKVector3 AGLKVector3LowPassFilter(
    GLfloat fraction,
    GLKVector3 target,        // target value to approach
    GLKVector3 current);      // current value
```

The target vector specifies a new value. The current vector specifies the current value. The fraction argument specifies how close the function's returned vector should be to the target vector or the current vector. For example, if fraction is 0.0, then the returned value is the same as current. If fraction is 1.0, then the returned value is the same as target. When fraction has values between 0.0 and 1.0, the returned vector is correspondingly a proportional mix of target and current producing a vector between the two.

Animation results from changing values over time and is accomplished by calling a filter function with a gradually changing fraction argument. The fraction argument is typically computed by dividing the elapsed time since the animation started by the total amount of time needed to complete the animation. For example, a cart completes its turn only when the total amount of time elapsed since the start of the turn equals or exceeds the amount of time allotted for the turn.

AGLKFrustum

Chapter 5, "Changing Your Point of View," introduces the mathematic notion of a frustum, the pyramid shape describing the volume of space made visible by coordinate system transformations. Chapter 9 introduces the AGLKFrustum data type and functions to perform calculations with it. AGLKFrustum stores the same information encoded in standard projection and modelview transformation matrices. AGLKFrustum.h declares functions to initialize the AGLKFrustum data type, convert back and forth between AGLKFrustum and matrices, and determine whether points or spheres are contained within a frustum. As a purely mathematic construct valid regardless of any particular View subsystem implementation, the AGLKFrustum type is declared in the Model subsystem. The AGLKFrustum type is used within the implementation of the UtilityCamera class and in the Model subsystem physics simulation.

TETerrain (modelAdditions)

The modelAdditions category adds methods to the TETerrain Core Data generated class. Added methods simplify calculations involving terrain. For example, the —widthMeters method returns the width of the entire terrain measured in meters as opposed to the units used to store values in Core Data. The
-calculatedHeightAtXPosMeters:zPosMeters:surfaceNormal: method applies functions declared in AGLKCollision.h to return the height of the terrain at the specified X and Z coordinates. The method also returns by reference a vector identifying the slope of the terrain at the point of collision. The slope plays a role in physics simulation and helps determine the influence of gravity on carts.

TECart

Each TECart instance has a corresponding 3D model, a 3D position, a velocity, and stores the current magnitude of any "boost" acceleration. Several other properties such as a vector defining the forward direction of the cart are calculated as needed from the position and velocity. Carts inform an optional delegate object about changes to the cart's position giving the delegate an opportunity to influence the change. For example, the OpenGLES_Ch12_1AppDelegate instance in the Controller subsystem serves as a delegate for carts and constrains their positions to prevent them from falling off the edges of the terrain. It's common in Cocoa Touch applications for Controller objects to serve as the delegates for Model and View objects.

TECart instances implement physics simulations within the - (void) updateWithController:(id <TECartControllerProtocol>)controller method. The following TECartControllerProtocol protocol declaration in TECart.h identifies methods that cart controllers must implement:

```
//////////////////////////////////////////////////////////////////
// Protocol for objects that control carts.
@protocol TECartControllerProtocol

- (NSTimeInterval)timeSinceLastUpdate;
- (TETerrain *)terrain;
```

```
- (UtilityBillboardParticleManager *)particleManager;
- (TECart *)playerCart;
```

@end

The -timeSinceLastUpdate and —terrain methods of TECartControllerProtocol enable carts to calculate positions along the surface of the terrain. The —particleManager method isn't used within the Model subsystem but enables generation of particle effects when TECart's -(void)emitParticlesWithController:(id <TECartControllerProtocol>)controller method is overridden by the TECart (viewAdditions) category within the View subsystem. TECart uses the —playerCart method to determine whether the cart is controlled by a player or by AI.

TEParticleEmitter

The TEParticleEmitter class stores a position property and declares an Objective-C Block type used to control particle emission. For carts, the emitter position is defined relative to the cart's position. A small triangular pyramid-shaped 3D model included with the cart 3D model identifies the emitter position. Using a small 3D model enables visual placement of the emitter position from within 3D model editing tools such as Google SketchUp.

TEParticleEmitter instances are initialized with the -(id)initWithModel:(UtilityModel *)aModel method. The geometric center of the aModel argument identifies the emitter position.

Actual generation of particles happens within a Block with the following type:

```
//////////////////////////////////////////////////////////////////
// Type for blocks called to emit particles
typedef void (^TEParticleEmitterBlock)(
    GLKVector3 position,
    UtilityBillboardParticleManager *manager,
    NSTimeInterval elapsedTime,
    id owner);
```

Passing Blocks to the TEParticleEmitter's -updateWithParticleEmitterBlock:manager:elapsedTime:owner: method enables flexible generation of multiple particle effects. Blocks enable variations in particle emission logic without requiring changes to the TEParticleEmitter class itself.

UtilityBillboardParticle

Each UtilityBillboardParticle instance stores position, velocity, force, initialSize, finalSize, lifeSpanSeconds, fadeDurationSeconds, minTextureCoords, and maxTextureCoords properties. Each of those properties enables animation: Changing the position moves the particle. The velocity and force properties enable calculation of new positions based on elapsed time and physics. Particles grow or shrink in size by gradually transitioning from initialSize to finalSize. When a particle's lifespan in seconds has elapsed, the particle no longer needs to be rendered. Particle translucency varies between fully opaque, 1.0, and fully transparent, 0.0, over fadeDurationSeconds. If fadeDurationSeconds equals 0.0, the particle never fades. If fadeDurationSeconds is greater than lifeSpanSeconds, the particle starts partially translucent the first time it's rendered.

UtilityBillboardParticle also calculates distanceSquared, isAlive, lifeRemainingSeconds, size, and opacity properties to provide the current state of the particle as needed. The distanceSquared property is calculated when the particle is updated via the –updateWithElapsedTime:frustum: method and used to sort particles based on signed distance squared from the viewing frustum eye position.

Particle rendering is performed by the UtilityBillboardParticleManager class implemented within the View subsystem. The View subsystem requires particle sorting to produce correct rendering results as explained in the "UtilityBillboardParticleEffect and UtilityBillboardParticleShader" section of this chapter.

Although not currently implemented, the available billboard properties enable calculation of collisions between billboards and other objects within the Model subsystem. For example, billboard-based particles could be used to represent bullets or laser rays in a shooting game. Collisions between billboards and other objects can be detected by the physics simulation within the Model subsystem.

UtilityTextureInfo

The UtilityTextureInfo class encapsulates raw texture data stored within binary .modelplist files. Within the Model subsystem, UtilityTextureInfo only provides simple storage. The class is extended by the UtilityTextureInfo (viewAdditions) category within the View subsystem to enable conversion of UtilityTextureInfo instances into GLKTextureInfo instances for use with GLKit and OpenGL ES.

UtilityMesh

Chapter 6 first introduced the UtilityMesh class, which manages large quantities of geometric vertex data and commands for processing sub-ranges of the data. Meshes are a critical data structure used for 3D graphics. Meshes define the shapes of 3D models. Although terrain data is represented by the TETerrain class instead of UtilityMesh, terrain also applies a variation of the mesh concept. Functions declared in AGLKCollision.h to detect collisions between 3D objects can be applied to detect collisions between any groups of triangles including meshes.

Methods for rendering meshes are provided by the UtilityMesh (viewAdditions) category implemented in the View subsystem. It's common to implement abstract, geometric, and mathematic methods along with data storage in the Model subsystem and then extend operations on the data within the View subsystem. The geometry remains valid no matter how rendering is performed and supports non-graphical calculations such as collision detection. Using categories implemented in the View subsystem decouples specific rendering approaches from generic geometry. For example, the geometric data composing a mesh could be displayed as coordinate values in a table. A View subsystem that uses a table could extend the `UtilityMesh` class with a category containing methods to supply information for a Cocoa Touch `UITableView` object instead of methods to render in 3D.

UtilityModel

Each instance of `UtilityModel` stores a `mesh` property defining the geometry for one or more 3D models. `UtilityModel` also stores a `name` property to identify the specific subset of the mesh needed by the 3D model. The computed `axisAlignedBoundingBox` property provides a bounding box containing all the mesh vertices included in a model. The `doesRequireLighting` property indicates whether to render the 3D model with or without using OpenGL ES lighting calculations on a case-by-case basis.

Chapter 6 introduces the `UtilityModel` class and its relationships with the `UtilityMesh` class. Meshes are optimized to store large quantities of vertex data in a format suitable for transfer to GPU-controlled memory. Sending all the mesh data to the GPU in one operation provides optimum performance. 3D models then coordinate rendering of subsets of the mesh vertex already stored in GPU-controlled memory. The `UtilityModel (viewAdditions)` category within the View subsystem implements rendering for `UtilityModel` instances.

The View Subsystem

The View subsystem contains code to display terrain, models, and user interface objects such as buttons. Several of the classes declared in the Model subsystem are extended by categories within the View subsystem to implement specific rendering capabilities. A key question must be asked to understand separation and decoupling between Model and View subsystems: "Can an entirely different View subsystem be implemented using the same Model subsystem, and can the implementation of the Model subsystem be changed without impact to the View subsystem?" Example OpenGLES_Ch12_1 is designed to answer "Yes."

For example, the Model subsystem can be changed to use a data storage mechanism other than Core Data without any impact to the View subsystem. The View subsystem can be completely omitted from the project without impact to the Model subsystem; the Model subsystem in Example OpenGLES_Ch12_1 contains no references or dependencies on the View subsystem.

The classes and categories explained in this section demonstrate how to implement relatively complex and full-featured 3D rendering for abstract geometric data supplied by a decoupled Model subsystem. Code in the View subsystem remains generic and applicable for many 3D applications comprised of textured 3D models, billboards, and particles.

UtilityEffect

Chapter 10 introduces the `UtilityEffect` class to load, compile, link, and validate OpenGL ES 2.0 Shading Language programs. `UtilityEffect` conforms to GLKit's `GLKNamedEffect` protocol. `UtilityEffect` implements two methods, `-bindAttribLocations` and `-configureUniformLocations`, to generate exceptions if they are ever invoked directly. Subclasses of `UtilityEffect` must override the two methods.

UtilityEffect's -(BOOL)loadShadersWithName:(NSString *)aShaderName method loads and compiles vertex and fragment Shading Language programs with the root name specified by the aShaderName argument, and the suffixes/extensions .vsh and .fsh. -loadShadersWithName: calls -bindAttribLocations and —configureUniformLocations as needed, returning NO if any problems are encountered and YES if successful.

The UtilityModelEffect, UtilityPickTerrainEffect, UtilityTerrainEffect, and UtilityBillboardParticleEffect classes in example OpenGLES_Ch12_1 all subclass UtilityEffect. They implement -bindAttribLocations and —configureUniformLocations to bind attributes and configure uniform value storage specific to their respective Shading Language programs.

UtilityModelEffect and UtilityModelShader

The UtilityModelEffect class coordinates execution of the UtilityModelShader.vsh vertex Shading Language program and the UtilityModelShader.fsh fragment Shading Language program. The UtilityModelShader programs are relatively simple and render submitted geometric data using just one texture, ambient light, and directional diffuse light. The simplicity enables efficient rendering of 3D models with a subset of the traditional OpenGL lighting calculations. Chapter 3, "Textures," explains textures. Chapter 4, "Shedding Some Light," explains lighting equations for ambient and diffuse lights.

The UtilityModelShader.fsh Shading Language program discards any fragments that are nearly transparent. Discarding them prevents invalid changes to the depth render buffer, which controls whether newly generated fragments replace previously generated fragments when fragments overlap. For example, if not discarded, when a nearly transparent fragment generated for one model is "in front" of an opaque fragment generated for another model, the nearly transparent fragment could prevent the opaque fragment from affecting the final pixel color render buffer contents resulting in an incorrect result. The opaque fragment should be visible through the nearly transparent fragment but won't be present at all in this scenario. Chapter 5 introduces the depth render buffer, and Chapter 3 explains operations affecting fragment colors. Discarding the nearly transparent fragment avoids the problem without reducing the quality of the rendered scene because nearly transparent fragments are hardly noticeable anyway.

UtilityPickTerrainEffect and UtilityPickTerrainShader

Chapter 10 explains the UtilityPickTerrainEffect class and related UtilityPickTerrainShader Shading Language programs used to render terrain and models in false color. The scene is rendered into a pixel color render buffer managed by a UtilityPickTerrainEffect instance. Terrain X and Z position coordinates are encoded in the red and green color components of fragments. For example, fragments generated from the terrain mesh at position {100, 50, 75} have the floating-point RGB color {100.0 / terrainWidth, 75.0 / terrainLength, 0.0}. The resulting pixel colors at specific positions in the pixel color render buffer identify the terrain coordinates corresponding to the positions. 3D model indices are rendered with false color encoded in the blue component of pixels in the pixel color render buffer. When reading a pixel color back from the pixel color render buffer, if the color has a non-zero blue component, the value of the blue component is an index used to look up which model contributed to the pixel color.

The `UtilityPickTerrainEffect` class is not used in example OpenGLES_Ch12_1 but is retained from the implementation of `UtilityPickTerrainEffect` in Chapter 10. Enhancing OpenGLES_Ch12_1 to take advantage of picking is left as an exercise for the reader. For example, touch events could be used to launch missiles from the player's cart to the position touched. The simulation becomes more of a game when players are able to destroy computer-controlled carts by carefully anticipating the positions carts will occupy when a missile arrives. The player might also need to dodge missiles fired by computer-controlled carts.

`UtilityTerrainEffect` and `UtilityTerrainShader`

Chapter 10 explains the `UtilityTerrainEffect` class and related `UtilityTerrainShader` Shading Language programs used to render textured terrain. The Shading Language programs mix four textures together to calculate colors of fragments generated for terrain geometry. Separate texture transformation matrices and blending weights apply to each texture, enabling tremendous variety within the final rendered result. Chapter 3 explains texture transformation. The weights applied to blend textures are stored in a fifth texture along with pre-calculated light intensity values. In other words, lighting is baked into the fifth texture, so the `UtilityTerrainShader` Shading Language programs do not need to perform lighting calculations.

Terrain rendering applies some of the most complex Shading Language programs used in this book and still retains good performance even on the oldest iOS devices. Achieving equivalent rendering results and performance using earlier OpenGL ES versions that don't support Shading Language programs is nearly impossible.

`UtilityBillboardParticleEffect` and `UtilityBillboardParticleShader`

The `UtilityBillboardParticleEffect` class and related `UtilityBillboardParticleShader` Shading Language programs render translucent particles. Particles require a somewhat unusual vertex attribute:

```
/////////////////////////////////////////////////////////////////
// Vertex attributes used in UtilityBillboardParticleShader
typedef struct
{
  GLKVector3 position;
  GLKVector2 textureCoords;
  GLfloat opacity;
}
BillboardVertex;
```

The `position` and texture coordinates, `textureCoords`, of each vertex are straightforward and similar to vertex attributes used with other effects like `UtilityModelEffect`. However, instead of using a vertex normal vector attribute or a vertex color attribute, billboard particle vertices store an `opacity` attribute. Opacity is used within the Shading Language programs to control blending of billboard fragments with existing colors in the pixel color render buffer. The opacity attribute is equivalent to the Alpha component of a Red Green Blue and Alpha (RGBA) color. By only storing the opacity of vertices instead of a full color, both memory and runtime performance are preserved.

Because particles are translucent, they need to be rendered after any other opaque objects like terrain, models, and the skybox have been rendered. Rendering them last enables the final colors in the pixel color render buffer to depict the result of looking through the billboard particle to the objects behind it. The particles must also be rendered in order from furthest away from the viewer to closest. Otherwise, it won't be possible to see distant billboard particles through nearby billboard particles. Figure 12.3 depicts the desired result of rendering. Management of billboard particle vertex attributes and sorting of particles by distance from the viewer occurs within the `UtilityBillboardParticleManager` class.

Figure 12.3   Rendering translucent billboards.

UtilityBillboardParticleManager

Each instance of the UtilityBillboardParticleManager class maintains an array of UtilityBillboardParticle instances and corresponding vertex data. Each time a UtilityBillboardParticleManager instance is prepared for drawing, it sorts the array of UtilityBillboardParticle instances based on the distance of each particle from the eye position of a frustum.

```
//////////////////////////////////////////////////////////////////
// Sort billboards in reverse order for rendering from furthest
// to nearest.
- (void)prepareToDrawWithCamera:(UtilityCamera *)aCamera;
```

UtilityBillboardParticleManager collects vertex attributes for live particles contained within aCamera's frustum and submits the vertex attributes for rendering as a single large collection of triangles. Live particles are the ones that return YES for the isAlive property. UtilityBillboardParticle returns NO for the isAlive property after the billboard's lifeSpanSeconds have elapsed.

The -addParticle: method adds a particle to the array of billboards maintained by a UtilityBillboardParticleManager instance.

```
//////////////////////////////////////////////////////////////////
// Adds aParticle to the end of the particles array. If a
// dead particle is available, then one dead particle is also
// removed so the total number of particles does not increase.
- (void)addParticle:(UtilityBillboardParticle *)aParticle;
```

Each UtilityBillboardParticleManager instance limits the number of living particles to UtilityMaximumNumberOfParticles, which defaults to 4000. Rendering more than 4000 billboard particles at a time reduces the display update rate by several frames per second on older iOS devices.

To save a step when creating a new UtilityBillboardParticle instance and then adding it to a manager, UtilityBillboardParticleManager provides the following method to accomplish it all at once:

```
- (void)addParticleAtPosition:(GLKVector3)aPosition
   velocity:(GLKVector3)aVelocity
   force:(GLKVector3)aForce
   initialSize:(GLKVector2)anInitialSize
   finalSize:(GLKVector2)aFinalSize
   lifeSpanSeconds:(NSTimeInterval)aSpan
   fadeDurationSeconds:(NSTimeInterval)aDuration
   minTextureCoords:(GLKVector2)minCoords
   maxTextureCoords:(GLKVector2)maxCoords;
```

UtilityModelManager

The UtilityModelManager class encapsulates a mesh, a texture, and a collection of named 3D models that can be rendered using portions of the mesh and the texture. Chapter 7 introduces UtilityModelManager and explains the methods available for loading a mesh and 3D models from binary data. UtilityModelManager, UtilityModel, UtilityMesh, UtilityModelEffect, and UtilityModelShader Shading Language programs all work together to process 3D models from the time they are loaded as binary data to final rendering in a pixel color render buffer.

UtilityModelManager serves as an overall manager or coordinator for 3D models and meshes. Calling UtilityModelManager's –prepareToDraw method also prepares the mesh to draw by configuring the current OpenGL ES context with the mesh's vertex data. The –modelNamed: method returns the requested model, which can then be rendered by preparing a UtilityModelEffect for drawing and then calling the 3D model's –draw method.

UtilityCamera

Chapter 10 introduced the UtilityCamera class to encapsulate a viewing frustum and provide convenient methods for moving and rotating the camera within a virtual 3D world. Cameras also inform an optional delegate object whenever the camera changes position. The delegate has an opportunity to overrule the change. Examples in Chapter 10 use the delegate to keep the camera above terrain. Example OpenGLES_Ch12_1 doesn't explicitly constrain the camera position because the example always positions the camera near the player-controlled cart, and carts are constrained to follow the terrain by their own delegates.

UtilityMesh (viewAdditions)

The UtilityMesh (viewAdditions) category extends the UtilityMesh class from the Model subsystem. The following methods are added by the category:

```
@interface UtilityMesh (viewAdditions)

- (void)prepareToDraw;
- (void)prepareToPick;
- (void)drawCommandsInRange:(NSRange)aRange;
- (void)drawBoundingBoxStringForCommandsInRange:
    (NSRange)aRange;

@end
```

The –prepareToDraw method configures the current OpenGL ES context to use the mesh's vertex attributes for subsequent rendering. The –prepareToPick method is similar to –prepareToDraw but configures the current OpenGL ES context to use a subset of vertex attributes applicable when rendering with UtilityPickTerrainEffect. The –drawCommandsInRange: method calls glDrawElements() one or more times to render triangles defined by mesh vertex attributes. The range typically specifies a single set of vertex indices identifying vertex attributes used by one 3D model, but drawing more than

one 3D model at a time is theoretically possible. Finally, the
–drawBoundingBoxStringForCommandsInRange: method is sometimes helpful for visually
debugging 3D model rendering. The method draws lines along all edges of a box enclosing the
vertices referenced by commands in the specified range. Like –drawCommandsInRange:, the
range specified typically covers only one 3D model, so the resulting box visually encloses the
model.

UtilityModel (viewAddition)

The UtilityModel (viewAdditions) category adds exactly one method to the
UtilityModel class from the Model subsystem. The added method calls the associated mesh's
–drawCommandsInRange: method specifying the range of commands applicable to the model.

@implementation UtilityModel (viewAdditions)

```
/////////////////////////////////////////////////////////////////
// This method draws the receiver using the receiver's
// UtilityMesh and a UtilityModelEffect that have both already
// been prepared for drawing.

- (void)draw
{
   [self.mesh drawCommandsInRange:NSMakeRange(
      indexOfFirstCommand_, numberOfCommands_)];
}


@end
```

TETerrain (viewAdditions) and TETerrainTile

Terrain meshes are too large to be drawn with a single call to glDrawElements(), and drawing
the whole terrain mesh including portions that can't be seen is wasteful anyway. Therefore,
terrain meshes are subdivided into tiles encapsulated by the TETerrainTile class. Each tile
references a small subset of the terrain mesh vertices composing the entire terrain encapsulated
by an instance of TETerrain. Chapter 10 introduces the TETerrainTile class, the TETerrain
class, and the TETerrain (viewAdditions) category.

In addition to the terrain mesh itself, instances of the TETerrain class reference
TEModelPlacement instances. Each model placement specifies the name, position, and
orientation of a 3D model within the terrain. Example OpenGLES_Ch12_1 uses model
placements to draw trees, bushes, rocks, and buildings. There's no reason to draw 3D models
located within tiles that can't be seen. For that reason, TETerrain (viewAdditions) provides
a method to draw only the models positioned within specified tiles.

```
- (void)drawModelsWithinTiles:(NSArray *)tiles
   withCamera:(UtilityCamera *)aCamera
   modelEffect:(UtilityModelEffect *)aModelEffect
   modelManager:(UtilityModelManager *)modelManager;
```

The `UtilityModelManager` object passed to `-drawModelsWithinTiles:`
`withCamera:modelEffect:modelManager:` coordinates 3D model rendering using the
specified `UtilityModelEffect` with transformation matrices provided by the specified
`UtilityCamera`. Similar methods draw the tiles themselves using a specified camera and
`UtilityTerrainEffect`.

TECart (viewAdditions)

The `TECart (viewAdditions)` category adds the `-(void)drawWithEffect:`
`(UtilityModelEffect *)anEffect` method to the `TECart` class from the Model subsystem:

```
////////////////////////////////////////////////////////////////
// Draw the receiver using anEffect.
- (void)drawWithEffect:(UtilityModelEffect *)anEffect;
{
   GLKVector3 position = self.position;

   // Move cart to position
   anEffect.modelviewMatrix = GLKMatrix4Translate(
      anEffect.modelviewMatrix,
      position.x,
      position.y,
      position.z);

   // Transform to cart's orientation
   anEffect.modelviewMatrix = GLKMatrix4Multiply(
      anEffect.modelviewMatrix,
      GLKMatrix4Transpose(self.orientationMatrix));

   [anEffect prepareModelview];

   [self.model draw];
}
```

The cart's orientation is computed within the Model subsystem to make the cart hover
over terrain even when the terrain is sloped. The cart tilts as needed. The cart's orientation
is defined by its `orientationMatrix` property relative to the cart itself, but that's not the
matrix needed to modify a `UtilityModelEffect`'s transformation matrix when rendering a
cart model. Instead, a corresponding orientation matrix in the effect's own coordinate system
must be used. To convert from the cart's own coordinate system to the effect's coordinate
system, inverting the cart's `orientationMatrix` is necessary. The `-drawWithEffect:` method
implementation takes advantage of the fact that for uniformly scaled coordinate systems, the
computationally inexpensive `GLKMatrix4Transpose()` is equivalent to the more complex
`GLKMatrix4Invert()` function. The minor optimization to transpose rather than invert
imposes the non-obvious restriction that cart model's should not be non-uniformly scaled.
Don't try to render a squished skinny cart.

The implementation of TECart (viewAdditions) also overrides the -(void) emitParticlesWithController:(id <TECartControllerProtocol>)controller method that's defined to do nothing by the main TECart implementation in the Model subsystem. The new implementation in the View subsystem uses the cart's particleEmitter property and UtilityBillboardParticleManager to create particles simulating rocket exhaust, blown dust, and smoke shown in Figure 12.4.

Figure 12.4   Particles emitted from carts.

UtilityTextureInfo (viewAdditions)

The UtilityTextureInfo class encapsulates a dictionary of attributes including the binary data defining a texture's image, but the attributes are not suitable for direct use with OpenGL ES. The UtilityTextureInfo (viewAdditions) category provides name and target properties needed by OpenGL ES to identify a texture for subsequent rendering. Chapter 3 explains texture names and targets. To generate the needed name and target, a new GLKTextureInfo instance is created behind the scenes and initialized with the UtilityTextureInfo's image data. The name and target are then obtained from the GLKTextureInfo instance.

To create GLKTextureInfo instances from UtilityTextureInfo instances, the GLKTextureInfo class is extended via a category as follows. The ability to add methods to framework classes is one of the most powerful features of the Objective-C programming language.

```objc
@implementation GLKTextureInfo (utilityAdditions)

/////////////////////////////////////////////////////////////////
// Returns a GLKTextureInfo instance initialized based upon
// information provided in aDictionary.
+ (GLKTextureInfo *)textureInfoFromUtilityPlistRepresentation:
   (NSDictionary *)aDictionary
{
   GLKTextureInfo *result = nil;

   const size_t imageWidth = (size_t)[[aDictionary
      objectForKey:@"width"] unsignedIntegerValue];
   const size_t imageHeight = (size_t)[[aDictionary
      objectForKey:@"height"] unsignedIntegerValue];

   // The imageData property is expected to be a Tiff image
   UIImage *image = [UIImage imageWithData:
      [aDictionary objectForKey:@"imageData"]];

   if(nil != image && 0 != imageWidth && 0 != imageHeight)
   {  // Create GLKTextureInfo corresponding to image.
      NSError *error;
      result =
         [GLKTextureLoader textureWithCGImage:[image CGImage]
            options:[NSDictionary dictionaryWithObjectsAndKeys:
               [NSNumber numberWithBool:YES],
               GLKTextureLoaderGenerateMipmaps,
               [NSNumber numberWithBool:NO],
               GLKTextureLoaderOriginBottomLeft,
               [NSNumber numberWithBool:NO],
               GLKTextureLoaderApplyPremultiplication,
               nil]
            error:&error];

      if(nil == result)
      {
         NSLog(@"%@", error);
      }
      else
      {
         glTexParameteri(GL_TEXTURE_2D,
            GL_TEXTURE_MAG_FILTER,
            GL_LINEAR);
         glTexParameteri(GL_TEXTURE_2D,
            GL_TEXTURE_MIN_FILTER,
            GL_NEAREST_MIPMAP_LINEAR);
         glTexParameteri(
```

```
         GL_TEXTURE_2D,
         GL_TEXTURE_WRAP_S,
         GL_REPEAT);
      glTexParameteri(
         GL_TEXTURE_2D,
         GL_TEXTURE_WRAP_T,
         GL_REPEAT);
   }
 }

 return result;
}

@end
```

Device Motion

Cocoa Touch includes the Core Motion framework, which provides the `CMMotionManager` class documented at https://developer.apple.com/library/ios/DOCUMENTATION/CoreMotion/Reference/CoreMotion_Reference/_index.html. `OpenGLES_Ch12_1ViewController` in example OpenGLES_Ch12_1 initializes its `motionManager` property and requests periodic motion updates via the following code called from `–viewDidLoad`:

```
self.motionManager = [[CMMotionManager alloc] init];
[self.motionManager startDeviceMotionUpdates];
```

`OpenGLES_Ch12_1ViewController` implements `–viewDidUnload` to discontinue motion updates and set the `motionManager` property to `nil`:

```
[self.motionManager stopDeviceMotionUpdates];
[self.motionManager stopAccelerometerUpdates];
self.motionManager = nil;
self.particleManager = nil;
```

Older iOS devices don't contain hardware to detect all motions. The following `–updatePlayerCartForDeviceMotion` method from `OpenGLES_Ch12_1ViewController` falls back to using built-in but imprecise accelerometer hardware when more sensitive motion detectors are unavailable:

```
/////////////////////////////////////////////////////////////////
// Factor used to dampen motion inputs controlling cart yaw
static const GLfloat TEDeviceRotationFactor = (0.03f);

/////////////////////////////////////////////////////////////////
// This method updates the player's cart orientation in response
// to device motion. Turning the device turns the player's cart.
- (void)updatePlayerCartForDeviceMotion
```

```
{
    TECart *playerCart = [self playerCart];

    // Update cart direction based on device motion inputs
    if(self.motionManager.isDeviceMotionActive)
    {
        self.rollAngleRadians = TEDeviceRotationFactor *
            self.motionManager.deviceMotion.attitude.pitch;
    }
    else
    {   // Use device accelerometer when other sources unavailable
        if(!self.motionManager.isAccelerometerActive)
        {
            [self.motionManager startAccelerometerUpdates];
        }

        self.rollAngleRadians = -TEDeviceRotationFactor *
            self.motionManager.accelerometerData.acceleration.y;
    }

    [playerCart turnDeltaRadians:self.rollAngleRadians];
}
```

Figure 12.5 illustrates the device motion used to steer the player's cart. CMMotionManager designates device rotation about the axis pointing out of the screen as "pitch". The accelerometer designates the axis pointing out of the device screen as "Y". Therefore, -updatePlayerCartForDeviceMotion looks for pitch changes to the device **attitude** when available and looks for rotational acceleration about the device Y axis otherwise.

Figure 12.5   Device rotation for steering.

The term *attitude* describes the orientation of an object in terms of three angles called pitch, roll, and yaw. If an object has a direction designated as "forward," then roll is rotation about an axis that points forward. Yaw is rotation about an axis that points up. Pitch is rotation about an axis perpendicular to both forward and up. Wikipedia provides a diagram and some animations illustrating pitch, roll, and yaw in the context of an aircraft at http://en.wikipedia.org/wiki/Yaw,_pitch_and_roll.

Summary

The chapters in this book introduce computer graphics concepts one by one, culminating with this chapter incorporating almost every covered topic in an overarching example. Apple applies the MVC software architecture within the Cocoa Touch frameworks, and most applications for iOS should adopt the MVC architecture, too. Partitioning classes and other source code into Model, View, and Controller subsystems imposes an organization expected by other programmers familiar with Cocoa Touch. Example OpenGLES_Ch12_1 benefits from the decoupling promoted by the MVC organization.

Many experienced graphics programmers accumulate libraries of reusable code over the course of years. Starting a new project from first principles and building all the way up to advanced features is seldom necessary. Nevertheless, understanding the technology involved is important. Staring out with high-level frameworks, such as GLKit, can be a huge advantage and make you more productive as a programmer, but might also conceal underlying theory and practice. With confidence in the underlying technology, higher-level frameworks such as GLKit and third-party game engines become more approachable. As a rule, programmers detest mysteries. Knowing how everything fits together is important.

Ultimately, every pixel color on an iOS device screen is controlled by the GPU, and the GPU is controlled using standard OpenGL ES 2.0 programming interfaces. Apple's Core Animation framework and GLKit simplify many common graphics programming tasks without impeding access to lower-level OpenGL ES 2.0 functions. This book explains how to use GLKit and Core Animation Layers to render 3D graphics, but more importantly, this book provides insight into the implementation of GLKit and interaction with Core Animation. Be empowered by the information to realize your creative goals.

Index

FREE
Online Edition

Safari Books Online

Your purchase of **Learning OpenGL ES for iOS** includes access to a free online edition for 45 days through the Safari Books Online subscription service. Nearly every Addison-Wesley Professional book is available online through Safari Books Online, along with over thousands of books and videos from publishers such as Cisco Press, Exam Cram, IBM Press, O'Reilly Media, Prentice Hall, Que, Sams, and VMware Press.

Safari Books Online is a digital library providing searchable, on-demand access to thousands of technology, digital media, and professional development books and videos from leading publishers. With one monthly or yearly subscription price, you get unlimited access to learning tools and information on topics including mobile app and software development, tips and tricks on using your favorite gadgets, networking, project management, graphic design, and much more.

Activate your FREE Online Edition at
informit.com/safarifree

STEP 1: Enter the coupon code: VHYRWBI.

STEP 2: New Safari users, complete the brief registration form.
Safari subscribers, just log in.

If you have difficulty registering on Safari or accessing the online edition,
please e-mail customer-service@safaribooksonline.com

Addison Wesley Adobe Press ALPHA Cisco Press FT Press IBM Press Microsoft Press New Riders O'REILLY

Peachpit Press PRENTICE HALL QUE Redbooks SAMS SAS Publishing vmware PRESS WILEY wrox